Age of Iron

Age of Iron

On Conservative Nationalism

BY COLIN DUECK

OXFORD
UNIVERSITY PRESS

OXFORD
UNIVERSITY PRESS

Oxford University Press is a department of the University of Oxford. It furthers
the University's objective of excellence in research, scholarship, and education
by publishing worldwide. Oxford is a registered trade mark of Oxford University
Press in the UK and certain other countries.

Published in the United States of America by Oxford University Press
198 Madison Avenue, New York, NY 10016, United States of America.

Library of Congress Cataloging-in-Publication Data
Names: Dueck, Colin, 1969– author.
Title: Age of iron : on conservative nationalism / by Colin Dueck.
Description: New York, NY : Oxford University Press, [2020] |
Summary: "Age of Iron attempts to describe the past, present,
and possible future of conservative nationalism in American foreign policy.
It argues that a kind of conservative US nationalism long predates the
Trump presidency, and goes back to the American founding.
Different aspects of conservative American nationalism have been
incorporated into the Republican Party from its creation.
Every Republican president since Theodore Roosevelt has tried to
balance elements of this tradition with global US foreign policy priorities.
Donald Trump was able to win his party's nomination and rise to the presidency,
in part, by challenging liberal internationalist assumptions. Yet in practice,
he too has combined nationalist assumptions with global US foreign policy priorities.
The long-term trend within the Republican party, predating Trump, is toward
political populism, cultural conservatism, and white working-class
voters — and this has international implications. Republican foreign policy
nationalism is not about to disappear. The book concludes with
recommendations for US foreign policy, based upon an understanding
that the optimism of the post-Cold War quarter-century is over.
Nationalism; conservatism; populism; Trump presidency;
American foreign policy; liberal internationalism; US diplomatic history;
geopolitics; American party politics; the Republican Party"— Provided by publisher.
Identifiers: LCCN 2019017395 | ISBN 9780190079369 (hardback) |
ISBN 9780190079383 (epub) | ISBN 9780190079376 (pdf)
Subjects: LCSH: Republican Party (U.S. : 1854–)—History. |
Conservatism—United States. | Nationalism—United States. |
Populism—United States. | United States—Foreign relations—Philosophy.
Classification: LCC JC573.2.U6 D8354 2020 | DDC 320.540973—dc23
LC record available at https://lccn.loc.gov/2019017395

1 3 5 7 9 8 6 4 2

Printed by Sheridan Books, Inc., United States of America

CONTENTS

ACKNOWLEDGMENTS

My understanding of contemporary US foreign policy challenges—and of related conservative traditions—has been enriched by discussions, interviews, panels, debates, and conversations with a wide range of people over the years. An incomplete list of such people would include Elliott Abrams, David Adesnik, Alex Alden, Michael Allen, Robert Art, Emma Ashford, Misha Auslin, Michael Barone, Peter Beinart, Peter Berkowitz, Russell Berman, Richard Betts, Dan Blumenthal, John Bolton, Anna Borshchevskya, Karlyn Bowman, Hal Brands, Christopher Bright, Cherise Britt, Ted Bromund, Chris Brose, Ian Brzezinski, Mark Brzezinski, Jonathan Burks, Joshua Busby, Dan Byman, Steve Cambone, Jim Carafano, Paul Carrese, Omri Ceren, Steve Chan, Dean Cheng, Eliot Cohen, Bridge Colby, Heather Conley, Zack Cooper, Ryan Crocker, Audrey Cronin, Ted Cruz, Ivo Daalder, Tom Davis, Jackie Deal, Rick Dearborn, Bob Deitz, Michael Desch, Daniel Deudney, Paula Dobriansky, Michaela Dodge, Giselle Donnelly, Michael Doran, Peter Doran, Michael Doyle, Daniel Drezner, Joseph Duggan, Mackenzie Eaglen, Nicholas Eberstadt, Eric Edelman, Jeff Engel, Drew Erdmann, Peter Feaver, Michele Flournoy, Jamie Fly, Richard Fontaine, John Fonte, Rosemary Foot, Chris Ford, Aaron Friedberg, David Frum, Francis Fukuyama, John Gaddis, Mike Gallagher, Nile Gardiner, Adam Garfinkle, Erik Gartzke, Jeff Gedmin, Michael Gerson, Derek Gianino, Jonah Goldberg, James Goldgeier, Lyle Goldstein, Seb Gorka, Ron Granieri, Kelly Greenhill, Chris Griffin, Jakub Grygiel, Nick Gvosdev, Richard Haass, Mary Habeck, Stephen Hadley,

David Hamon, Jerad Harper, Will Hay, Michael Hayden, Yoram Hazony, Jacob Heilbrunn, Tom Henriksen, Jon Herrmann, Roger Hertog, Charles Hill, John Hillen, Jordan Hirsch, Rachel Hoff, Frank Hoffman, Kim Holmes, Brian Hook, Michael Horowitz, Mike Hunzeker, Will Inboden, Bruce Jentleson, Bob Jervis, Fred Kagan, Roy Kamphausen, Maya Kandel, Robert Kaplan, Tom Karako, Robert Karem, Mark Katz, Robert Kaufman, Richard Kauzlarich, Zachary Keck, Charles Kesler, Zalmay Khalilzad, Yuen Khong, Jamie Kirchick, Greg Koblentz, Richard Kohn, Julius Krein, Andrew Krepinevich, Sarah Kreps, Bill Kristol, Matt Kroenig, Charles Kupchan, James Kurth, Jim Lacey, Mark Lagon, Ellen Laipson, Chris Layne, Richard Ned Lebow, Derek Leebaert, Melvyn Leffler, Daniel Leger, Paul Lettow, Scooter Libby, Robert Lieber, Tod Lindberg, Fred Logevall, Becky Lollar, Rich Lowry, Alan Luxenberg, Tom Mahnken, Peter Mandaville, Harvey Mansfield, Peter Mansoor, Dan Markey, Damir Marusic, John Maurer, Andrew May, Walter McDougall, Eric McGlinchey, Bryan McGrath, John McIntyre, H.R. McMaster, Walter Russell Mead, Benjamin Miller, Myra Miller, Paul Miller, Joshua Mitchell, Wess Mitchell, Bert Mizusawa, Mark Moyar, Mitch Muncy, Joshua Muravchik, Chuck Myers, Henry Nau, Daniel Nexon, Hung Nguyen, Michael Noonan, Grover Norquist, Michael O'Hanlon, Meghan O'Sullivan, Henry Olsen, Josiah Osgood, Rich Outzen, John Owen, Mac Owens, Roland Paris, Jim Pfiffner, Peter Pham, Danielle Pletka, Ken Pollack, Alina Polyakova, Ionut Popescu, Patrick Porter, Chris Preble, Maud Quessard, Jeremy Rabkin, Brian Rathbun, Mitchell Reiss, Stanley Renshon, Michael Reynolds, Ed Rhodes, Peter Rightmyer, Joe Riley, Nadege Rolland, Gideon Rose, Stephen Rosen, Robert Ross, Joshua Rovner, Mark Royce, Michael Rubin, Will Ruger, Donald Rumsfeld, Dan Runde, Paul Saunders, Phil Saunders, Nadia Schadlow, Kori Schake, Gabe Scheinmann, Gary Schmitt, Randy Schweller, Derek Scissors, Zachary Selden, James Sherr, Keith Shimko, Jim Shinn, Kristen Silverberg, Dmitri Simes, Michael Singh, Kiron Skinner, Lee Smith, Marion Smith, Henry Sokolski, Elizabeth Spalding, Matt Spalding, Luke Strange, Jeremi Suri, Ray Takeyh, Jim Talent, Jordan Tama, Ashley Tellis, Jim Thomas, Trevor Thrall, Peter Trubowitz, John Unger, Dan Vajdich, Kelley Vlahos, Ming Wan, Vin Weber, George Will, Ryan Williams, William Wohlforth, Woj

Wolfe, Paul Wolfowitz, Joe Wood, Leet Wood, Thomas Wright, Ali Wyne, John Yoo, Paul Zajac, Dov Zakheim, Roger Zakheim, Robert Zarate, and Philip Zelikow. My thanks to all of them.

In the end however, the specific arguments contained in these pages—including with regard to the current administration—are mine alone.

It has been a real pleasure to work again with Editor David McBride, as well as Holly Mitchell and the staff of Oxford University Press on this book. My sincere thanks to them all.

Thank you to Andrew Wylie for representing me as a client, a task he performed with impressive capability, efficiency, and precision. I look forward to similar projects together in the future.

Thanks to Dean Mark Rozell, the faculty, staff, and students of the Schar School of Policy and Government at George Mason University for providing a supportive, stimulating, and excellent environment within which to study US foreign policy.

While writing this book in 2017–19, I was a Jeane Kirkpatrick visiting fellow at the American Enterprise institute. Thanks to Dany Pletka, the scholars, staff, administration, and research assistants Taylor Clausen and Max Frost of AEI for their marvelous assistance during that time. This book is in many ways a defense of conservative nationalism. I think the fact that AEI was willing to back it, demonstrates its openness to a range of ideas.

Portions of various chapters are drawn and revised from my own articles in *Orbis, The National Interest* online, and at the Foreign Policy Research Institute. My thanks to the editors and publishers of those journals and websites for permission to reprint these sections.

Finally, greatest thanks go to my wife Kirsten. This book is dedicated to our son Jack. Jack is American by birth. His father is American by choice.

Introduction:
On Conservative Nationalism

The rise of populist nationalism on the right is one of the most striking trends of our time. Critics on both sides of the Atlantic fear that we are witnessing a return to the 1930s, including the resurgence of fascism, authoritarian forms of governance, and possibly catastrophic wars. In relation to the Trump administration's foreign policy, these same critics contend that the United States is now deliberately undermining what they call the rules-based liberal international order. Yet in relation to the United States, observers have misunderstood both the nature of American nationalism—past and present—and the foreign policy of the Trump administration. Conservative American nationalism is arguably the oldest US foreign policy tradition in existence, and is neither fascistic nor undemocratic. On the contrary, it is meant to preserve the very right of American citizens to self-government. Nor is a conservative US nationalism historically incompatible with American engagement overseas, including the promotion and defense of democracy. However, accumulated US foreign policy frustrations of the twenty-first century—both military, political, and economic—have led to the resurgence of a distinct form of American nationalism on the Right, emphasizing the need for allied burden-sharing, US sovereignty, and the promotion of material American interests. And because this resurgence is based upon domestic and international factors much larger than Donald Trump, it is probably not about to disappear simply when and because the president leaves the scene.

Conservative nationalism is a democratically oriented and civic form of patriotism: a love of a particular place, maintaining that the world is best governed by independent nation-states, and that only within the context of such states can a free citizenry experiment with constitutional forms of self-rule. In relation to foreign policy, conservative nationalists focus on preserving and promoting their own country's interests, rights, values, security, traditions, and way of life, believing it is entirely legitimate to do so. Within the United States, a kind of conservative American nationalism was the mainstream bipartisan political and foreign policy tradition for most of the country's history. But America's founders also hoped that the nation's example of popular self-government would eventually spread worldwide, and they saw no contradiction between holding out that hope, or even pressing it forward, and preserving US national sovereignty.

In the heat of World War I, President Woodrow Wilson offered a fundamental alternative to the American nationalist foreign policy tradition by arguing that the United States adopt global, binding, multilateral security commitments in order to best promote progressive liberal values internationally. And while he lost that argument in the short term, he won it posthumously one generation later, when American presidents Franklin Roosevelt and Harry Truman picked up the liberal internationalist or "globalist" banner during the 1940s, adapting it for the most part skillfully to new geopolitical, economic, and domestic conditions.

Republicans, for their part, had grave concerns about Wilson's foreign policy vision from the very beginning, along with its domestic implications. But they disagreed over how far exactly to correct or resist it. Three main GOP foreign policy options or groupings were already visible during the great debates surrounding Wilson's policies in response to World War I:

1. *Nonintervention.* Republicans like Senator Robert LaFollette (R-WI) argued for peace, disarmament, nonintervention, and strict disengagement in response to the First World War.

2. *Hawkish or hardline unilateralism.* Republicans like Senator William Borah (R-ID) argued for robust national defenses and firm responses to any intrusion on the nation's honor, while attempting to remain apart from Old World hostilities or alliances.

3. *Conservative internationalism.* Republicans like Senator Henry Cabot Lodge (R-MA) argued for vigorous responses to German aggression and postwar alliance with France and Great Britain, without making any sweeping commitments to worldwide collective security.

The interaction between these three factions or schools of thought has determined the history of Republican foreign policy approaches, whether in or out of office.

As of 1918–1919, the most common foreign policy view among Republican senators was that of Lodge, in favor of a Western alliance. But the final outcome of the League debate was essentially a victory for GOP unilateralists and noninterventionists like Borah and LaFollette. That victory informed Republican foreign policy approaches throughout the 1920s, and into the opening years of World War II. Then conservatives again divided, with one side arguing for US aid to Great Britain against Nazi Germany, and the other side opposing it. The Japanese attack on Pearl Harbor settled that debate in favor of the GOP's internationalists.

The rise of the Soviet Union after World War II only reinforced the new predominance of conservative internationalists within the GOP. Strict noninterventionists were marginalized. But in reality, hardline conservative nationalists and unilateralists had to be dragged kicking and screaming into a set of postwar US commitments overseas, and the only thing that ensured their support was a fierce anti-Communism. No subsequent Republican president was able to entirely ignore the continued force of hardline nationalism at the grassroots level, and most achieved political and policy success precisely by incorporating aspects of it into their overall approach. The specific manner in which they did so varied considerably from one president to the next. Those who failed to strike effective balances on this score—such as Senator Barry Goldwater (R-AZ)—tended to lose elections, whatever their other virtues.

In the immediate aftermath of the Cold War, the most common Republican feeling with regard to the party's foreign policy record was one of satisfaction. But already in the 1990s, noninterventionists resurfaced, led by Pat Buchanan on the one hand and libertarian Ron Paul on the other. Though they seemed marginal at the time, over the long run Buchanan in particular was prophetic. President George W. Bush managed to rally most hardline GOP nationalists to his policy of a war on terror, combined with the 2003 invasion of Iraq and a freedom agenda for the Middle East. But frustrations in Iraq raised some obvious criticisms, and once Bush left office the GOP again splintered into its most basic divisions. In 2016, insurgent candidate Donald Trump took advantage of these divisions to do what had previously seemed impossible, and upend the dominance of internationalists in favor of the other two groupings. The actual practice of the Trump administration, however, has been a hybrid or mixture of all three tendencies.

In the following chapters, I flesh out these arguments in order to trace the past, present, and—possibly—future of conservative American nationalism.

Chapter 1 sketches the outlines of US nationalism prior to the twentieth century; the liberal internationalist or globalist alternative offered by Woodrow Wilson, including subsequent variations from FDR to Barack Obama; and conservative nationalist responses since World War I. The latter includes a fuller definition of the nature and varieties of conservative American nationalism, including its recurring breakdown into the three distinct tendencies mentioned here.

Chapters 2 and 3 explore GOP presidencies from Theodore Roosevelt to George W. Bush, along with periods in opposition, to demonstrate how different Republican leaders have each combined or balanced nationalist with internationalist impulses to craft their own unique foreign policy approach. And while each GOP president has expressed it differently, conservative American nationalism—along with a repeating tension between the national and the global—has always been a powerful theme in Republican foreign policy.

The Trump phenomenon is best understood as a resurgence of one specific form of conservative American nationalism against liberal internationalism. While researching this book, I found it surprisingly difficult to locate a brief summary of the Trump administration's foreign policy, free from invective. So I decided to write one. It can be found in the middle of chapter 4. That section is preceded in the same chapter by a brief analysis of Donald Trump's incoming foreign policy assumptions, decision-making style, and 2016 presidential campaign, including how he was able to turn national security and transnational issues to his advantage in both the Republican primaries and general election. The final section of the chapter offers my own analysis of the Trump doctrine as a set of international pressure campaigns, along with some advantages and disadvantages of each. Here I make no pretense other than having a particular point of view, and simply offer my own thoughts as to the strengths and weaknesses of his chosen approach. This includes issues of alliance management, strategic unpredictability, and orientations toward world order.

Chapter 5 explores issues of populism, foreign policy, and the Republican Party—past, present, and future. A close look at public opinion polls over the past ten years reveals that a new conservative nationalism began to coalesce among many GOP voters during Barack Obama's first term in the White House. At that time, the median Republican voter remained supportive of aggressive counterterrorism and strong defense spending, while revealing increased ambivalence toward economic globalization and protracted US military interventions overseas. Internationalist candidate Mitt Romney won the 2012 GOP nomination in spite of this ambivalence. Four years later, Donald Trump tapped into and encouraged the new conservative nationalism in his own direction with distinct stands on foreign policy, trade, and immigration. Yet Republican voter opinion has remained surprisingly stable on international issues throughout this time. Even on the now highly politicized matter of US–Russia relations, most Republican voters retain a negative image of Vladimir Putin. And on free trade, the base of the party is not so much protectionist as divided.

Viewed over the longer term, however—say, by comparison with the New Deal era—there has indeed been a profound shift in the composition

of the Republican Party toward political populism, cultural conservatism, and white working-class voters. And again, Trump is not so much
the cause of this trend as an effect. What Trump has done, to an unusual extent, is to bring the policy preferences of newly empowered populist supporters into tension with orthodox conservative economics on
selected key issues. For now, he retains the support of the vast majority of
GOP voters, whether traditionally conservative or populist. But because
certain internal party differences over foreign policy, immigration, free
trade, and domestic economic issues predate his candidacy, and have now
been brought into the open, these divisions will likely outlast him as well.

The long-term future of Republican foreign policy will therefore involve and require striking effective and appropriate balances between conservative internationalist, hardline, and noninterventionist concerns. The
specific character and substance of how this is done will be up to future
conservative leaders. Donald Trump has cracked existing orthodoxies and
opened up previously latent foreign policy options. Yet his very ability to
do so indicates that he acts upon structural forces bigger than he is, and
therefore likely to persist. Or to put it another way, whether in one form
or another, conservative nationalism is here to stay.

In the concluding chapter, "Age of Iron," I describe some of the
advantages of a US-led alliance system and strategic forward presence,
along with key reasons that both the theory and practice of an associated liberal international order has come under question. The leading
reasons for this discontent are categorized and described in more detail as
economic, national, and geopolitical. I argue against any deep US disengagement overseas, and make the case for a forward-leaning conservative
American realism based upon regionally differentiated strategies of pressure against authoritarian competitors. In some ways, at least, the current
administration has pursued such an approach, and deserves credit for it.
I then outline three main areas of concern regarding the president's foreign
policy approach, centering on trade, alliances, and decision-making style.

Liberals on both sides of the Atlantic today argue that the rules-based
global order is under grave assault from the United States. But world order
has never been simply a framework of liberal rules. Rather, it has rested on

certain geopolitical underpinnings—notably, American power—which liberals themselves have regularly critiqued. There was indeed a kind of golden age of US liberal internationalism, stretching from FDR's leadership during World War II through the opening of John F. Kennedy's presidency, and it did considerable good. But that age ended over fifty years ago, in Vietnam. Ever since then, American liberals have struggled to develop robust approaches to US national security, erring on the side of excess optimism. Conservative Republicans, for their part, have made some similarly optimistic errors, most notably during 2003 in Iraq. Indeed the entire post–Cold War period may be viewed as one of excessive Wilsonian idealism. But now that Wilsonian quarter-century is definitely over. Both the United States, its allies, and its adversaries appear to have entered a new era of geopolitical competition. The new era is characterized by intensified great-power rivalry, resurgent nationalisms both authoritarian and democratic, popular skepticism regarding the benefits of globalization, shifts in focus from the Atlantic to the Pacific, and severe challenges to American primacy from multiple directions. Donald Trump's presidency is more an effect of all these trends than their primary cause. In truth, the golden age of liberal internationalism ended some time ago. This is the age of iron.

Nationalism, Internationalism, and American Conservatives

Prior to Woodrow Wilson's presidency, the mainstream and bipartisan US foreign policy tradition was one of American nationalism. This tradition valued the strict preservation of US national sovereignty, and the expansion of republican forms of government, preferably by example, but also through US territorial and commercial expansion. Key figures such as George Washington, John Quincy Adams, and Abraham Lincoln showed a kind of geopolitical awareness regarding America's international surroundings. Out of the catalyst of World War I, President Woodrow Wilson offered a fundamental alternative to the US nationalist tradition. He argued that only through a new set of global, binding, and multilateral commitments could liberal values be served. This Wilsonian or US liberal internationalist tradition lost politically in the short term, but eventually became a leading influence on American foreign policy over the course of the next century. In particular, Presidents Franklin Roosevelt and Harry Truman adopted and revised it during the 1940s in a more hard-nosed direction to counter first the Axis powers and then the Soviet Union. American frustrations in Vietnam led to a liberal splintering, and a new school of thought emphasizing international accommodation. Most conservative Republicans, for their part, never entirely embraced all aspects of the Wilsonian tradition, but wrestled with how far to correct or resist it. Conservative American nationalism is essentially the GOP's answer to Woodrow Wilson, and it has come in multiple varieties.

AMERICAN NATIONALISM

Nationalism is a form of collective identity with both cultural and political aspects. Academics tend to emphasize the way in which it is imagined, invented, or subject to manipulation. They also tend to emphasize the grave dangers of nationalism. And of course there are certain versions of nationalism that really are exceptionally violent, aggressive, and authoritarian, based upon the image of a single ethnic group as racially superior and imperial by right. The memory of the 1930s and of the wartime struggle against fascists has informed all reflection on nationalism ever since.

Yet the mainstream Western tradition, going back to the ancient world, includes a civic conception of nationalism that is far more benign. In this civic conception nationalism is essentially patriotism, or love of country, based upon an affectionate identification with a particular place, a particular way of life, and a particular set of lawful institutions that sustain the common liberty. For civic nationalists the enemy is not ethnic contamination, but rather domestic tyranny, corruption, and any foreign adversary who threatens the republic. In the early modern era, European philosophers in this civic tradition argued that the world was best governed by independent nation-states, precisely in order to protect the freedoms of both countries and individuals. The belief was that every nation had its own traditions worth preserving—and that only within the context of a sovereign nation-state could individual citizens experiment with versions of republican or constitutional rule. This belief eventually had immense impact worldwide, helping to reorder the international system along lines of national sovereignty and self-determination. And whatever the limitations of the nation-state, in terms of allowing for democratic forms of popular self-government, no superior form of political organization has yet been found.[1]

American nationalism, properly understood, is a form of civic nationalism. To be sure, as a matter of historical record, the original American
colonies were founded by English Protestant settlers, and this specific cultural and religious heritage was the context for US founding principles.
Over the years, some US nationalists have defined their identity mainly
in religious or ethnic terms. This has long encouraged tensions between
an ethnic definition of the American nation and a civic one.[2] Yet in their
declaration of independence the American revolutionaries said that "all
men are created equal," and they said so deliberately. In other words, they
justified their rebellion in part by claiming natural rights based upon universal truths, and these claims were informed by beliefs well described as
classically liberal. There has consequently been within the United States,
from the very beginning, a kind of "American creed," civic religion, or
national identity with classical liberal elements, including the rule of law,
individual freedom, majority rule, equality of right, enterprise, progress, and limited government. As nineteenth-century Marxists such as
Frederick Engels noted, that classical liberal creed made it very difficult
to promote socialism within the United States. This is what Engels meant
by American exceptionalism, and he found it exceptionally frustrating.[3]

In terms of its worldwide implications, the leaders of the American
Revolution hoped that it would encourage the spread of republican forms
of government and the creation of a new international system characterized
by peaceful commercial exchange, individual liberty, the rule of law, and
human progress. They rejected the eighteenth-century European state
system as corrupt, militaristic, warlike, and autocratic. Of course, the
question was inevitably how to interact with states still a part of that Old
World system. To varying degrees, the Founders and succeeding generations embraced America's westward continental expansion, to create what
Thomas Jefferson described as an "empire of liberty." They also embraced
commercial opportunities overseas. In this sense, US economic and territorial expansion beyond existing boundaries long predated America's
later rise to global power. Simultaneously, however, these very same early
statesmen cherished the preservation of US national sovereignty, and for
that matter held to a policy of disengagement from European alliances, a

policy best laid out formally by George Washington in his 1796 Farewell Address when he said that "the great rule of conduct for us in regard to foreign nations is in extending our commercial relations, to have with them as little political connection as possible." This emphasis on avoiding what Jefferson called "entangling alliances" became a key component of US foreign policy throughout the nineteenth century. Early American statesmen saw no contradiction between expanding the sphere of republican governments, and preserving US national sovereignty.[4]

Partisan political debate over the precise foreign policy implications of American nationalism was evident from the very start. Thomas Jefferson and Alexander Hamilton agreed on American exceptionalism, US national sovereignty, and the long-term expansion of republican governments. They did not agree on its exact foreign policy implications. Whereas Jefferson envisioned the United States as a vast, decentralized, agrarian republic, Hamilton looked to encourage a centralized treasury and nascent US manufacturing, along with other apparatus of state power in the international arena including professional standing armed forces. During the 1790s Jefferson tended to sympathize with revolutionary France; Hamilton, with Great Britain. It was precisely these differences between Jefferson and the Federalists that Washington hoped to quell in issuing his Farewell Address. To his mind, one advantage of US nonentanglement overseas was the avoidance of domestic factional controversies inside the United States.

Each round of nineteenth-century US territorial expansion was typically characterized by some significant internal debate over whether said expansion was constitutional, cost-effective, or appropriate. These genuine philosophical differences were often bound up with sectional interests and party politics—along with support of, or opposition to, individual presidents. And presidents sometimes acted aggressively to direct American territorial expansion. Jefferson, for example, decried the centralization of executive authority, but when the opportunity presented itself in 1803 to purchase the vast Louisiana territory from France he did so, admitting he stretched the constitution until it cracked. Later waves of attempted territorial expansion and US warfare against Britain, Mexico, and Native

American tribes brought intense controversy and debate, pitting those Americans who favored expansion against those who did not. Both sides often argued that the other was untrue to America's founding principles.

Early American expansion was therefore powered by a number of central factors. It was powered by land-hunger. It was powered by the search for commercial opportunity. It was powered by the relative weakness of surrounding neighbors. It was powered by a common Anglo-American belief, at the time, in their own superiority as a people. It was powered by sectional interests, partisan debate, and genuine differences over the relative merits of specific acts of national self-assertion. And it was powered by the desire to promote the spread of a republican form of government. In practice, early American nationalism encompassed all of these things. Nor were US ambitions limited to their own continent. Americans hoped to see the creation and encouragement of a friendly system of republican regimes throughout Latin America. The 1823 Monroe Doctrine, conceived primarily by Secretary of State John Quincy Adams, clarified that the United States would at least in principle oppose any further European colonial interventions or annexations within the Western hemisphere.

It would be a mistake, however, to think that the United States in these early years was entirely immune from geopolitical pressures and national security anxieties—or that early American statesmen were utterly unaware of such considerations. America's position in between two great oceans did make it relatively safe and secure, but only by a difference of degree. The United States had no absolute security, and as Americans rediscovered in 1814 when the White House was burnt down by the British, the loss of control over nearby waters could be a pathway for attacks upon the United States. Even the idealistic Jefferson understood that the security of the New World depended upon a division and balance of power within the Old. Moreover, early American continental expansion was sometimes driven as much by security concerns—or fear of great-power encirclement—as by any other consideration, and this fear had deep roots in colonial experience, for example during the French and Indian wars. Early nineteenth-century Americans feared that the still-mighty British Empire could use surrounding military and naval bases in Canada and the Caribbean to occupy, raid, harass, and blockade the United States, and of course during the War of 1812 this is precisely what happened. The argument for war against Mexico in 1846—like the argument for the annexations of Florida, Oregon, and Texas—was at least partly defensive. The westward continental expansion of American explorers, hunters, trappers, and settlers was encouraged by the federal government partly to ensure that US citizens reached and occupied these vast trans-Mississippi territories before any European power did. Americans were determined to prevent any balance of power from forming on their own continent. Hamilton and Jefferson did not disagree on this point. The United States would be predominant in North America. There would be a balance of power in the Old World—not in the New.[5]

The tension between liberty and union, and the exact meaning of American national identity, were brought into sharp relief by the question of whether newly acquired western territories would be open to slavery. The Republican Party was founded on the understanding that slavery be confined to the South. More broadly, Republicans shared an ideology that emphasized social harmony and order, mercantilism, economic growth, free labor, and American nationalism. Abraham Lincoln ran and won on this platform in 1860, triggering the secession of Southern states from the Union. The resulting Civil War opened up the possibility of renewed European intervention in the Americas, and to some extent such interventions actually happened. France took advantage of America's wartime disunity to intervene in Mexico—a spectacle that very much worried Lincoln. Skillful Union diplomacy helped stave off more direct European aid to the Confederacy, and in truth the British had little interest in going to war with the United States. The war itself resolved some central questions: slavery would be abolished. In effect, the American creed was redefined to include a fuller application of declared US founding principles to African Americans. As Lincoln noted in his second inaugural address, neither the North nor the South had initially sought this outcome. Yet the war revealed a new American nation in other ways as well. Under Lincoln's leadership the Union was revealed as a newly coherent, organized nation-state, heavily armed, capable of fielding extensive and successful battle-hardened armies with broad popular support. In this sense the Civil War resolved not only the issue of slavery and the issue of union, but also the issue of which great-power or assortment of powers would be dominant on the North American continent—an issue of evident concern to Lincoln. With the North's victory in 1865, any possibility of a balance of power on that continent was removed. Paradoxically, this eventually led to somewhat improved relations with the British Empire, since London had to recognize the resulting power imbalance within North America as well.[6]

In 1898, American nationalism was expressed in yet another form. President McKinley had not previously possessed any notion of going to war with Spain. But when the USS Maine exploded in the harbor of Havana that February many Americans concluded that Spain was the culprit, and demanded US military action to liberate Cuban rebels from Spanish rule. McKinley oversaw and channeled this determination effectively, leading a war effort that ended in US military victories over Spanish forces located in Cuba, Puerto Rico, and the Philippines. On the question of what to do with these newly seized territories, most Americans were happy to see US influence extended over Cuba and Puerto Rico in the Caribbean. The case of the Philippines was more controversial. This was far more of a stretch geographically, and to determined anti-imperialists such as Mark Twain and William Graham Sumner, the whole exercise seemed an abandonment of US foreign policy and constitutional traditions. In this sense, Sumner described the war's outcome ironically as the "conquest of the United States by Spain."[7] Anti-imperialists often argued that the Filipinos were racially inferior, and therefore unfit to be brought into an American system of rule. But a new wave of US nationalists, led by figures like Theodore Roosevelt, argued that the acquisition of the Philippines was indicative of America's new international role; necessary to secure access to the vast China market, while staving off Japanese or European advances in the region; potentially beneficial to the Filipinos themselves, under enlightened rule; and the logical extension of previous US expansion westward across the North American continent. In the end McKinley was convinced of these arguments, and so assumed US control over the Philippines under

a peace treaty with Spain. Most Americans quickly tired of the momen-
tary enthusiastic outburst for war and empire, and the Philippines was
left as something of a strategic liability for the United States, practically
indefensible if attacked—a weak spot in the US posture with long-term
consequences. Nevertheless, the Spanish-American War had indeed revealed the United States as a potential global power with some impressive
military capabilities and the ability to project them across oceans. No new
multilateral commitments were made.[8]

Even as it was consolidating its overseas acquisitions from Spain, the
McKinley administration issued a new US foreign policy principle in
relation to China, with broad implications. The American fear was that
Europe's great powers—together with Japan—would join in formally
partitioning China, as Europeans had already partitioned Africa. This
would shut out US exports, and violate American hopes for the Chinese.
Secretary of State John Hay responded by issuing a series of notes in 1899,
calling upon other nations to respect the territorial integrity and independence of China, together with open and equal economic access for
all. Hay's declaration of this "Open Door" policy was viewed as a great
success within the United States, gaining immediate and bipartisan support for the principle. US diplomatic historians have tended to see it as
tremendously significant. And to be sure, it captured longstanding US
aspirations toward a kind of benign informal empire of commercially interdependent sovereign nations, not only in East Asia but beyond. But in
reality, Hay's Open Door declaration had limited impact on the ground
inside China, where European colonial powers, the Japanese empire, local
nationalists, and Qing dynasty officials wrestled for influence amidst increasingly chaotic conditions. The Open Door policy was certainly indicative of American national ambitions, but at least in relation to China, the
United States had little ability to enforce them.[9]

Taken as a whole, the United States entered the twentieth century
with a foreign policy posture characterized by the aggressive promotion of US trade and investment overseas; an intense belief in American
exceptionalism; a small standing army; a growing blue-water navy; effective hegemony on the North American continent; an increasingly

preponderant role within the Caribbean; declared special interests in China, the Philippines, and Latin America; and a strict detachment from European wars and alliances. For the most part, politically influential Americans in both major parties still revered George Washington's Farewell Address, John Quincy Adams's Monroe Doctrine, John Hay's Open Door, and saw no need to radically overhaul these organizing principles—or any contradiction between them. The strict protection of US national sovereignty was viewed as incompatible with neither the promotion of republican forms of government overseas, nor the promotion of US strategic and economic interests. These were some of the central tenets of a broadly held American nationalism in relation to the country's foreign policy as the United States entered the twentieth century.

LIBERAL INTERNATIONALISM

The classical liberal tradition in international relations has deep historical roots, but first flourished intellectually during Europe's Enlightenment. Toward the end of the eighteenth century, the German philosopher Immanuel Kant suggested that a "perpetual peace" might eventually be attained through the spread of cosmopolitan law and republican forms of government. This vision gained strength among liberals over the course of the nineteenth century and into the twentieth. The liberal internationalist tradition maintains that popular self-government, growing economic interdependence, and international law act as three mutually reinforcing factors in favor of peace between nations. According to liberals, democratic governments do not go to war with one another because their publics restrain them from doing so, and because they see one another as no threat. Growing material interdependence, through peaceful civilian commercial exchange, also creates economic ties between trading nations that are costly to break. And international legal institutions encourage predictability, normative restraint, and reasonable recourse with regard to interstate disputes. At least these are the traditional liberal internationalist claims, and of course they have had tremendous impact worldwide,

especially over the past century. Liberals believe that positive change, progress, and evolution in the very nature of international order is possible—
perhaps even inevitable—away from the power politics of the past. It is a
vision that is essentially universalistic, hopeful, and cosmopolitan.[10]

Within the United States, as we have already seen, hopes for the worldwide spread of popular government go back to the nation's founding.
Having taken the Philippines from Spain, American officials did try to
democratize it. They further believed that the spread of peaceful commercial exchange and US economic influence would help transform the
international system in a peaceful, democratic direction. By the end of
the nineteenth century there was growing upper-middle-class interest
in concepts of international arbitration, arms control, and an organized
peace movement. At the same time, contemporary American statesmen
placed a very high priority on the strict preservation of US national sovereignty. In practice they had little interest in binding America's freedom
of action through multilateral organization. Nor did they have the capacity to authorize massive US military interventions on behalf of liberal ideals over a truly global scale—or any interest in doing so. American
foreign policy therefore remained predominantly nationalist, rather than
globalist, well into the early twentieth century. The real break came with
Woodrow Wilson and the American response to the First World War.[11]

President Wilson entered the White House determined to pursue domestic progressive reforms, with no interest whatsoever in taking part in
European conflicts. But after several years of trying to avoid deepening US
intervention across the Atlantic, in the wake of German submarine attacks
against American shipping, Wilson finally led the United States into war.
He explained and conceived of this decision in terms of America's ability
not only to help defeat Germany militarily but to lead in the creation of a
transformed global order characterized by democratic governments, national self-determination, collective security, open trading arrangements,
freedom of the seas, multilateral organization, the peaceful settlement of
disputes, and general disarmament. A new League of Nations was to be
the capstone of this new US-led order, containing at its heart what Wilson
envisioned as a "virtual guarantee of territorial integrity and political

independence" for every member state.[12] Wilson's great innovation was not simply to argue that American liberal values needed to be vindicated by force on the European continent, though this was dramatic enough in itself. Nor was it simply to tie his League project to the achievement of progressive reforms inside the United States, though he did that as well. His innovation was also to say that only through binding, universal, and formal multilateral commitments on the part of the United States could progressive liberal values be vindicated—worldwide. In the end, the US Senate refused to pass the Versailles Treaty by the required two-thirds vote. But Wilson had laid down a marker, ideologically, that would not disappear. In fact, the Wilsonian vision would become an animating force in American foreign policy, both politically and internationally, over the course of the next hundred years.[13]

The next Democratic president, Franklin Roosevelt, was largely preoccupied with the Great Depression and New Deal reforms during his early years in office. But the onset of war in Europe led FDR into a series of foreign policy initiatives effectively bringing the United States into informal alliance with Winston Churchill's Britain, against Nazi Germany. Even before the Japanese attack on Pearl Harbor, with the August 1941 Atlantic Charter, Churchill and Roosevelt described their overall wartime purpose as that of saving and promoting a humane international order based upon democratic governance, freedom of the seas, national self-determination, open trading arrangements, and the punishment of territorial aggression. In other words, America's declared wartime goals were essentially Wilsonian, and at least in FDR's case, there is every indication that he meant it.[14] However, Roosevelt was considerably more pragmatic and canny than Woodrow Wilson—both at home and abroad—in pursuing these ultimate goals. At home, he cultivated GOP support where he could find it, and anticipated Republican concerns regarding any postwar erosion of US national sovereignty in part by making serious accommodations to these concerns. This helped put American support for a new League—the United Nations—on more solid footing, both politically and on its own merits.[15] For the most part, FDR's management of the overall US war effort was strong. The one major exception was in his unrealistic expectation for postwar cooperation with Josef Stalin's USSR. FDR and many other contemporary US officials privately hoped and believed that Stalin could be eased into a great-power concert based upon "open," liberal spheres of influence for every major power.[16] Stalin certainly looked for a Soviet sphere of influence in Eastern Europe, and was willing to bargain pragmatically for it, but he had no intention of leaving this sphere open to liberal American designs. Moreover, as a true Marxist-Leninist, Stalin viewed long-term conflict with the United States and other capitalist powers as inevitable.[17] After FDR's death in 1945, it was left for Harry Truman to decide how to handle the inevitable tension between American postwar aims and Soviet ones.

Like Roosevelt, President Truman initially hoped to continue postwar cooperation with Moscow. But Stalin's refusal to allow free and fair elections in occupied Poland, and his aggressive probing of Western positions around Turkey and Iran, convinced Truman that such cooperation was impossible. The new hard line was best articulated by US diplomat George Kennan, who argued for the containment of Soviet influence through a series of moving counterpressures.[18] As implemented by the Truman administration incrementally over time, containment involved a set of unprecedented economic, diplomatic, and military commitments by the United States in Europe, the Middle East, and the Asia-Pacific. These commitments included new peacetime military alliances (NATO, Japan, South Korea, ANZUS), extensive foreign aid programs (e.g., the Marshall Plan), membership in a wide range of international organizations, and the long-term maintenance of a large standing army for the first time in American history. The overall purpose of the strategy was both to counterbalance Soviet power, and to nurture the eventual development of an integrated American-led bloc of allied and market-oriented liberal democracies outside of the Soviet sphere. US anti-Soviet containment therefore had a strong Wilsonian component. But it also had a clear balance-of-power aspect, as well as an ideologically anti-Communist one, and without these other aspects it is highly unlikely that most Americans or their political leaders would have found the need for such expensive commitments to be necessary and persuasive. For Truman administration officials, including the president, the primary purpose of containment and its associated commitments was ultimately to promote US national security.[19]

No less important than US security commitments under the Truman administration's strategy of containment was American leadership in a new set of multilateral economic organizations designed to help promote open international order. Even in the depths of the Great Depression, after an initial sharp emphasis on trade protection, FDR had initiated significant reductions in US tariff barriers—a longstanding Democratic Party preference—by signing bilateral free-trade agreements with multiple countries. Congress meanwhile began to defer more to executive leadership on trade, revealing a certain degree of self-restraint. Both institutionally and ideologically, the dominance of protectionist ideas was broken. This movement toward American leadership of a more open global order was accelerated by the events of the Second World War, during which Britain and the United States agreed to establish a novel international economic framework at Bretton Woods. The new International Monetary Fund would manage exchange rates and payment imbalances. The new World Bank would provide loans to governments in need. And beginning in 1948, the new General Agreement on Tariffs and Trade (GATT) would work to reduce worldwide tariff barriers through successive rounds of multilateral negotiation. Altogether, the United States—through this system—would aim to promote a more open international economic order outside of the Soviet sphere, characterized by convertible currencies, freer trade, and fixed exchange rates. The United States would now play the role of stabilizing economic hegemon, by offering allies and partners improved access to its vast domestic market; through generous foreign assistance programs; and by utilizing the dollar as the key international currency. Under this new system, it was understood that allies including the United States would retain ample ability to protect domestic autonomy, escape provisions, and nationally distinct economic objectives. A strict abandonment of all barriers to trade would have been unacceptable to every major participant. Under these new arrangements, international activity by US multinationals once again flourished, and foreign trade grew in its relative importance to the American economy. The United States was hardly all-powerful under this system. America could not achieve everything it wanted. Still, after a generation of delay including two world wars, the United States finally replaced Great Britain as the world's leading actor in finance and trade.[20]

Truman's foreign policy involved not only international political shifts, but domestic ones as well. Specifically, mainstream liberal Democrats had to be enlisted behind a hawkish anti-Communist foreign policy. Since mainstream Democrats were able to observe Soviet international behavior about as well as Truman, for the most part this was no great challenge. Those on the far left of the Democratic Party, however, led by Henry Wallace, continued to champion a comprehensive accommodation with Stalin. Indeed Wallace went so far as to secretly meet with the NKVD station chief in Washington, DC, in the naïve hope of easing such accommodation.[21] After being let go as Secretary of Commerce, Wallace broke with Truman to run as a third-party Progressive presidential candidate in 1948, on the premise that the emerging Cold War was primarily America's own fault. Even the American socialist Norman Thomas realized and openly said at the time that this premise was mistaken, since democratic socialists frequently understood better than anyone how murderously flawed the Stalinist system actually was. It was important politically for mainstream liberal Democrats to be disabused of the notion that US foreign policy was more of a threat than Soviet Communism. This was one of Truman's most significant accomplishments. Indeed, within the context of the early Cold War, many anti-Communist New Deal and Fair Deal Democrats positively demanded it.[22]

In retrospect, the 1940s was a golden age of US liberal internationalism, though it certainly seemed tumultuous and difficult at the time. The very disillusionment of the interwar era had produced a chastened and toughened idealism in the end, resting on more solid footing than Wilson's earlier version. Two Democratic presidents in a row now provided effective foreign policy leadership more often than not. Both made mistakes, to be sure. And like any other, their approach carried the seeds of its own weaknesses. Still, FDR and Truman successfully built broad popular support for their preferred foreign policy initiatives—including Republican support where possible—and led the public, rather than simply following it. Indeed their sensitivity to GOP concerns actually made their policies better. The new foreign policy paradigm earned broad popular support, informed by the lessons of the 1930s, cemented by a growing elite consensus, and made plausible by international events.

FDR, Truman, and many of their leading foreign policy advisers possessed an instinctive geopolitical sensibility and an explicit understanding that totalitarian powers could not be permitted to dominate the landmass of Eurasia. Both presidents also said and understood that the American experiment in constitutionalism at home might not survive a world dominated by dictatorships. Both made sure to follow national security strategies that did not create an authoritarian garrison state within the United States. Both presidents pursued multilateral solutions where possible, but had no qualms about unilateral action when necessary—as it often was. Nor did the Democratic presidents of the 1940s entirely reject the American nationalism of preceding generations. On the contrary, in certain ways they built upon it. FDR and Truman shared the traditional national belief in American exceptionalism, and in a special mission for the United States, when formulating their international agenda. Truman in particular had a straightforward, border-state Jacksonian sensibility that he incorporated into his bold foreign policy approach. In practical terms, neither president ruled out regime change as one possible solution to severe international security dilemmas, either in relation to the Axis powers, or—after 1946—toward the Soviet Communist bloc. Democracy promotion was a key aspect of their policies. But they also tried to be prudent about how best to pursue such long-term possibilities. Sometimes, prudence ultimately dictated the forcible defeat and occupation of intransigent forces, such as Nazi Germany. Sometimes it recommended containment, rather than direct military rollback. The long-term hope for a more benign world order remained the same. Clearly, in the process FDR and Truman abandoned Thomas Jefferson's ancient warning against entangling alliances. But in a way their purpose was to help encourage internationally what Jefferson himself favored. Namely: an empire of liberty.[23]

President John F. Kennedy maintained and pushed forward a version of liberal internationalism at least as ambitious as that of Harry Truman. Indeed Kennedy and his leading foreign policy advisers had high expectations that the United States could help midwife positive social change in developing countries, by force if necessary, away from Communism and toward a liberal democratic model. Vietnam was to be a test case for this theory, a cause embraced by Kennedy's successor Lyndon Johnson, however reluctantly.[24] Subsequent wartime frustrations in that country—combined with new political alignments within the United States over issues such as civil rights—helped to tear apart the old New Deal coalition and break down America's Cold War consensus. Northern liberal Democrats, in particular, began to seriously question the premises of anti-Communist containment as an organizing principle for US foreign policy, not only in relation to Vietnam but beyond. A new school of thought developed with regard to American foreign policy, variously described by political scientists as post–Cold War liberal internationalism or "accommodationism."[25] Accommodationists believed that a militant anti-Communism had steered the United States wrong in Vietnam and beyond. They argued for a demilitarization of US foreign policy, strict constraints on the CIA, diplomatic accommodation of onetime adversaries, and a new emphasis on issues such as human rights, Third World development, and the environment. Following Richard Nixon's inauguration in 1969, this school of thought was free to flourish on the center-left. With the notable exception of a few US senators such as Henry "Scoop" Jackson (D-WA), Northern liberal Democrats moved in a decidedly dovish direction. The nomination of George McGovern for president in 1972 confirmed the ascendance of this new direction within the Democratic Party.[26] Four years later, Georgia Governor Jimmy Carter ran for and won the presidency on a platform that straddled internal Democratic Party divides. While he had a few very capable advisers—notably national security advisor Zbigniew Brzezinksi—Carter never managed to create or sustain a successful overall foreign policy strategy. The essential problem was that while post–Cold War liberal internationalists might want to move beyond superpower competition, the Soviet Union did not. As this realization sank in, Carter himself shifted back toward a more traditional Cold War stance. But by the time he ran for re-election, it was too late to restore lost impressions of solidity. This image of weakness on national security issues would continue to plague Democratic presidential candidates throughout the 1980s. All things considered, a specifically progressive internationalism went through some severe challenges from the mid-1960s until the end of the Cold War.[27]

The collapse of the Soviet Union allowed new opportunities for post-Vietnam liberal internationalists to argue that their moment had finally arrived. Beginning in 1993, President Bill Clinton pursued a foreign policy emphasizing international engagement, continued US forward presence, democracy promotion, institution-building, assertive multilateralism, peacekeeping, globalization, open markets, and humanitarian intervention. Clinton made it clear there would be no dismantling of America's world role in the wake of the Cold War's end. Indeed his administration championed the concept of expanding or enlarging a US-friendly zone of market democracies worldwide. At the same time, he regularly attempted to pursue ambitious liberal internationalist goals at minimal cost, creating significant US policy gaps or contradictions in numerous cases. Defense spending was cut even as missions proliferated. With regard to cases of peacekeeping, nation-building, and humanitarian intervention in Somalia, Haiti, Bosnia, and Kosovo, Clinton met several bumps in the road, resolved more successfully in the Balkans than elsewhere. With regard to China, Clinton soon dialed back his initial rhetoric on human rights, instead stressing diplomatic and economic engagement. In relation to Russia, Clinton also stressed engagement in the hopes of nudging forward a post-Communist democratic transition. With regard to foreign economic policy, Clinton initially sustained serious political costs in order to champion free-trade initiatives such as the North American Free Trade Agreement (NAFTA), allowing further advancements to stall once the depth of anti-globalization feeling on the Left became evident. And with regard to rogue states such as North Korea and Iran, eventually relabeled states of concern, the United States embraced diplomatic efforts while trying to uphold containment. Only in relation to Saddam

Hussein's Iraq did the Clinton administration reject diplomacy and formally embrace the goal of regime change. In the end, Clinton managed to straddle internal Democratic Party divides between hawks and doves more successfully than Carter had done, and to improve his foreign policy management skills over time, thus ending his two terms with relatively solid public approval ratings on international issues.[28]

The terrorist attacks of 2001 temporarily threw liberal Democrats off-balance on issues of national security. But President Bush's decision to invade Iraq—together with subsequent wartime frustrations—eventually rallied Democrats around a new foreign policy message. Barack Obama ran for president in 2008 on the premise that a more multilateral and less militarized US approach would reap benefits internationally, permitting what he called nation-building at home. As president Obama engaged in diplomatic outreach toward numerous foreign autocracies, with mixed results. An attempted reset with Russia ended in frustration, as Vladimir Putin pocketed the gains and proceeded to fresh aggressions. Engagement with China did not prevent that rising colossus from asserting itself economically worldwide, or militarily in nearby waters. The administration soon cycled back to reassuring US allies through a stated "pivot" to Asia, but engagement with China remained the American baseline. In relation to Iran, the Obama administration concluded a nuclear arms agreement. Longstanding US sanctions on Cuba were partially lifted. American defense spending was cut, in agreement with Congress, under the Budget Control Act of 2011. Politically, Obama's aversion to new large-scale US military interventions fit with public preferences, and the successful raid on Osama Bin Laden's secret compound allowed the president to solidify a winning foreign policy message heading into his re-election campaign. But second-term foreign policy frustrations and setbacks with regard to Syria, Ukraine, and the Islamic State undermined the impression of strength, especially on matters of counterterrorism. In the end Obama's foreign policy record was viewed favorably by Democrats, much less so by Republicans or independents.[29]

Finally, during the late twentieth and very early twenty-first century US liberal internationalism was intellectually buttressed and revised through the development of new scholarly schools of thought in its favor. Beginning in the 1970s, and in keeping with post-Vietnam liberal internationalist thinking, authors such as Robert Keohane and Joseph Nye argued that the rise of nonstate actors, nontraditional issues, and transnational ties under conditions of economic interdependence had led to a world in which the use of force would be less relevant. A chief imperative would henceforth be to manage this complex interdependence through the agenda-setting power of international institutions.[30] Keohane expanded on this line of thought in the 1980s by laying out in greater detail the argument that multilateral regimes and institutions might allow for the persistence of international cooperation even after the decline of American hegemony. Nation-states would be able, he argued, to pursue their own self-interest—along with global public goods—at less cost, with better information, and with more predictability, by acting through multilateral regimes and institutions.[31]

The classical liberal optimism of the post–Cold War moment was best captured by Francis Fukuyama, who described a long-term trend wherein every ideological-political alternative to liberal democratic capitalism had been defeated or exhausted.[32] Liberal internationalist scholars within the United States emphasized new possibilities for collective security, global governance, peacekeeping, humanitarian action, democracy promotion, assertive multilateralism, cuts in US defense spending, international economic development efforts, and a strengthened United Nations. The European Union was frequently held up as an example of where the nature of international politics could, should, and likely would be headed. John Ruggie suggested that a multilateral foreign policy approach, grounded in a cosmopolitan US domestic identity, was the one way to secure American engagement overseas and overcome the traditional logic of balance of power.[33] John Ikenberry argued that by restraining and binding itself through multilateral practices, making its power more acceptable and less fearful to others, the United States could help to promote and maintain a cooperative and liberal world order.[34] And in response to the George W. Bush presidency, Joseph Nye added the concept of "soft power" to the internationalist lexicon. Specifically, Nye argued that by working through multilateral institutions, setting a good example domestically, worrying less about US sovereignty, and avoiding unilateral actions unless absolutely necessary, the United States could avert international counterbalancing coalitions and better promote its own influence overseas.[35] Altogether, liberal internationalist scholars in the post–Cold War era placed great emphasis on the need for the United States to act multilaterally. Moreover, this emphasis had some practical implications, as it was taken up by leading policymakers in both the Clinton and Obama administrations. Secretary of State Hillary Clinton spoke for most liberal internationalists when she emphasized in a 2009 address to the Council on Foreign Relations the prioritized need to help solve common global problems through institutionalized multilateral cooperation on the part of the United States.[36] The fact that this position was long since viewed by that time as simply common sense only indicated its conceptual predominance. In essence, liberal internationalists argued that the very nature of world politics had progressed, changed, or evolved in a liberal direction.

CONSERVATIVE NATIONALISM

American conservative nationalism only emerged explicitly in response to Woodrow Wilson's foreign policy innovations. Prior to that there was no need for it, since its central tenets were held by the vast majority in both major US political parties. In practice, there have been multiple versions of conservative US nationalism, and their waxing and waning helps to explain the particular shape of the GOP at any point in time. Some versions owe more to classical conservative beliefs and assumptions, historically common throughout the Western world. But all US versions wrestle with the distinctly American question of how best to promote popular forms of self-government overseas. All versions furthermore tend to place greater emphasis than do liberal internationalists on the preservation of US national sovereignty. This may be defined as a condition by which the people of the United States—through their elected delegates in government, and under existing American laws—are self-governing, independent, in

effective control of their own territory, able to autonomously form relations with other countries, free from external interference, and recognized
as such.

The Danish scholar Carsten Holbraad points out that conservative
nationalism regarding foreign policy has been one prominent strain of
thought in Europe for roughly two hundred years. According to Holbraad,
the defining characteristics of a defensive conservative nationalism are
adherence to the European state system, political realism, and concepts
of nationality against progressive forms of supranational governance.
European conservative nationalists favor nation-state sovereignty, the
existing international order, and the pursuit of national interests, rights,
values, and security as lodestones of foreign policy. Leading historical
examples of conservative nationalists include George Canning, Benjamin
Disraeli, Charles De Gaulle, and Margaret Thatcher. This strain of thinking
developed in two great waves, first in the nineteenth century, and again in
the wake of World War II. In its post-1945 form, as with Thatcher and De
Gaulle—and even earlier, in the case of Disraeli's Britain—it is entirely
compatible with democratic forms of government.[37]

A democratically oriented nationalism often relies upon classical
conservative assumptions. Classical conservatives in both Europe and
America tend to have a limited or skeptical vision of what government
action can achieve. This flows from a belief that human nature is for all
practical purposes both imperfect and fixed, rendering perfectionist or
utopian political visions not only unachievable but positively dangerous.
Classical conservatives note the negative unintended consequences that
often follow major political or social reforms. They emphasize tradition
and custom, by suggesting that the wisdom of generations is worth at
least as much as individual reason. They stress social and political order
as an underlying bulwark of freedom. They believe in a central buffering
and supporting role for intermediate social institutions such as church
and family between the lone individual and the state. Traditionally,
conservatives do not believe that democracy should be unconstrained.
They distrust unchecked power in all directions, and therefore look for
filters on popular majorities as well as on elites, notably through the rule

of law and legal forms. They place special emphasis on the preservation of private property. They may very well support equal rights under the law, but have little interest or belief in the possibility of socioeconomic equality of condition. They look to history for inspiration and instruction. They generally respect the public role of religion, regardless of private belief. And they invariably embrace love of country or patriotism as a healthy and worthwhile passion.[38]

With regard to international politics, classical conservatives tend to be skeptical of transformational possibilities, and doubtful that international organizations, political reforms, or written treaties will bring about an era of perpetual peace. They place great emphasis on protecting their own country's particular interests, along with its way of life, and see this as quite legitimate. In fact they believe you must first love your own country, along with what Edmund Burke called the "little platoons" of local community, in order to properly embrace broader human affections. This leaves classical conservatives as instinctive civic nationalists in many respects. They endeavor to defend their nation's independence of action in relation to external challenges. They frequently resist major cessions of their country's sovereignty to transnational institutions. They view the international arena as a rather dangerous place, and believe the threat of force unlikely to be eliminated from it altogether. As a result, they place importance on the maintenance of military preparedness and reputation. Classical conservatives respect both the constraints and traditions of professional soldiers. And they are often reluctant warriors, cautious in resorting to armed intervention, and disinclined to see the military as a tool for social or political transformation.[39]

The American Revolution contained some classically conservative elements, in the sense that many revolutionaries believed they were fighting for their traditional rights as Englishmen. Most of America's founders did not reject their country's premodern Western inheritance, including common law, biblical, and civic republican legacies. Yet the United States also grew out of a revolutionary experience partly rooted in classical liberal concepts.[40] The country's founders believed—and many Americans have subsequently believed—that human beings are capable of

at least some political progress, and that the United States has a special interest and role to play internationally in promoting that progress through
the spread of popular self-government. This is what is generally meant by
the phrase "American exceptionalism" with reference to US foreign policy.
In a sense this is a classically liberal belief, rather than a classically conservative one, and it has been a powerful component of US foreign policy
from the very beginning. All efforts to develop a distinctly conservative
US foreign policy approach consequently wrestle with balancing traditional conservative insights and classical liberal ones. And there has never
been any one lasting solution to this challenge.

Conservative American nationalism therefore contains some distinctive features. It starts from a desire to preserve the American republic,
in a form not impossibly distant from the one created by its founders.
This includes key elements such as the rule of law, individual liberty,
constitutionalism, and a limited form of government. In other words, it
is an overall foreign policy perspective linked to a broadly conservative
view on key political questions. Abroad, conservative US nationalists
have always harbored the hope that the American example of popular
self-government would spread. Yet precisely how to encourage that has
always been a matter of lively debate within the conservative nationalist tradition. Far more so than most countries, America embodies
an idea—an idea of freedom. But America is also a particular place,
peopled by living human beings, citizens who hope for a certain minimum of prosperity and physical security. Obviously, when formulating
US foreign policy, their interests must be considered fundamental.
The United States is a separate nation-state, with a material integrity, boundaries, autonomy, and internal order worth protecting. And
its citizens have their own distinct national culture, society, identity,
traditions, and way of life worth defending. Conservative nationalists
therefore recognize that while the United States must stand for freedom
internationally, it cannot do so while undermining the very material,
human, and autonomous foundations of the American republic. This
would be self-defeating. Furthermore, some foreign interventions may
actually undermine the US global position rather than bolstering it.

Conservative nationalists look to maintain and preserve America's international position. They look to promote US national interests. Conservative nationalists therefore attempt to weigh the likely costs of any given intervention overseas against the likely benefits. And the answers they arrive at vary greatly, from one time, place, and individual to another. Broadly speaking, the typical answers come in three categories: noninterventionist, hardline unilateralist, and conservative internationalist. Each is its own tradition.[41]

Conservative internationalists believe in an active US role overseas— economically, militarily, and diplomatically. In the twenty-first century they support existing US alliances and military commitments, along with free-trade agreements, foreign aid programs, and relatively high levels of defense spending. Yet conservative internationalists differ from their liberal counterparts in placing less overwhelming emphasis on the significance of multilateral institutions.[42] At the elite level, conservative internationalism has been the dominant tendency within the Republican Party since World War II. Every Republican president between Eisenhower and George W. Bush was in this vein. There are of course significant differences between various types of conservative internationalists. Some, in the tradition of Richard Nixon, emphasize great-power realpolitik. Others, like George W. Bush, emphasize democracy promotion and rogue state rollback. Yet both Nixon and Bush 43 were—like Eisenhower, Reagan, and Bush 41—Republican internationalists who favored a forward American presence overseas. This basic commonality is worth keeping in mind, since not all Republicans share it.

The success of Donald Trump in the 2016 Republican primaries encouraged the impression that broadly internationalist policies have no support whatsoever at the grassroots level within the GOP. This is a mistaken impression. In reality, even among those who voted for Trump in the primaries, select internationalist policies still carry considerable grassroots support. Just to take one example, Trump's own supporters are far more likely to look favorably upon NATO than unfavorably.[43] More will be said about this point later on. Yet Trump did campaign on a foreign policy platform dramatically different from any successful Republican candidate since the 1940s, and his nomination represented a challenge to GOP internationalists of all kinds.

Noninterventionists oppose US military commitments overseas. Many members of this school do support commercial opportunities and diplomatic engagement with other countries. But their defining feature is a deep resistance to American military intervention, bases, and alliances abroad. This was a dominant sentiment within the Republican Party during the 1920s and 1930s. In the US context, it often flows from a libertarian commitment to limited government at home—along with the conviction that said government tends to be undermined by international military entanglements. During the Cold War, this strain of thinking was marginalized among conservative Republicans, as anti-Communist policies won out. Noninterventionists were also temporarily subdued by the commonly recognized need to respond to the terror attacks of September 11, 2001. But frustrations in Iraq after 2003 gave anti-interventionist arguments a new lease on life, and indeed such arguments had been percolating on the edges of the GOP ever since the collapse of the Soviet Union, for example in the repeat presidential runs of former Nixon speechwriter Pat Buchanan.

Noninterventionists believe that America's war on terror has been overly militarized and a threat to civil liberties under every president since 9/11. Some of the leading GOP noninterventionist candidates in recent years include former US Representative Ron Paul (R-TX) and his son, Senator Rand Paul of Kentucky. Both have run for president, and have a core following of libertarians, but both have been unable to expand their support beyond that limited core. One reason is that while libertarian noninterventionists represent a clear and principled point of view within the Republican Party, they are still very much a minority faction—including on foreign policy issues.[44] The median Republican voter today is not so much noninterventionist, as hardline.

Conservative hawkish or hardline unilateralists arguably make up a plurality of GOP voters at the grassroots level these days, but are badly underrepresented among the US foreign policy elite. This sometimes leaves them with few articulate proponents. Those few GOP foreign policy experts who are not internationalist tend to be noninterventionist. In reality, however, hardline unilateralists are a recognizable third grouping, distinct from either of the other two. And during the Obama era, they rose to new prominence.

Conservative hardliners have no objection to either high levels of US defense spending, or to the most aggressive measures against terrorism. They are not remotely pacifist. At the same time, hardliners disdain nation-building exercises, nonmilitary foreign aid programs, humanitarian intervention, and international institutions designed to promote global governance. For hardliners, the maintenance of American sovereignty is paramount, and diplomatic engagements with known US adversaries are generally unwelcome. The basic hardline instinct is to maintain very strong defenses, punish severely any direct threat to US citizens, refuse international accommodations, and otherwise remain detached from multilateral commitments. This mentality is well captured by the words of the coiled snake on the yellow Gadsden flag, a favorite of Tea Party supporters: "Don't tread on me."

The foreign policy attitudes of hardline unilateralists are well captured by Walter Russell Mead, who describes them as "Jacksonian."[45] According to Mead, the Jacksonian temperament has its base in the American heartland, particularly among Southern, Western, and white rural or working-class voters. These hardline unilateralists take the exceptional nature of the US political system as a given, view the global arena as a dangerous place, and are often skeptical of elite projects for progressive improvements overseas. Hardliners favor an American military sufficiently strong to overmatch any possible enemy. They take great pride in the US armed forces, and are overrepresented in its ranks. Jacksonian hardliners believe that reputation matters, and that weakness invites abuse. They have no objection to the use of force when necessary, and are characteristically ferocious when they see their country as threatened. Yet their first instinct in most circumstances is not to intervene overseas. Hardliners are typically persuaded into action not by globalist abstractions, but by the existence of concrete and visible adversaries. This particular combination of qualities makes conservative hardliners a poor match for the usual scholarly foreign policy categorization. Mead is right to characterize Jacksonians as nationalists. The only qualification to add is that American nationalism has also expressed itself, at various times and places, through either noninterventionist or conservative internationalist tendencies—tendencies described by Mead as Jeffersonian or Hamiltonian, respectively.[46]

Historically, it is Jacksonian hardliners who have acted as the crucial pivot players within the GOP on foreign policy issues. When convinced of threats to the United States, they can be unyielding. During the Cold War, for example, the GOP's hardliners worked with its internationalists to press back against the Soviet Union and its allies overseas. Indeed a chief complaint of conservative hardliners for much of the Cold War was that the United States was not doing enough to roll back Communism worldwide. After September 11, 2001, Republican hardliners again supported the most assertive measures taken by President George W. Bush in the war on terror, including the 2003 invasion of Iraq. Over the years, however—and particularly since Barack Obama became president—many conservative hardliners have come to think twice about well-intentioned pro-democracy interventions in the Muslim world. This change of heart was significant in allowing for the rise of Donald Trump.

All told, Republican internationalists dominated the party's foreign policy ideas and practices after 1940–1941, with conservative hardliners in a crucial but secondary supporting role. Noninterventionists were long marginalized. Put simply, what Trump did during the 2016 primaries was to unite the GOP's hardline unilateralists with many of its noninterventionists in a full-blown and politically successful assault on the party's dominant internationalist faction. The significance of this upset can hardly be overstated. There was really no precedent for it since World War II.[47]

So we see that noninterventionists, hardliners, and conservative internationalists have sometimes competed, sometimes cooperated, and sometimes come together in differing coalitional combinations. Each of the three tendencies has risen or fallen for a time. Still, what explains the waxing and waning of these three traditions? One possible explanation, championed by scholars of international political economy, is to look at the shifting economic interests of key party constituencies. For example, during the 1920s and 1930s, conservative Midwestern Republicans represented import-competing rather than export-oriented districts. Even the great US manufacturing firms of the Northeast had limited interest in overseas sales.[48] After the Second World War, on the other hand, US multinationals developed a greater interest in overseas exports, as did Midwestern farmers. Moreover, America's rising Sunbelt states possessed a growing material interest not only in international markets, but in US defense expenditures disproportionately concentrated in those very states. Under these circumstances it was probably not a coincidence during the early Cold War that the GOP's long-term trajectory was toward a more hawkish internationalist stance.[49]

Yet while shifting economic interests are helpful in explaining long-term changes, such explanations are hardly all-determining or sufficient on their own. Just to take one example, the divide within the GOP between competing foreign policy visions during the great debates of 1939–1941 had as much if not more to do with competing ideological visions, than with economic differences per se. There were Midwestern conservative internationalists as well as Northeastern GOP noninterventionists. Foreign policy ideology—together with party—was actually a better predictor than either region or economy of foreign policy preferences.[50] Consequently we need an understanding of shifting conservative foreign policy traditions that takes ideas seriously.

In the 1970s and 1980s, political scientists such as Eugene Wittkopf and Ole Holsti discovered certain powerful underlying differences in opinion between liberals and conservatives within the United States. Liberals, these scholars found, had largely abandoned the military aspects of anti-Communist containment, but remained committed to nonmilitary and cooperative aspects of liberal internationalism including arms control treaties, multilateral agreements, the United Nations, foreign aid, environmental initiatives, human rights promotion, transnational governance, peaceful diplomacy, and the nonviolent resolution of international conflict. Conservatives, meanwhile, remained firmly committed to US military spending, covert action, and the use of force overseas—including preventive strikes—against Communist countries. In other words, within a post-Vietnam context, conservatives tended to be hawks, whereas liberals tended to be doves. But conservatives in the 1970s and 1980s disagreed among themselves as to the utility of nonmilitary foreign policy tools. Some—hawkish internationalists— supported both military and nonmilitary components of American internationalism. Others—unilateralist hardliners—supported the military aspects, but opposed the nonmilitary ones.[51] And although this particular configuration of opinion was specific to that time, it hints at broader and more enduring differences between left and right on foreign policy matters. Liberals may support military intervention of various kinds, but in the end prefer to emphasize possibilities for international cooperation and peace via multilateral coordination. American conservatives, for their part, may shy away from intervention, but seem more inclined to view the world as a dangerous place, and to view US military power as essential in staving off various security threats. These basic differences in perspective leave conservatives more likely to embrace hardline national security policies, and liberals more likely to embrace a kind of dovish internationalism, across different historical eras.[52]

Yet the conservative nationalist tradition in the United States is even bigger than this. For all practical purposes, prior to the First World War, the conservative nationalist tradition within the United States was the American tradition writ large. In spite of heated debates over specific foreign policy issues, such as whether to annex the Philippines from Spain, there remained a broad consensus within and between both major parties regarding fundamentals hardly open to discussion—including the preservation of US national sovereignty. Only with America's reluctant entry into World War I, and President Wilson's proposed agenda for a new League of Nations, were these fundamentals really challenged. At the opening of the twentieth century the United States had achieved astonishing economic growth, and was already an economic giant in relation to Europe's imperial powers. But the United States was not yet a diplomatic or military giant, and it did not play a great role in Old World alliance politics. This was the situation when Theodore Roosevelt unexpectedly assumed the presidency on September 14, 1901.

Global versus National

From TR to Eisenhower

Conservative nationalism has always been a major theme in Republican foreign policy. When the GOP holds the White House, the precise expression of that nationalism has long been determined primarily by the chief executive. Every Republican president has combined noninterventionist, hardline, and internationalist impulses and policies to craft their own unique approach—some more successfully than others. In this sense, at least, the Trump administration is not that unusual. Yet periods out of power have also been significant in permitting conservatives to rethink the appropriate relationship between American nationalism and US foreign policy specifics. For Republican conservatives the tension between the global and the national is persistent, allowing for various possible balances and combinations. A brief look at GOP presidencies from Theodore Roosevelt to Dwight Eisenhower, along with some periods in opposition, helps to illustrate the point.

Theodore Roosevelt's legacy is shaped by the lasting impression he made as a cavalry volunteer during America's 1898 war with Spain: a former Dakota Badlands rancher and war hero, in love with empire and eager for battle. Ohio Senator Mark Hanna reacted to Roosevelt's ascension to the presidency by bemoaning the rise of "that damned cowboy." Yet the common image of an aggressive, bombastic Rough Rider bears little resemblance to Roosevelt's actual foreign policy record as president—a record characterized by considerable skill, care, and restraint. This practical restraint was all the more impressive, since it was obviously in tension with some of TR's personally combative instincts. Roosevelt had learned a lesson from the Badlands that he found useful internationally as well: "Don't bluster, don't flourish your revolver, and never draw unless you intend to shoot."[1]

TR's version of Republican politics was activist and reform-minded, willing to nurture a robust central government in order to promote national stability and cohesion. To his mind, these were public goods that rose above the interests of any particular group or class.[2] For the same reason, he supported what he called "unhyphenated Americanism," or the successful integration of new immigrants into the United States. As he put it: "We should insist that if the immigrant who comes here in good faith becomes an American and assimilates himself to us, he shall be treated on an exact equality with everyone else, for it is an outrage to discriminate against any such man because of creed, or birthplace, or origin. But this is predicated upon the person's becoming in every facet an American. . . . There can be no divided allegiance here."

Foreign policy was one of TR's foremost concerns, because in foreign policy one saw most clearly the necessity for pursuing national as opposed to individual or subnational group interests. TR believed in a leading, active role for the United States in world affairs. He viewed American national security as best protected in a competitive great-power environment by a more forward US presence overseas. And he believed the United States had a duty to exercise a kind of international police power in combination with other Western nations. Yet domestic political constraints at the time pressed against these ambitions.

The overarching characteristic of American public opinion in the opening years of the twentieth century was its basic indifference to foreign affairs. Domestic political issues dominated both popular concern and partisan debate. Whatever enthusiasm existed for imperialism in 1898 had since dissipated. Public opinion could still be hawkish when visible threats to US interests emerged, such as in the Caribbean. But in general, the preference of the American public was for nonintervention overseas. Congress also tended to be very skeptical of new foreign commitments, and of any conceivable infringements on US national sovereignty. Organized business interests with ties to the Republican Party sometimes had strong preferences on selected international matters, such as the issue of protective tariffs. TR supported the traditional Republican policy of trade protection, alongside a willingness to consider tariff reform. But the influence of specific business interests on TR's broader foreign policy was actually quite limited. For one thing, the primary foreign interest of American business was in international peace and stability, not costly imperial adventures. Nor did corporate interests usually have strong, united, or well-formed views on particular questions of US intervention or diplomacy. In any case, TR was contemptuous of policies formulated to satisfy narrow economic interests. He intervened overseas when he saw broader US national, strategic, ideational, and economic interests at stake.[3]

TR responded to domestic political constraints not by leapfrogging them, but by pushing the boundaries of what was possible through energetic action and forceful appeals, while ultimately respecting those limits the American public would tolerate. His policy was—insofar as possible— to encourage balances of power in the Old World, and American predominance in the New.

In Latin America, TR worked to secure US naval and diplomatic predominance within the Caribbean, against any possibility of great-power competition. He deployed US forces to both Cuba and the Dominican Republic, reluctantly, on this very basis—so that civil or financial disorder in those countries would not become an excuse for European intervention. He warned the Kaiser's Germany off from any intervention in Venezuela, for similar reasons. And in a move that really was popular within the United States, however controversial, he secured effective US control over a new Panama Canal Zone, ensuring speedier US naval access between the Pacific and Atlantic Oceans. In the Asia-Pacific region, TR worked to bolster regional balances first against Russia, then Japan, notably via the 1905 Portsmouth peace conference. And in Europe and North Africa, he did what little he could to support Britain and France diplomatically, and check Germany, again by helping to mediate a 1906 peace conference at Algeciras.[4]

On a day-to-day level, the most striking feature of TR's diplomacy was its realistic understanding of certain perennial truths regarding effective statecraft. He summarized these truths in his pithy maxim, which he borrowed from an African saying: "Speak softly and carry a big stick."[5] When Roosevelt said speak softly, he meant it. He understood that a tactful style or tone makes a difference in foreign policy. In most crisis situations, he went out of his way to allow opponents to save face. He typically conducted international negotiations with considerable patience, skill, and care. And when he had to issue a warning to another country, over some vital interest, he would do so firmly but diplomatically and in private. Speaking softly also meant refusing to make any threats or promises that could not actually be kept. Roosevelt hated bluff and buster in diplomacy. He tried to avoid making new commitments that might overstrain America's limited military capabilities. And he avoided sending US armed forces into circumstances where the intervention would be half-hearted or ineffective.

Carrying a big stick was the other half of Roosevelt's maxim. This meant, quite simply, possessing the power—especially the military power—to support one's stated interests. Roosevelt understood that in the arena of world politics, diplomacy is ineffective unless backed by power. He scorned what he called the "world gush creatures" and "maudlin sentimentalists" of the growing American peace movement, because they refused to see that international tribunals and world public opinion were no substitute for military strength.[6] In Roosevelt's mind, military preparedness was not only a necessary complement to American diplomacy—it was actually the best guarantee of peace, since a strong armed force would deter aggressors and prevent wars from occurring in the first place. As he put it in his 1906 Nobel peace prize acceptance speech:

> As yet there is no likelihood of establishing any kind of international power . . . which can effectively check wrong-doing, and in these circumstances it would be both a foolish and an evil thing for a great

and free nation to deprive itself of the power to protect its own rights and even in exceptional cases to stand up for the rights of others. Nothing would more promote iniquity . . . than for the free and enlightened peoples . . . deliberately to render themselves powerless while leaving every despotism and barbarism armed.[7]

A strong US navy was a natural and necessary component of this approach. To his way of thinking, a first-class navy was needed to keep the peace, meet existing commitments, and support an active foreign policy within the Pacific as well as the Caribbean. TR regularly called upon Congress to increase naval expenditures, and he tried to rally popular support for a bigger navy. During his last two years in office, this naval building program met serious resistance from a bipartisan coalition of fiscal conservatives, anti-imperialists, and noninterventionists in Congress. In the end, after lengthy negotiations, TR was able to get much of what he wanted: two new dreadnaughts each year, along with a dramatic and successful world cruise of American battleships. But the struggle over the navy illustrated the limits of support for military sending, even within the Republican Party.[8]

As a younger man, Roosevelt had welcomed the prospect of serving in combat. But after assuming the presidency, he showed no eagerness to launch the United States into any new armed conflict. As he wrote in a 1906 letter to the English author George Trevelyan: "I have no sympathy with those who would lightly undergo the chance of war in a spirit of mere frivolity." TR's ideal was not the pacifist, but "the just man armed who wishes to keep the peace." His actual conduct of American diplomacy as president was characterized by a desire to prevent and avoid war.[9]

Altogether, Roosevelt navigated international and domestic foreign policy pressures with considerable success, striking useful and effective balances along multiple fronts. He was an instinctive national defense hawk who, as president, avoided either open warfare or strategic overextension. He was a natural foreign policy realist with a powerful sense of moral responsibility for himself and his country. And he was a fierce American nationalist who laid the groundwork for modern Republican

internationalism. Mark Hanna need not have worried about this particular Rough Rider. In the end, TR's presidency was a successful exercise in
cowboy diplomacy.

The Roosevelt years witnessed a growing divide between conservatives
and populist progressives within the Republican Party over issues of domestic political economy. But as long as Roosevelt was president, this division had limited impact on foreign affairs. TR had his own distinct foreign
policy views agreeable to conservatives; populist progressives liked him
personally, supported his domestic policy program, and had not yet developed an alternative international vision of their own. During the tenure
of Roosevelt's successor in the White House, William Howard Taft, the
intraparty Republican divide between conservatives and populists finally spilt over into foreign policy matters. Conservative Northeastern
Republicans continued to view US military intervention overseas as oc-
casionally necessary in order to protect American strategic and economic
interests. Western GOP populists, on the other hand, began to develop a
critique of imperialist interventions as powered by the same narrow financial and corporate interests that progressives were battling at home.
This intraparty divide would also help shape Republican foreign policy
debates during the presidency of Woodrow Wilson, including throughout
the First World War.[10]

Republicans were initially deeply divided over how to respond to the
titanic conflict in Europe. Eastern, establishment Republicans—like the
sardonic patrician Henry Cabot Lodge (R-MA)— tended to be deeply
sympathetic to the British, hostile toward Germany, and supportive of
increased military spending or preparedness, along with extended credit
to the Allies. Western GOP populists or progressives—such as Senators
William Borah (R-ID) and Robert LaFollette (R-WI)— were adamantly
opposed to US intervention, viewing the war as nothing but a distant,
morally indifferent contest between rival militaristic empires. Such pas-
sionate anti-interventionist sentiments were only reinforced by the fact
that many western GOP leaders represented heavily German American
constituencies, resistant to the idea of going to war against their ancestral

home. However, Borah and LaFollette diverged on their specific responses. LaFollette opposed increased defense expenditures as well as any US military response to the war whatsoever. Borah, on the other hand, favored a built-up US navy, precisely in order to protect American neutral rights— and to punish any violation of them by either Germany or Great Britain. Here was an early indicator of a new divergence between conservative internationalists, hardline unilateralists, and GOP noninterventionists over the coming century.[11]

Wilson, for his part, prepared for re-election by initiating a series of domestic and foreign policy adjustments in the opening months of 1916. At home he tacked to the left, sending progressive legislation through Congress on matters such as taxation. On foreign policy, he co-opted the issue of military preparedness while embracing the concept of an international league to enforce the peace. Republicans had a hard time matching this performance, especially since they themselves were profoundly divided over both foreign and domestic matters. The party's 1916 campaign platform called for limited reforms at home, and a "thorough and complete national defense" alongside "strict and honest neutrality" in relation to all European combatants. The resulting double straddle on both foreign and domestic issues was awkward rather than compelling, and nominee Charles Evans Hughes compounded the problem with a colorless and ineffective campaign. The combination of peace, economic prosperity, and domestic reform was sufficient to tilt key Western states as well as normally Republican Ohio into Wilson's electoral column.[12]

With his re-election secured, Wilson laid out an extremely ambitious vision as to how the conclusion of the First World War might serve broad liberal goals worldwide. In a January 1917 address to the Senate he called for a "peace without victory," in which a new League of Nations would underwrite the spread of democracy, collective security, national self-determination, freedom of the seas, and international disarmament. On April 2 of that year, he asked Congress to declare war. LaFollette was one of only six senators to vote against this declaration. Lodge was relieved to vote in favor. Borah, for his part, was reluctant to see the United States dragged into this conflict. But he had come to view German submarine assaults on US civilian shipping as an intolerable attack on American lives, honor, and neutral rights. So he voted in favor of war against Germany, noting: "I join no crusade, I seek or accept no alliance. . . . I obligate this government to no other power."[13]

Once Germany finally sued for peace, in November 1918, Wilson traveled to Versailles to help formulate a peace treaty. The outcome was negotiated among the various Allies over the spring of 1919, and presented to Berlin as a fait accompli. In exchange for victor's terms, Britain, France, and Japan agreed to sign on to Wilson's version of a new League of Nations. This included a collective promise to uphold the integrity and independence of all League members and to combat any international aggression, preferably through sanctions and arbitration, but by force if necessary—a promise enshrined in Article 10 of the League covenant. Most Democratic senators supported Wilson on the League, but with only forty-seven members, still fell far short of the two-thirds vote required for treaty passage. Wilson needed a significant number of GOP votes.[14]

Most Republicans had supported US military efforts against Germany wholeheartedly, once at war, but held deep misgivings about Wilson's League of Nations and the Treaty of Versailles. In the Senate, GOP senators again split into noninterventionist, hardline unilateralist, and conservative internationalist factions. Hardliners like Borah and noninterventionists like La Follette objected to the Versailles Treaty and the League altogether, preferring postwar US strategic disengagement from Europe. Most such senators were Western populists or progressives, capable of mustering anywhere from five to twenty Senate votes, depending upon the issue. LaFollette opposed the Treaty of Versailles as insufficiently progressive and bound to militarize US foreign policy. Borah shared these concerns, along with some practical strategic ones. As he put it: "What will your League do if it does not contain powers that no one dreams of giving it?"[15] Above all, Borah looked to maintain a free hand for the United States. Yet a majority of Republican senators were conservative internationalists, open to some version of the League. These conservative internationalists, like Lodge— by this time, chairman of the Senate Foreign Relations Committee— actually supported a firm US postwar commitment to Europe, including

a straightforward alliance with Britain and France, but viewed as imprac-
tical the notion that Americans would commit to defend the territorial
integrity of virtually every other country on earth. In the words of former
Secretary State Elihu Root, an ally of Lodge:

> If it is necessary for the security of Western Europe that we should
> agree to go to the support say of France if attacked, let us agree to do
> that particular thing plainly, so that every man and woman in the
> country will understand that. But let us not wrap up such a purpose
> in a vague universal obligation, under the impression that it really
> does not mean anything [is] likely to happen.[16]

Amazingly, in order to secure French support for the League, Wilson
agreed to a specific US commitment defending France against any future
German attack. Republican reservationists were therefore willing to support both the League and the Treaty of Versailles, so long as Wilson also
removed some of its more unlikely provisions, including the promise of
universal collective security under Article 10. This, Wilson would not do.
Determined to maintain the purity of his foreign policy vision, while punishing his critics—and with his physical and mental agility undermined by
a series of strokes—Wilson simply refused to bend. Instead, he went on a
public speaking tour to drum up support for the League. These speeches,
while well received, did not alter political realities in the Senate: GOP
senators would not accept an unaltered Treaty of Versailles, and Wilson
would not accept a modified one. Moreover, many leading conservative
Republicans such as Lodge had their own domestic political concerns,
feeding into this deadlock. They were reluctant to give Wilson sole credit
for a major new policy initiative, heading into the elections of 1920. They
genuinely disliked significant components of that initiative. They viewed
the League as part of an overall and unwelcome expansion of federal
government power that Wilson and the Democrats had supported since
1912. And eastern GOP conservatives looked to maintain party unity with
western GOP populists, so far as possible. The simplest way to meet all of
these concerns was to oppose Wilson's particular version of the League. So

that is exactly what Lodge did. As he told Elihu Root in 1920, "I am much more interested in getting the whole party to fight together against Wilson and the League than I am in myself or anything else." Over a period of several months, Lodge marshalled opposition toward Wilson very skillfully from all quarters in the Senate, while maintaining a "reservationist" stance. The preservation of US national sovereignty was central to that stance. Republicans rallied around the position laid out by RNC Chairman Will Hays: "While we seek earnestly and prayerfully for methods lessening future wars, and will go far indeed in an honest effort to that end, and will accomplish very much, we will accept no indefinite internationalism as a substitute for fervent American nationalism." Or as Lodge put it before the Senate: "I would keep America as she has been—master of her own fate."[17]

Under these conditions, no one version of the treaty could make its way through the Senate. Wilson continued to withhold his support for any modified version of the League throughout 1920, hoping Democratic success in the presidential election that fall might resuscitate the League's chances. But the public had grown tired of the League debate, tired of international policy controversies, and tired of the sociopolitical experiments of the Wilson era. With this as the prevailing mood, Republicans nominated Warren Harding for president, a well-liked US Senator from Ohio who promised the country what he called a "return to normalcy." Lodge, for his part, hoped this might entail a modified League commitment, including a Western alliance with Britain and France.

Harding was—and is—often underestimated. While solidly conservative, his own private view of the League was closest to that of GOP noninterventionists. Yet he issued vague, bland statements throughout most of his election campaign, to reassure potential supporters on all sides that he had no fixed position against them. Once well on his way to a landslide electoral victory, he confirmed that his administration would resuscitate American commitment toward neither the Treaty of Versailles, nor the League of Nations, nor any postwar alliance with European powers. As Harding put it, "I do not want to clarify these obligations. I want to turn my back on them." In this way, the new Republican foreign policy direction was fixed. By quietly killing off any remaining chance of a foreign policy direction he did not support, the genial Harding appears to have outmaneuvered a great many famous figures considered more brilliant than him.[18]

The death of the League in the US Senate is generally considered a great tragedy, and in some ways it was, although not for the reasons usually ascribed. Wilson's insistence on a literal interpretation of Article 10 truly was unrealistic, since as events would later reveal, nations do not generally sustain great costs on behalf of universal collective security principles unless it is in their interest to do so. However, where Wilson and Lodge actually agreed was around the notion that Britain, France, and the United States would have to cooperate in the postwar era to check any future German aggression. In fact, this—and not a global collective security system—was Lodge's number-one concern. What Lodge and most Republican senators wanted to see in 1919 was something like the later North Atlantic Treaty Organization. And if Wilson had compromised on his more universalistic ambitions, he could have had it. This would have meant a solid US postwar strategic commitment to European peace and stability, including a specific pledge to defend France against Germany if attacked. At the very least, this would have complicated Hitler's calculations during the late 1930s, and possibly deterred him. It would have been a commitment worth making. So the real tragedy was not the death of Wilson's vision. The real tragedy was the death of Lodge's—namely the very real prospect of an earlier creation of NATO, to help deter a second world war.

In many respects Republican foreign policy during the 1920s was strikingly modern, carrying as it did a strong emphasis on the pacifying effects of globalization. Leading politicians, bankers, and businessmen within the Republican Party believed that a combination of arms reductions, open markets, and worldwide economic growth would help to transform the international system in a peaceful, democratic direction.[19] At the same time—and partly because of their very optimism—Republican officials placed clear limitations on American obligations overseas. In the military-diplomatic realm they would accept no binding commitments, and no entangling alliances in relation to the defense of particular countries. No one represented this combination of assumptions more completely than Herbert Hoover.

Throughout his early life, Hoover impressed virtually everyone he met with his exceptional (if humorless) ability, intelligence, honesty, and efficiency. Considered a potential candidate for president in 1920, he was made Secretary of Commerce the following year by Warren Harding, who called Hoover "the smartest 'gink' I know." President Harding left Hoover—together with the very capable and onetime Republican presidential nominee Charles Evans Hughes as Secretary of State—broad leeway over the making of US foreign policy. Harding's successor Calvin Coolidge would do the same for Hoover, albeit with greater Yankee skepticism regarding the man he called "wonder boy."[20]

Hoover proved to be an unusually strong, active Secretary, with informal influence over all areas of American diplomacy. He sought energetically and successfully to promote US exports abroad. He generally opposed the use of military force by the United States—indeed he opposed increased military spending, and called for multilateral disarmament instead. He allowed the private sector to take the lead in promoting economic development overseas. He believed that these policies would encourage the liberalization of the international system.[21]

Hoover was also a firm supporter of high tariffs against foreign competition—a policy that still carried broad support within the Republican Party. He opposed the cancellation of war debts, in the absence of dramatic concessions by European states on issues such as disarmament. And while he promoted American exports with unprecedented energy, at the end of the day he knew that the American economy was far more self-sufficient than most other major powers, and he looked to domestic production as the key to American prosperity. He was therefore a kind of peaceful nationalist on foreign economic policy, combining a genuine commitment to the pacification of the international system with a hard-nosed pursuit of relative national advantage on international economic matters.[22]

Hoover's broad foreign policy preferences, though genuinely held, were well aligned with domestic political pressures. Western agrarian populists and progressives in Congress such as Senators Borah, LaFollette, Gerald Nye (R-ND), and George Norris (R-NE) tended to be strongly opposed to international political or financial entanglements, imperialism, arms expenditures, and US military intervention. Republican administrations frequently tacked in the progressives' direction on foreign policy, precisely in order to help maintain an already somewhat tenuous party unity on domestic issues.[23]

Business interests were another domestic factor of immense impor-tance to US foreign policy during the 1920s. Indeed, through the mech-anism of proxy diplomats and unofficial economic diplomacy, it was often literally private bankers and businessmen that represented the United States abroad. The great majority of US business leaders agreed upon an overarching foreign policy framework that simultaneously included high tariffs, a search for exports, arms limitations, strategic nonentanglement, debt repayment, and the use of surrogate diplomats from the private sector to promote international cooperation on financial matters. This for-eign policy framework, in turn, permitted a regime of low taxes, balanced budgets, and limited government interference at home, which after all was the primary concern of American business.[24]

Peace groups of various kinds also carried unprecedented influence during this period.[25] Altogether, a broad domestic political coalition was built and sustained in favor of a foreign policy platform based upon eco-nomic nationalism, strategic nonentanglement, and anti-interventionist assumptions. This was an approach that progressives, farmers, urban professionals, businessmen, pacifists, industrial workers, ethnic minorities, and conservatives at the time could all support. It was an immensely pop-ular approach, and it provided a focal point around which Republicans could rally, effectively eliminating foreign policy as a particularly contro-versial, salient or damaging political issue.[26]

From 1921 to 1928, the business-oriented and dovish diplomacy of Hoover and his associates played out in three major regions: Europe, East Asia, and Latin America. In relation to East Asia, the Harding ad-ministration signed a series of naval disarmament treaties with Tokyo and London—the Washington treaties of 1921–1922—setting limits on each nation's warship tonnage, and agreeing to respect Chinese independence. These arms control arrangements had the support of multiple GOP constituencies including agrarian progressives, fiscal conservatives, peace reform lobbies, and business leaders.[27] In relation to Europe, the Coolidge administration deployed Chicago banker Charles Dawes to help renegotiate German war debt reparations with Paris and London. The Dawes Plan, as it was called, encouraged a budding détente between Germany and France, whereby the two sides mutually guaranteed their border at the 1925 conference of Locarno.[28] And in relation to Latin America, Republican administrations scaled back the interventionism of the Wilson era, by starting to wind down US military deployments in Nicaragua and the Dominican Republic.[29] The noninterventionist trend in Latin America was possible, in part, because no major powers threatened basic US interests in the region at the time. But US influence in Europe and East Asia was far more limited, resting on hopeful declarations and treaty systems that were essentially unenforceable by Washington.[30]

Once Hoover became president in 1929, he had the opportunity to exercise even greater influence over US foreign policy than as Secretary of Commerce. His basic foreign policy priorities from the start of his administration were to promote American commercial interests, pursue arms control agreements, and avoid US military intervention abroad, while keeping costs to a minimum. He resisted new naval construction altogether, and signed a naval disarmament treaty with Britain and Japan in 1930—ill-fated, because Japan withdrew almost immediately. He further hoped to promote peaceful economic and political cooperation in Latin America, Europe, and East Asia. At the same time he "had no desire to see the United States involved" in Old World "power politics" and "rival imperialisms," especially in relation to the European continent, which he described as a "boiling social and economic cauldron" producing "miasmic infections." In the final analysis, Hoover believed there to be two basic alternatives for the United States: the first was to "stand on moral forces alone in support of law between nations," while the second was "to use economic and inevitably military force against aggressors." Hoover was careful to stand on moral force alone.[31]

In Latin America, Hoover accelerated the trend toward nonintervention begun in the 1920s. The lesson that he took from America's continuing military entanglement in Nicaragua was to avoid such engagements in the future. None of this constituted a surrender of America's position as the predominant outside power in Latin America. Preponderant influence was simply exercised a little more tactfully.[32] But Latin America was something of an exception.

In Europe, where US influence was far from predominant, Hoover's decision to avoid significant international costs or commitments meant the effective surrender of America's ability to help stave off deteriorating political and economic conditions. The administration's European policy began promisingly enough in 1929, with a new renegotiation and reduction of German reparations debt—the Young plan, named after American businessman and proxy diplomat Owen Young. The onset of the Depression that autumn, however, threw a wrench into the transatlantic financial order. Private US loans to Germany and the rest of Europe soon dried up. Debtor countries were unable to make their payments. American popular and congressional attention focused entirely on domestic economic conditions. The United States Congress followed in 1930 with the infamous Smoot-Hawley tariff, a highly protectionist measure that further shut out European exporters from the US market. In effect, the international economic order was breaking down, and the tenuous cycle of loans and repayments between the United States, France, Britain and Germany was simply no longer viable.[33]

Hoover had privately come to realize that all of these issues were interrelated, and that war debt, reparations and disarmament might only be handled together, but there were still strict limits on what he was willing or able to offer. In the end the Germans defaulted on their foreign debt payments altogether, as eventually did Britain, France, and virtually every other debtor country. The international trading and monetary system continued to spiral downward into regionally autarchic blocs, creating material hardships worldwide and further undermining support for democratic political elements in Germany and Japan. By the time Hoover left the White House, Adolf Hitler was Chancellor of Germany.

A similar pattern was evident in East Asia, where the rickety basis of the Washington treaty system was fully revealed. In September 1931, freelance elements of the Japanese army invaded the Chinese province of Manchuria. But Hoover was adamantly opposed to any American response beyond a purely moral one. Even sanctions, he insisted, would only lead to "the development of incurable hatreds."[34] He did however place great faith in what he called "the moral reprobation of the world," and was unwilling to let Japanese actions stand without some sort of formal declaration. He therefore agreed to let Secretary of State Henry Stimson issue a series of statements condemning the Japanese attacks.[35] In January 1932 Stimson released what became known as the "Stimson doctrine," declaring that the United States would not formally recognize Japanese conquests or puppet governments within Manchuria. Of course the Stimson doctrine did nothing to alter the situation in East Asia, or to help the Chinese, but it was extremely popular within the United States, with peace groups, Congress, and public opinion for its thundering condemnations of international immorality. The lesson drawn in Tokyo was that the United States would chastise and remonstrate but not act concretely to oppose Japanese expansion. At the same time, Washington's legalistic condemnation of Tokyo's behavior infuriated Japanese opinion. The result was really the worst of all possible outcomes: the United States had openly displayed its irrelevance within the region, while promising long-term hostility toward Japan over an issue that Tokyo obviously deemed vital and the United States did not. Yet American opinion did not sour on the Stimson doctrine; far from it. Incredibly, the issuance of that doctrine was widely viewed for several years within the United States, including elite circles, as having been a great foreign policy success, and one that would inevitably force a Japanese retreat through the sheer pressure of economic interdependence and international opinion. Herbert Hoover shared this view.[36]

As Hoover left office in 1933, both the Washington treaty system in Asia and the Locarno treaty system in Europe were clearly in shambles. The preceding twelve years had been characterized by a Republican foreign policy approach so optimistic that it finally dissolved into air. Certainly, Hoover and many of his leading associates during this period were not lacking in intelligence, vision, or good intentions. Nor were they isolationists in the sense of wanting to avoid international involvement altogether. The question, however, is whether their relatively pacifist approach secured its own objectives, and here the answer must be overwhelmingly negative outside of Latin America. Hoover and other Republican foreign policy leaders at the time declared and apparently believed that the United States would successfully promote a more democratic, prosperous, and peaceful world order simply through the combined effects of international law, arms negotiations, commercial exchange, and public opinion. This was no strategy of offshore balancing; on the contrary, it was an attempt to transcend and escape international power politics altogether. The goals were extremely ambitious, idealistic, and global. Yet the unwillingness to back up those goals with significant material commitments—whether economic or military—left the United States with minimal practical leverage over most foreign policy questions outside the western hemisphere. America's home markets were not opened to potential allies; foreign aid was not utilized; international economic leadership was not provided. This determination to avoid costs or expenditures of virtually any kind left US officials with precious few sticks or carrots on international economic matters, despite America's great wealth. In terms of military capabilities, the lack of diplomatic leverage was even more obvious. With a constabulary Army, a treaty-limited Navy, and an absolute avoidance of new security commitments in Europe or Asia, the United States could not expect to have much influence over international questions that might involve the use of force. Overall, whatever its ambitions, the Republican foreign policy approach between 1921 and 1933 did little to contribute to international order. The nascent democratic systems of the era were fragile and unstable enough as it was. Without concrete American support, they hardly stood a chance against the coming storm.

Throughout the mid-1930s, while Democrats and Republicans debated the merits of FDR's New Deal, they agreed on the need to avoid international entanglements. In 1939–1940, however, the outbreak of war in Europe—and even more shocking, the fall of France—triggered a great debate among Americans over how to respond. For Republicans, this was arguably the most fateful and divisive foreign policy disagreement in the history of their party.

On one side of the debate were GOP unilateralists and noninterventionists, like US Senator Robert Taft of Ohio. The son of former president William Howard Taft, Robert was a rather stern, honest, intelligent champion of balanced budgets, sound credit, and individual liberty. Like many GOP conservatives, he viewed FDR's New Deal as nothing less than revolutionary in eroding American traditions of limited government. His great fear regarding US foreign policy was that America's involvement in overseas wars would further erode these domestic traditions. Moreover, he believed the United States to be essentially invulnerable and self-sufficient—geographically, economically, and strategically—allowing for a posture of continental or at most Western hemispheric defense. As he put it:

> I believe the peace and happiness of this country can best be secured by refusing to intervene in war outside the America and by establishing our defense line based on the Atlantic and Pacific Oceans. I believe that the difficulty of attacking America across these oceans will forever prevent any such attack being even considered, if we maintain an adequate defense on the sea and in the air. I believe that airpower has made it more difficult, not easier, to transport an army across an ocean and that conquest must still be by a land army.[37]

Taft's views were the dominant ones not only among Midwestern conservatives, but among congressional Republicans. Most GOP House and Senate members therefore lined up against any measures that might deepen American involvement in this new European war. They found likeminded support from import-competing, small- and medium-sized business interests; Christian pacifists; the publishing empires of Robert McCormick and William Randolph Hearst; and celebrity spokesmen like aviator Charles Lindbergh. Noninterventionist foreign policy organizations sprang up, notably the America First Committee, attracting a certain number of conspiracy theorists, anti-Semites, and Anglophobes. FDR used the resulting implication of fascism to wiretap his political opponents, and to suggest—wrongly—that GOP noninterventionists as a whole were led by Nazi sympathizers. But the weightiest share of support for views like Taft's simply came from a sincere desire to avoid war, and to protect American liberties at home.[38]

On the other side of this great debate were Republican hawks and internationalists, arguing for increased US military and economic aid to Great Britain. GOP hawks found much of their elite leadership among deeply conservative, urban, Northeastern, upper-income Anglo-Saxon Protestants with international diplomatic, financial, and legal experience. They feared that German victory in Europe would threaten vital sea lanes, collapse the international balance of power, close off vast regions from US trade and investment, and encourage Nazi influence in Latin America. They often worked with New York banks, export-oriented industries, internationalist organizations such as the Council on Foreign Relations, and conservative publishers like Henry Luce to press for US aid to Britain. But GOP internationalism was hardly limited to Wall Street. Millions of Republicans nationwide, even within the Midwest, shared this perspective, favoring a more assertive US posture against Nazi Germany. If anything Republican internationalists were underrepresented in Congress, relative to their popular numbers. In January 1941, for example, a solid majority of Republican voters said they supported "all-out" aid to Great Britain. Some congressional Republicans such as Senators Warren Austin (R-VT), Styles Bridges (R-NH), and Warren Barbour (R-NJ) could be relied upon to make the case for intervention even more aggressively than the president. These GOP hawks provided Roosevelt with political cover, allowing him to argue that his preferred policies against Nazi Germany had bipartisan support. He brought key Republicans into his cabinet—Secretary of War Henry Stimson, and Secretary of the Navy Frank Knox—for that very same reason.[39]

With Republicans divided, FDR nudged the United States toward informal wartime alliance with Churchill's Britain in a way that was politically dexterous, incremental, frequently misleading, and ultimately successful. In 1939 he proposed that Britain be allowed to purchase American war materials, so long as it could pay for them—a program known as "cash and carry." In 1940, he traded fifty American destroyers to the UK on his own authority, in return for leasing rights over a number of British Caribbean bases. That same year, Congress and the administration reintroduced military conscription—the first peacetime draft in the history of the United States. Republicans debated these various measures, some in favor, some opposed. Conservative noninterventionist senators like Robert Taft and Arthur Vandenberg (R-MI) contended for their party's presidential nomination, opposing the drift to war. But in the wake of France's collapse, Republicans decided to nominate for president a likeable utilities executive and moderate internationalist, Wendell Willkie, as the best chance to beat Roosevelt. FDR responded by reactivating his winning New Deal coalition—and by reassuring Americans that "your boys are not going to be sent into any foreign war."[40]

Having secured re-election, Roosevelt proceeded to suggest that the United States could lease, grant, or loan weapons to Great Britain with no need for instant repayment—in effect a massive military aid program, known as Lend-Lease. In 1941 he extended a security zone across the North Atlantic, providing US Navy convoys for merchant ships crossing the ocean, and ordering American warships to shoot German submarines on sight. And in 1940–1941 he imposed tough economic sanctions on Japan, demanding its withdrawal from Chinese territory. Unintentionally, these sanctions helped trigger a desperate Japanese gamble for supremacy within the Western Pacific, including a surprise attack on the US naval base at Pearl Harbor. That attack of course unified Americans against Japan more effectively than anything else, and Hitler obliged with a formal declaration of war upon the United States that was immediately reciprocated. The great intra-GOP foreign policy debate of 1940–1941 thus came to a dramatic close. Senator Vandenberg spoke for many Republicans on December 8, 1941, when he wrote in his diary, "Now we are in it. Nothing matters except victory."[41]

After Pearl Harbor, Republicans rallied to the common US war effort against the Axis. However, they continued to debate the shape of America's postwar global commitments. The war itself rendered isolationism a losing stance, politically. Elite opinion in both parties had shifted in favor of overseas engagement. Moreover, a solid majority of Republicans—like a solid majority of Americans as a whole—were now convinced of the need for some kind of revived League of Nations, combined with a larger place for the United States in world affairs. This still left open a variety of possibilities. On one end of the GOP spectrum, in his bestselling 1943 book *One World,* Wendell Willkie embraced an especially idealistic liberal internationalism, arguing for "a new society of interdependent nations" characterized by "effective organization of world unity." Publisher Henry Luce of *Life* magazine called for the United States to seize the lead in creating an open international postwar economic order in a new "American Century," and "assume the leadership of the world." On the other end of the spectrum, Senator Taft worried that all such international schemes would turn the United States into a "meddlesome Mattie, interfering in every trouble throughout the world." As he said of Luce's position: "It reminds me of the idealism of the bureaucrats in Washington who want to regulate the lives of every American along the lines that the bureaucrats think are best for them." Taft and the GOP nationalist bloc in Congress looked to keep America's postwar entanglements to a minimum.[42]

It was left to Senator Vandenberg, with his impeccable conservative, Midwestern, and prewar noninterventionist credentials, to navigate these intraparty differences. At Lake Huron's Mackinac Island, in September 1943, prominent Republican met to hash out a combined position on the question of a new league of nations. The resulting statement, mediated by Vandenberg, supported "responsible participation by the United States in a postwar cooperative organization among sovereign nations to prevent aggression." It also protected the prerogatives of Congress in foreign affairs. This was a stance virtually all Republicans could support heading into the 1944 elections, and indeed it was adopted by GOP presidential nominee Thomas Dewey. The Mackinac declaration, together with

Dewey's own position on the matter, also permitted FDR to move ahead with broad bipartisan support for a new United Nations. At the same time, it shaped the limit of America's commitment, since Republicans clarified they would accept no radical cession of US national sovereignty under the new organization. Unlike Woodrow Wilson, FDR was pragmatic enough to accept this condition. The final vote for a new United Nations sailed through Congress in July 1945, with the support of every senator but two. Even Taft voted in favor, while clarifying that Congress retained the right to declare war, apart from the UN.[43]

On the question of postwar international economic arrangements, Republicans were clearly divided. FDR had already begun moving toward reduced US tariff barriers during the mid-1930s. In 1944, US officials met with their British counterparts at Bretton Woods. They agreed that Washington and London take the lead in developing both a new World Bank and an International Monetary Fund to nurture global trade, stable currencies, international development, and investment, along with postwar reconstruction. The moderate Northeastern wing of the GOP, along with key figures like Dewey and Vandenberg, were convinced by their wartime experience of these arrangements' utility. Robert Taft was not so convinced. The Ohio senator and other conservative Midwestern nationalists remained committed to a more traditional mercantilist approach, including high US tariff barriers, independent national economic development, "freedom of action," and bilateral or regional commercial and monetary agreements where appropriate. Roosevelt and his successor Harry Truman moved forward on the Bretton Woods agenda, supported by one wing of the GOP but opposed by its other half.[44]

As the Soviet Union expanded its postwar influence throughout Eastern Europe and beyond, Republicans were as alarmed as anyone. From 1946 to 1948, GOP members of Congress largely cooperated with the Truman administration in adopting a firm US policy against the USSR, albeit with concern over the cost of such initiatives. As chairman of the Senate Foreign Relations Committee, Senator Vandenberg helped shepherd supportive legislation through Congress, nudging GOP internationalists along. The 1948 GOP nominee for president, Thomas Dewey, also took a foreign policy stance largely indistinguishable from that of Harry Truman. Senator Taft, for his part, worried that anti-Soviet containment would lead to indefinite big-government deficits, inflation, taxation, and centralized planning at home. He also feared that massive US foreign aid programs like the Marshall Plan were simply a "policy of scattering dollars freely around the world." Yet he voted for it in the end, concerned as he was about the Soviet Communist threat. Midwestern conservative nationalists did not block most anti-Communist policies. They did, however, insist upon keeping certain limits on taxation and government spending—including foreign aid and defense expenditures—as well as on coercive measures such as universal military training. In this way, they had a significant impact upon the unfolding US strategy of containment.[45]

Dewey's unexpected loss to Truman, combined with a series of shocking Cold War setbacks the following year, infuriated GOP conservatives and undermined any bipartisan US foreign policy consensus. Over the course of 1949, the test of a Soviet atomic bomb, the victory of Mao Zedong's Communists on the Chinese mainland, and continuing revelations around Soviet spies inside the United States convinced many staunch conservatives like Taft that the Truman and Roosevelt administrations had actively indulged Communist gains within Europe, Asia, and even the United States itself. It was within this tinderbox context that the previously obscure Senator Joseph McCarthy (R-WI) gave a February 1950 speech in Wheeling, West Virginia, drawing massive attention to allegations of Communist spies inside the State Department. As a matter of fact during and before the Second World War there really had been a broad Moscow-backed espionage ring inside the United States, including not only hundreds of US Communist Party members but government officials like Alger Hiss, as well as sympathetic American scientists and engineers secretly aiding a Soviet atomic bomb project. McCarthy's special contribution to this debate, so to speak, was to generate a number of specific accusations out of thin air, imply treason on the part of the president himself, and accuse the entire Northeastern liberal elite of disloyalty: those, as he put it, "who have had all the benefits that the wealthiest nation on earth has had to offer—the finest homes, the finest college educations, and the finest jobs in Government we can give." This new posture of populist outrage helped the GOP to appeal to fresh constituencies, such as Irish Catholics, in the short term. In the long term, however, the sheer irresponsibility of McCarthy's behavior actually diverted focus away from Soviet espionage as a genuine threat.[46]

The outbreak of war on the Korean peninsula in June 1950, and Truman's decision to respond with the deployment of US forces, again rallied Republicans to a major American war effort. But costly setbacks in that effort, combined with mounting US casualties, soon triggered popular dissatisfaction within the United States—not only with the bloodshed in Korea, but with the entire strategy of containment. General Douglas MacArthur openly suggested the United States bomb Chinese bases in Manchuria. Leading conservative nationalists like Taft seized the opportunity to support MacArthur, while offering their own overarching foreign policy alternatives. In 1951 Taft published his book, *A Foreign Policy for Americans*. In it, Taft recognized the deadly threat from the Soviet Union and its Communist allies, including to Western Europe. In fact he argued that the Truman administration had not taken this threat seriously enough. Yet Taft also felt that Truman's strategy of indefinite containment threatened America's system of limited government, and could very well "wreck the country's economy and, in time, its morale." Consequently the Ohio senator argued for a less costly approach, emphasizing US geographic and technological advantages, with "occasional extensions of action into Europe, Asia, or Africa, as promise success in selected areas." Under Taft's strategy the United States would rely primarily on its maritime and atomic airpower, together with a ring of bases in the Atlantic and Pacific Oceans, while avoiding major ground commitments on the mainland of either Europe or Asia. Simultaneously, it would ramp up rollback efforts against the entire Communist bloc, through covert action, psychological subversion, support for Chinese Nationalists, and military escalation against mainland China. In this way, Taft hoped to retake the initiative from the USSR and its allies, while avoiding the frustrations and costly entanglements of containment. These recommendations bore some resemblance to those of former president Herbert Hoover, who called for a return to "Fortress America."[47]

Concerned by the apparently endless growth in the expenditure and authority of the federal government, Taft took the opportunity in 1952 to again run for the Republican presidential nomination. This time he had the solid backing of the party's Midwestern and conservative wing. But the GOP's Northeastern moderates found an unusually compelling candidate in General Dwight Eisenhower, a staunch internationalist and fiscal conservative with unmatched credibility on security issues. In a very close and hard-fought convention contest, key party delegates came down in favor of Eisenhower as the more electable candidate. Midwestern conservative nationalists thus failed four times in a row, between 1940 and 1952, to nominate one of their champions. Yet Taft quickly recognized that Eisenhower was a genuine economic conservative who would endeavor to keep federal expenditures in check. In fact, the two men agreed on a great deal by this time. Both, for example, believed in emphasizing US atomic airpower, in order to keep a lid on military spending. Both looked to limit costly commitments overseas, including foreign aid. And of course both were fierce anti-Communists. These underlying commonalities allowed Taft to play a remarkably constructive role in relation to the new administration, until his death in July 1953. Taft personally never managed to locate a politically winning or satisfactory alternative to the liberal internationalist policies he opposed. By the 1950s, like most Republicans, he had moved far from strict nonintervention. But the conservative nationalism he embodied quite sincerely left a significant impact on US foreign policy even under Democratic administrations, and would continue to reverberate in different forms on the Republican side.[48]

Dwight Eisenhower's chief foreign policy goal as president was to preserve the new US world role—and to counteract international Communist advances—without bankrupting America's economy or its traditional ways of life. Raised in small-town Kansas, the gregarious "Ike" entered on a professional military career, and after 1941 experienced a meteoric rise, eventually becoming commander of Allies forces in Europe.

Demonstrating effective success and goodwill in this role, by the end of the war he won international renown. Drafted by moderate Northeastern GOP internationalists, Eisenhower ran for the presidency in 1952 as a Cold Warrior and a fiscal conservative. He promised to halt the domestic US drift toward what he called "creeping socialism"; resolve the bloody stalemate in Korea; press back more aggressively against world Communism; and refocus America's foreign policy toward "liberating captive nations" by "peaceful means." Indeed the 1952 GOP platform condemned Truman's existing strategy of containment as "negative, futile, and immoral."[49]

The November electoral outcome was a landslide personal victory for Eisenhower—notably, eating into Democratic support among middle-income Southern suburbanites—even as Republicans took back a narrow majority in Congress. On domestic issues, Eisenhower agreed with GOP conservatives that centralized government planning, high taxes, inflation, budget deficits, and regulation—what he called the New Deal "gravy train"—were all undermining US economic growth and individual liberty. At the same time, he viewed a full-blown return to the model of the 1920s as unrealistic, both politically and on its own merits. In practical terms he therefore embraced a center-right posture on matters of domestic political economy, a consensus-building approach he described as "modern Republicanism" or "the middle way."[50]

Eisenhower was entirely convinced that international Communism posed a terrible threat to the United States, and that this threat had a moral component along with a strategic one. As he framed it in his inaugural address, "Freedom is pitted against slavery; lightness against the dark." He therefore supported a strengthening and consolidation of US-led, anti-Communist alliances worldwide. Yet he feared that indefinite expenses on the scale of the Korean War were unsustainable in either fiscal or constitutional terms: "We must not destroy what we are attempting to defend." He consequently looked for lower-cost alternatives to conventional military expenditures, including nuclear deterrents, covert action, and psychological warfare. With regard to multilateral institutions such as the United Nations, Eisenhower welcomed international support for US foreign policy goals whenever possible, but had no objection to unilateral action when necessary. In the words of one historian regarding Eisenhower and the UN, "the administration . . . embraced the multilateral forum when it was perceived to best serve American interests, but ignored it with virtual impunity when it chose to act unilaterally."[51]

Eisenhower's first international task was to resolve the Korean War deadlock. He signaled to Beijing that US escalation of the war into mainland China was a real possibility. Mao's concern over this possibility—together with Stalin's death in March 1953—opened up diplomatic opportunities for an armistice that formally partitioned the Korean peninsula in two. Most Americans were relieved to see the war ended. Eisenhower further initiated a thorough review of US national security strategy, considering all of the various options, to determine how best to achieve his goal of "security without paying the price of bankruptcy." The answer he hit upon, known as the "New Look" or "massive retaliation," was to emphasize America's ability to respond with nuclear airstrikes against any Communist bloc aggression. This reliance on nuclear deterrence rather than more expensive conventional forces—combined with the conclusion of the Korean War—allowed Eisenhower to cut manpower levels and hold US defense spending under $50 billion in fiscal year 1954, a limit to which it was kept for the rest of his presidency.[52]

As commander-in-chief, Eisenhower emphasized allied burden-sharing. He was a staunch supporter of NATO, including the stationing of US ground forces in Europe. Yet out of concern for the resulting budgetary cost, he did not mean for such forces to be deployed indefinitely: "We cannot be a modern Rome guarding the far frontiers with our legions." For this reason he favored rearming West Germany, even up to and including shared control over US tactical nuclear weapons. His hope was that Western European integration and rearmament would create a "third great power complex in the world," capable of resisting the Soviet Union, thereby allowing the bulk of American forces to come home.[53]

Eisenhower's strategy toward the Soviet Union was one of relentless competition, coupled with a genuine desire for arms control. He understood that new technological developments such as the hydrogen bomb made the prospect of full-scale atomic warfare so horrendous, that if it occurred "you might as well go out and shoot everyone you see and then shoot yourself." He looked to reduce that risk, and to keep the cost of new weapons under check, partly through the pursuit of realistic arms limitation initiatives. Fundamental policy differences between the two superpowers, including Soviet objections to aerial inspection, made any such agreement difficult to achieve. Nevertheless, Eisenhower continued to hold that "you don't promote the cause of peace by talking only to people with whom you agree."[54]

In relation to Soviet-occupied Eastern Europe, Eisenhower emphasized "liberation," including through Radio Free Europe as well as covert action programs, but he ruled out direct or preventive warfare against Soviet forces as impossible. When the chance of liberation was finally tested in Hungary by that country's citizens during 1956, Eisenhower was forced to clarify that the United States would do nothing materially to help them. As he admitted, "We have excited Hungarians for all these years, and [are] now turning our backs on them when they are in a jam." But strategically, Hungary was "as inaccessible to us as Tibet."[55]

In Congress, Eisenhower was usually able to count on the foreign policy support of a significant bloc of Republican internationalists, along with many Democrats. In fact the most significant early opposition came from within his own party. During the opening years of Eisenhower's presidency, a powerful congressional bloc of largely Midwestern, conservative GOP nationalists led by Senators like John Bricker (R-OH), Everett Dirksen (R-IL), William Jenner (R-IN), William Knowland (R-CA), and William Langer (R-ND) gave the president trouble on numerous foreign policy issues. As a group, they tended to oppose free trade; backed Joseph McCarthy; favored Western European self-help; resisted presidential authority; safeguarded US national sovereignty jealously; supported "rollback" against the Communist bloc; criticized US foreign aid; emphasized the possible uses of atomic airpower; championed Taiwan; opposed contact with Communist countries; and were deeply suspicious of the State Department, the United Nations, and the FDR-Truman policy legacy. Some of this was compatible with Eisenhower's preferred approach. Some of it was not. For the most part, however, he responded not by fighting

the nationalists head-on but by consulting with them on policy substance, tacking in their direction where possible, and when necessary
outmaneuvering them behind the scenes. It worked. For example, when
Senator Bricker proposed a constitutional amendment scaling back the
expanded use of executive agreements with other countries, Eisenhower
did not fight the proposed Bricker amendment openly, but encouraged its
defeat from backstage. In relation to Joseph McCarthy, Eisenhower did
something similar, first holding his tongue, and then quietly working toward the Wisconsin senator's censure and self-destruction in 1954. At the
same time, as a hawkish anti-Communist and economic conservative, in
practical terms Eisenhower gave mainstream Republicans a good part of
what they wanted, mixed into his own preferred approach. Midwestern
GOP nationalists faded as a distinct faction. By 1955–1956, the great majority of Republicans in Congress and around the country—including key
figures like Senator Dirksen—came to support Eisenhower's hybrid foreign policy, deferring to the president's leadership in multiple crises. His
success in helping to convert most rank-and-file Republicans to a con-
sensual posture of activist Cold War internationalism was one of his most
striking and lasting political achievements.[56]

Eisenhower also succeeded in leading an historic change in GOP
priorities on trade and foreign assistance. Historically, of course,
Republicans had resisted free-trade initiatives, and in the early 1950s congressional Midwestern conservatives continued to do so. Eisenhower,
however, was committed to the promotion of an open international trade
regime and to US foreign aid programs, as two parts of an anti-Communist
global strategy. Under pressure from congressional conservatives he did
not dismantle but instead pruned US foreign aid, while agreeing that private investment would be the main vehicle for economic development
overseas. Meanwhile, heartland GOP farmers and businessmen grew increasingly export-oriented. Reflecting on the lessons of the 1930s—and
staunchly anti-Soviet in any case—most mainline Republicans gradually
accepted the premise of US foreign policy activism, including with regard to free trade. As the ideological and economic bases for protection
declined within the Midwest, Republicans came to defer in the direction

of Eisenhower's leadership on foreign economic policy, extending his authority over reciprocal trading arrangements. In this little-noticed but remarkable shift, Eisenhower helped convert the GOP to free trade from protection.[57]

In the developing world, Eisenhower's greatest priority was the containment of Communism. This often meant backing autocratic regimes when the most likely alternative was Marxist autocracy. It also entailed opposing radical nationalist movements, including non-Communist ones, when Eisenhower feared the Soviet bloc might benefit indirectly from their success. So in 1953–1954, for example, Eisenhower agreed to lend CIA support to coups against the Iranian nationalist government of Mohammed Mossadeq as well as the Guatemalan Marxist government of Jacobo Arbenz. In both cases the impression created was of CIA omnipotence, when in reality the outcome on the ground was primarily the result of local traditionalist forces mobilizing against increasingly erratic radical regimes. In other cases, Eisenhower was indifferent to or even supportive of anti-colonial nationalists, when convinced they might promote anti-Communist goals. This did not always end happily. In the case of the 1956 Suez crisis, notably, Eisenhower sided with Egypt's Nasser against the British. But he eventually came to regret this decision, believing he had been duped by Nasser, and concluding that the safest course was simply to support plausible regional allies and partners such as Israel.[58]

In East Asia, Eisenhower signed a formal defense pact with Taiwan, backing its Nationalist government against Communist China. He oversaw the creation of a new Southeast Asian Treaty Organization, with Britain, France, the United States, Australia, New Zealand, Pakistan, Thailand, and the Philippines as members. With regard to the war between France and the Communist-led Viet Minh, Eisenhower decided against bailing out the French at Dien Bien Phu, saying he "simply could not imagine the United States putting ground forces anywhere in Southeast Asia." This entailed the de facto acceptance of a 1954 partition of Vietnam into a Communist North and an independent, non-Communist South. But Eisenhower followed up with a great deal of American economic and military assistance to South Vietnam, while reserving the right to intervene in that country militarily. He did not doubt that Communist success in Vietnam would represent a severe blow to America's alliances worldwide.[59]

Ike ran for re-election in 1956 on a record of economic growth, peace, strong foreign policy leadership, and "modern Republicanism." He had ended the war in Korea, dampened domestic controversies such as McCarthyism, and halted the previous growth of federal government powers, while recognizing that most Americans did not actively look to dismantle the New Deal. This combination of appeals, together with own unique personal credibility, was more than enough to secure re-election.[60]

Eisenhower's second term was preoccupied by a sense of Cold War setbacks and foreign policy crises. In 1957 the Soviet Union launched the satellite Sputnik, creating great popular alarm inside the United States over a "missile gap" with the Soviet Union. In the Middle East, Eisenhower deployed troops to Lebanon to bolster a pro-US government. In relation to Berlin, Eisenhower faced down Khrushchev in a protracted contest over Western access rights. In Cuba, he initially reached out diplomatically to the revolutionary government of Fidel Castro. But once Castro turned Cuba's foreign policy in a pro-Soviet direction, Eisenhower initiated plans to overthrow the leftist dictator. On the subject of effective covert action against Castro, Eisenhower's one warning to his advisers was: "Boys, if you don't intend to go through with this, let's stop talking about it."[61]

By the late 1950s, critics offered two main lines of argument against Eisenhower's distinct foreign policy approach. One was that he paid insufficient attention to the anti-colonial and socioeconomic aspirations of newly independent peoples within the developing world. The other was that he did not spend enough on defense. These two lines of argument were skillfully combined by Senator John F. Kennedy (D-MA), who ran for president in 1960 on the premise that Eisenhower had been overly passive in the face of worldwide Communist advances. Kennedy and his team were determined to boost US foreign aid, strengthen counterinsurgency programs, increase defense expenditures including on conventional forces, and invigorate nation-building efforts in the developing world, on the assumption that the United States would help engineer Third World modernization in a non-Communist direction.[62]

Unlike Kennedy's best and brightest, Eisenhower was appropriately skeptical of America's ability to engineer social change in the developing world. Kennedy was not wrong to look for more calibrated alternatives to massive retaliation. But for the most part, his depiction of Eisenhower's international record was off-base. Contrary to contemporary academic and political caricatures, the Eisenhower archives reveal a foreign policy leader far from passive and instead highly diligent, calculating, and commanding behind the scenes. Eisenhower did indeed limit his own military options, but the limits were deliberate. He relied on implicit nuclear threats in cases such as Berlin and Quemoy-Matsu precisely to deter aggression, and to prevent gradual escalation toward full-scale warfare, while keeping US military spending under control.

The argument that Eisenhower was passive in the face of Communist expansion is untenable. He was really the opposite. He did however look to place certain limits on US military expense, and to preserve America's traditional forms of limited government, while simultaneously leading anti-Communist efforts overseas. And in this, he succeeded. Within the context of the late 1950s, keeping defense spending at just under 10 percent of GDP was not insufficiently high. In fact the only missile gap was one in favor of the United States. Eisenhower balanced domestic economic and constitutional purposes with international imperatives. He was a fierce anti-Communist and Cold War activist who believed fervently in the US political model. At the same time, he looked for peaceful outcomes, was genuinely open to diplomacy, did not believe the American model easy to export, was skeptical of preventive warfare, and understood from personal experience how quickly military entanglements could spin out of control. Precisely by respecting the limits of conservative nationalism, he internationalized the Republican Party.

Global versus National

From Goldwater to Bush

While Eisenhower led the GOP to accept a global foreign policy, some of the most conservative Republicans remained unreconciled to existing continuities with FDR and Truman. Indeed the modern conservative intellectual movement grew in reaction to Eisenhower's balancing acts. Classical liberals or libertarians, conservative traditionalist authors, and anti-Communist writers all agreed that Marxist-Leninism represented the antithesis of common American values. Those with personal experience as former Marxists—such as James Burnham and Whittaker Chambers— described quite persuasively the implacable expansionist nature of Soviet-backed Communism, and recommended strategies of rollback or liberation rather than of containment. This was enough to convince most conservative intellectuals of the need for an aggressively anti-Communist US foreign policy. Classical liberal and traditionalist writers remained deeply concerned by the spectacle of expanding federal government power, but crucially, most of them walled off anti-Communist efforts from a continuing opposition to the domestic welfare state. The various strains of a synthesized self-conscious American conservatism were brought to-gether by William F. Buckley in his new journal, *National Review*, which announced its position on the Cold War struggle: "We consider coexist-ence with communism neither desirable nor possible, nor honorable; we find ourselves irrevocably at war with communism and shall oppose any substitute for victory." Many grassroots conservatives by the end of the 1950s agreed, and believed they had located their champion in Senator Barry Goldwater of Arizona.[1]

Since his election to the US Senate in 1952, Goldwater had acquired a reputation as an honest, crisp, uncompromising spokesman for the right wing of the GOP. Even Eisenhower's relative fiscal conservatism was inadequate for Goldwater, who opposed the entire direction of expanded federal government powers since the 1930s as incompatible with the system of the American founding—a "system of restraints against the natural tendency of government to expand." He proposed not to accommodate this expansion but to drastically roll it back, removing the federal government from areas "in which it has no legitimate business." He was skeptical of federal legislation to enforce school desegregation in Southern states, for the very same reason—not out of racial bigotry, but because of his thoroughgoing commitment to local self-government, including on issues of civil rights.[2]

With regard to US foreign policy, Goldwater felt that neither Eisenhower nor Kennedy had pushed back hard enough against Communist advances in Cuba, Indochina, and Berlin. The Arizona senator favored a hard tug in a conservative nationalist direction, combined with a more aggressive anti-Communist approach. He criticized the United Nations as an "international debating forum" potentially "leading to an unconditional surrender of American sovereignty," and US foreign aid as largely "waste and extravagance." He was, however, willing to offer limited loans to those allies prepared to better defend themselves. International Communism Goldwater described as "a revolutionary world movement that possesses not only the will to dominate absolutely every square inch of the globe, but increasingly the capacity to do so." He dismissed containment, peaceful coexistence, arms control, and superpower summitry as futile, defensive, and mainly advantageous to the Soviet Union. He recommended alternative US strategies, "primarily offensive in character ... to engage the enemy at times and places, and with weapons, of our own choosing." On defense spending, he was "not in favor of economizing." Rather, the goal was to "achieve and maintain military superiority." His preference was "a war of attrition . . . to bring about the internal disintegration of the Communist empire." Under strategies of rollback, liberation, and "victory" in Asia, Cuba, and Eastern Europe, the United States would "encourage the captive peoples to revolt," and "be prepared to undertake military action against vulnerable Communist regimes," while at the same time "discouraging premature uprisings." Washington would further withdraw formal recognition from the USSR, as an "outlaw" power "neither legitimate nor permanent."[3]

Goldwater's fierce anti-Communism and hard-edged conservatism had considerable support not only among the new intellectual movement on the right, but within the nation's emerging Sunbelt. Rapidly expanding suburbs in states like Florida, Texas, California, Arizona, and Virginia had created an overlooked demographic and regional base for a potentially powerful faction of the Republican Party—more hawkish than the old Taft wing, but equally conservative, and used to local success. At the same time, the Northeastern moderate to liberal wing of the GOP remained significant throughout the 1960s, led by figures such as New York Governor Nelson Rockefeller. Aided by a network of leading foundations, newspapers, banks, law firms, and corporations, Northeastern GOP moderates like Rockefeller tended to be staunch internationalists, favorable toward NATO, the UN, and foreign aid programs. They joined this international stance to one supportive of civil rights and welfare expenditures at home. Traditional Midwestern congressional conservatives like Senator minority leader Everett Dirksen (R-IL) were caught in between the party's Sunbelt and Northeastern wings, but under Eisenhower's tutelage the Illinois senator no longer opposed either a strong presidency, a mixed economy, or a global foreign policy. And as a matter of fact Dirksen, Rockefeller, and Goldwater all concurred on foreign policy fundamentals of hawkish anti-Communism and high defense expenditures. The main question was implementation.[4]

In 1963, a group of well-organized conservative businessmen, politicians and strategists drafted Goldwater to run for the Republican presidential nomination. Unlike most observers at the time, they understood that the rise of the Sunbelt, new alignments on civil rights, and local party weaknesses—combined with continuing grassroots conservatism—might allow a more hardline candidate to defeat the GOP's relatively moderate northeastern internationalist wing for the first time in a generation. And on this basis, they proceeded to do so. In the 1964 Republican primaries, Eastern moderates like Rockefeller were divided, outmaneuvered, and defeated. Having captured his party's nomination, Goldwater proceeded to run as Barry Goldwater. He denounced diplomacy with Moscow, and recommended a more aggressive anti-Communist worldwide strategy of "eventual liberation," including support for "freedom fighters," along with decisive "victory" in South Vietnam. He made offhand remarks about the possible use of nuclear weapons. He called for a rollback of FDR's New Deal. He took a clear stance against the 1964 civil rights bill, even as most congressional Republicans supported it. And he clarified his view that "extremism in the defense of liberty is no vice." Stunned by this shift in tone and substance, numerous GOP liberals and moderates deserted their party's nominee altogether. Some of them even went so far as to compare Goldwater and his supporters to Nazis—a false comparison also made by leading journalists, Democrats, and civil rights activists. The politically savvy presidential incumbent, Lyndon Johnson, had little difficulty portraying his opponent as a dangerous, unstable, and possibly warmongering radical. And since Goldwater really did offer a conservative nationalist alternative outside the postwar bipartisan consensus of the time, the portrayal had teeth.[5]

Apart from significant losses in the Deep South, Johnson won reelection in a landslide. In the immediate aftermath, it was hardly clear that Goldwater's brand of conservatism would recover. But in the long run, the Arizona senator had indicated the late-twentieth-century direction of the Republican Party. The Goldwater campaign made explicit a new GOP coalition based in Southern and Western states: racially and economically conservative, insurgent, sharp-edged, and hawkish on national security. Nor were these new Sunbelt grassroots networks about to disappear. The eventual result was to bundle together support for military intervention, defense spending, the Republican Party, social and economic conservatism, more tightly than ever before, with significant consequences for both US party politics and conservative foreign policy.

The years immediately after Goldwater's defeat saw a rapid change in the national temper, destructive of existing consensus on domestic and international issues. Frustrations in Vietnam, race riots, student radicalism, rising crime, antiwar demonstrations, an emerging counterculture, controversial judicial rulings, increasingly unpopular welfare programs, and a pervasive sense of social disorder all combined to alienate culturally traditional Democrats from their own party's liberal wing. This sense of alienation was especially severe among conservative white Southerners, but it also included many working-class Catholics in the North. Meanwhile an insurgent antiwar movement gained increasing strength among mainstream liberal opinion. In 1968, Democrats nearly tore themselves apart over these divisions before nominating a traditional Cold War internationalist and New Deal liberal, Vice President Hubert Humphrey, for president. Deep South segregationists bolted to support Alabama's former Governor George Wallace in his independent bid for the White House. Wallace ran as a furious economic populist, an anti-Communist hawk, right-wing on cultural issues, and a bitter enemy of the country's social elite across party lines. The main beneficiary of all this intra-Democratic disharmony was of course the GOP, and specifically Richard Nixon.[6]

Amidst the turmoil of 1968, Nixon emerged as the favored Republican candidate. Born to parents of modest means in Southern California, he served in the Pacific during the Second World War, then as Congressman, Senator, and Eisenhower's vice president, before finally capturing the White House. Critics found Nixon shifty and uncharismatic, yet even they admitted his political skill, brainpower, and sheer work ethic. His instinctive politics were those of Middle American pragmatism, rather than ideological conservatism per se. He looked to build a new center-right coalition, populist on both cultural and economic issues, including what he called "the great majority," the "forgotten Americans, the non-shouters, the non-demonstrators . . . decent people; they work and they save and they pay their taxes and they care." He had no particular objection to governmental involvement in the economy, but truly resented the social positioning of what he called the country's "leader class" or "Eastern establishment," including on national security issues. Nixon's 1968 election platform emphasized a relatively middle-of-the road position on both civil rights and Vietnam, including an "honorable end to the war." He stressed the need for law and order, nailed down support from the GOP's rising Sunbelt wing, and presented himself as a capable foreign policy hand. On this basis, running particularly well with white-collar suburbanites nationwide, he scraped by with a narrow electoral win in November.[7]

Foreign policy tended to bring out Nixon's better qualities, and here he showed impressive skills and abilities, including bold innovation, tactical skill, and a readiness to defy conventional wisdom. By the late 1960s he possessed his own distinct and emerging vision for the redirection of American diplomacy. This entailed what he called a new "era of negotiations," along with a "complete reappraisal" of existing US commitments. Ever the pragmatist, Nixon had an instinctive feeling for international power politics. Yet as his Quaker mother's son, Nixon also regularly and privately expressed a keen desire to play the role of "peacemaker." He favored US diplomatic outreach toward Moscow and Beijing, both to bring China into the existing international order, and to improve America's geopolitical options. He understood that Cold War competition would continue, but after years of costly struggle in Vietnam, looked to place America's international commitments on a more sustainable basis—partly by playing on Sino–Soviet tensions, and partly through the "progressive de-Americanization" of the war in Vietnam. In Nixon's view, the post-1945 diffusion of economic dominance away from the two superpowers permitted and required fresh possibilities for allied burden-sharing. As a staunch anti-Communist and longtime Republican internationalist, he had the credibility to pursue these creative departures. As president, Nixon would be ably assisted by his national security adviser, Henry Kissinger, a brilliant Harvard professor with an instinct for bureaucratic maneuver and a rich foreign policy worldview compatible with Nixon's own. Skeptical of the State Department as an institution, the two of them would initially run US foreign policy strategy largely out of the White House.[8]

The domestic political context for Nixon's foreign policy was a break-down in America's Cold War consensus. Especially among mainstream liberals, the war in Vietnam triggered a sweeping reconsideration of anti-Communist policies overseas, in favor of a more dovish internationalism. The new doves rejected Cold War policies of anti-Communist interven-tion, including in Southeast Asia, and recommended a shift toward altered international priorities including the environment, Third World develop-ment, diplomatic accommodations, and human rights. With a few no-table exceptions such as Senator "Scoop" Jackson (D-WA), most Northern liberal Democrats in Congress were increasingly drawn toward the new doves, as were a significant minority of liberal Republicans. Conservative Republicans and Southern Democrats however tended to remain staunch Cold Warriors, which gave Nixon a base of support in Congress. The conflicted general public opposed any precipitous American surrender over Vietnam, and tended to resent antiwar demonstrators, but was coming to view the war itself as a mistake. Consequently, over the course of the early 1970s, political and popular momentum was clearly with the doves, both inside Congress and out. This domestic political reality constrained and informed Nixon's manner of regrounding Republican and US commitments.[9]

Beginning in 1969, Nixon and Kissinger sent out careful diplomatic overtures to Moscow, Beijing, and Hanoi, even while continuing broader US policies of anti-Soviet containment. Under the newly announced "Nixon doctrine," regional allies such as Israel, Iran, and Saudi Arabia were provided with generous American aid, but also expected to do more without direct US interference. In relation to Hanoi, through a policy of "Vietnamization," Nixon looked to bolster the South—and pressure the North into a favorable peace agreement—simultaneously with a slow withdrawal of US troops from the region. In relation to China, Nixon looked to balance against the Soviet Union. As he put it: "We're not doing this because we love the Chinese. We just have to see to it that we play both sides." And in relation to Moscow, the United States began serious negotiations over the status of Berlin as well as nuclear arms control. By 1972, all of these overtures bore fruit. Visiting Mao Zedong's China, Nixon concurred on the basic outlines of a "One China" policy, agreeing to disagree over the precise status of Taiwan. Beijing and Washington now formed a kind of tacit partnership against the USSR. Visiting the Soviet Union, Nixon concluded the Strategic Arms Limitation Talks (SALT), agreeing to freeze the two superpowers' nuclear arsenals at existing levels. And after employing US airpower to knock back repeated North Vietnamese military offensives in 1972, Nixon agreed to a cease-fire settlement in January 1973—the Paris peace accord—that kept Saigon's non-Communist government in power. By reaching out to China, pursuing détente with the USSR, and re-establishing US policy in Southeast Asia as part of an overall global strategy, Nixon and Kissinger looked to create a new triangular great-power arrangement, leaving the United States with more diplomatic leverage in multiple directions. This by no means indicated the end of anti-Soviet containment, but rather a more disciplined version of it, using carrots as well as sticks, at less cost to Americans and less risk of nuclear war.[10]

In foreign economic policy, as in national security, Nixon took a turn in a less globalist direction. He and many of his leading advisers believed the United States could no longer afford its traditional financial obligations under the Bretton Woods system. They preferred to emphasize America's autonomous economic health and freedom of action. Nixon therefore encouraged a short-term economic boom and won domestic political points in 1971 by unilaterally suspending the convertibility of the American dollar into gold.[11]

By the following year Nixon's overall foreign policy approach was politically popular within the United States, as he well understood, though he unnerved some US anti-Communist hawks as well as America's Asian allies in the process. The average American voter gave Nixon credit for a kind of fighting retreat from Vietnam, and with military conscription ended and US troops home from the war, the issue of Vietnam lost some of its sting. Meanwhile, the Democrats nominated for president their most liberal, dovish candidate, Senator George McGovern (D-SD), in effect vacating the center of the American political spectrum. Nixon responded with a hard-hitting campaign that emphasized right-of-center popu- list stands on issues such as amnesty, crime, drugs, and national secu- rity, while pointing to increased government spending and regulation on popular programs related to education, healthcare, and consumer safety. This mixed platform, while leaving conservative purists unhappy, was broadly effective politically. That November, center-right Democrats— including anti-Communist hawks, Catholics, white Southerners, and union households—deserted McGovern in droves, delivering a landslide win for Nixon.[12]

Nixon and Kissinger continued to seek anti-Soviet containment, even while pursuing détente. In Chile, they helped to destabilize the elected Marxist Salvador Allende, for fear of allowing "another Cuba" in Latin America. In the Middle East, they supported Israel during the Yom Kippur war, while using its resolution to begin weaning Egypt away from a Soviet alliance. But domestic political pressures made it increasingly dif- ficult for Nixon and Kissinger to implement their grand design. First, an ever-more dovish Congress continually cut back US aid to Saigon, making it harder to enforce the Paris peace accords. Second, liberal human rights advocates and hardline anti-Communists in both parties began joining together in politically powerful critiques of détente, notably through the Jackson-Vanik amendment, insisting that any new trade agreement with Moscow permit the emigration of Soviet Jews to Israel. And third, the Watergate scandal hobbled and distracted Nixon, finally forcing his resig- nation in August 1974. Kissinger's foreign policy realism was being chal- lenged left and right. Interestingly, both hawks and doves agreed that it paid insufficient attention to human rights inside the Soviet Union.[13]

Nixon's successor Gerald Ford brought a very different personality to the White House, but maintained the broad outlines of his predecessor's foreign policy approach, including Kissinger as a leading adviser. Liberal congressional doves performed well in the 1974 midterm elections, fur- ther empowering them to block US Cold War policies overseas. This in- cluded, for example, shutting down covert American operations against the Marxist government of newly independent Angola. Sensing an opportunity in their own region, North Vietnamese conventional military forces moved southward with stunning success in 1975, reaching Saigon that spring. To Kissinger's dismay, the US Congress made clear its complete lack of interest in an American military response, and in the end President Ford agreed. There was simply no popular appetite within the United States for renewed combat in Vietnam, and the South was allowed to fall.

At the 1975 Helsinki accords, Ford and Kissinger agreed to formally recognize Europe's postwar territorial settlement, in exchange for Soviet guarantees of political dissent and human rights within its sphere of influence. Neither Kissinger, nor Soviet negotiators, nor anti-Communist Western critics took these guarantees seriously at first, but in the long run Helsinki did help to encourage political dissent inside Eastern Europe. Liberals critiqued Kissinger's policy of détente as secretive, cynical, ignorant of humanitarian considerations, and supportive of right-wing dictatorships. Conservatives critiqued the very same policy as far too accommodating of the Soviet Union. National security hawks—including figures inside the Ford administration, like Secretary of Defense James Schlesinger—mounted an increasingly vigorous campaign against any further concessions to the Soviet Union on nuclear arms control. Indeed former California Governor Ronald Reagan almost captured the 1976 Republican nomination, running against his own party's president, as a staunchly conservative anti-Communist hawk. Reagan's challenge forced Kissinger and Ford to drop further use of the word "détente," and the Republican platform that summer in effect renounced its own president's foreign policy by condemning both "secret agreements" and the Helsinki accords.[14]

Georgia Governor Jimmy Carter, the 1976 Democratic nominee for president, denounced the Nixon-Kissinger foreign policy legacy as amoral, overly militarized, insufficiently free from Cold War assumptions, and at the same time too accommodating toward the Soviet Union. Ford for his part managed to bungle a discussion of US Soviet policy during the fall TV debates. In spite of this, public opinion polls revealed that voters continued to give Ford, Kissinger, and the Republicans the edge on foreign policy issues that year. Carter won, very narrowly, as a fresh face on the issues of Watergate, the economy, and on the basis of traditional Democratic strength in party identification. In particular, Kissinger's capabilities on foreign policy matters continued to play well with the general public, though less well with opinion elites in both parties.[15]

Between 1969 and 1976, as most voters realized at the time, two successive Republican administrations had a fair amount of success in regrounding America's global role on a more solid and realistic basis. Nixon and Kissinger, in particular, conducted a necessary fighting retreat from Vietnam, while developing careful and creative new strategies for containing the Soviet Union at reduced expense. Only within this improved strategic context did Jimmy Carter have the luxury to suggest that human rights should henceforth be of the highest concern. Yet there really was a sense in which Nixon and Kissinger underestimated the significance of Marxist-Leninist ideology for their Soviet counterparts. Events over the course of the 1970s would reveal that with or without détente, the USSR continued to promote socialist revolutionary regimes within the developing world. The United States was thereby forced to choose how to respond. Carter offered one alternative. Reagan offered another.

Ronald Reagan worked as a Depression-era sports announcer in his native Midwest before making his way to California, signing on as an actor with Warner Brothers. Originally a New Deal Democrat, he drew upon affable communication skills to become president of the Screen Actors Guild and then spokesman for General Electric. These real-life experiences, combined with wide reading, turned him into a staunch anti-Communist, an effective negotiator, and an economic conservative on issues of taxation, free enterprise, and government regulation—so much so, that he had to part ways with General Electric as he became more and more political. In 1964 Reagan delivered a very well-received TV address on behalf of Barry Goldwater, warning of the dangers to individual liberty from Communism abroad and government planning at home. Brought in this way to the attention of Republican conservatives nationwide, Reagan ran for governor of California two years later, easily defeating the incumbent Pat Brown among middle-of-the-road voters on pocketbook as well as law-and-order themes. Re-elected to a second term in 1970, Reagan fast became a favored presidential candidate on the right wing of the Republican Party. In 1976 he challenged President Ford for his own party's nomination, running especially well with grassroots conservatives in Southern and Western states. Reagan hit on themes of American nationalism and hardline anti-Communism to power through a string of Southern primaries, attacking détente, arms control, and US defense cuts, along with Ford's proposal for ceding control of the Panama Canal to Panama. As Reagan described the canal: "We bought it, we paid for it, we built it, it's ours and we intend to keep it." A narrow loss to Ford at the convention that summer neverthe-less clarified that Reagan would be the GOP's leading candidate four years later—and that the party was moving in his direction.[16]

Reagan spent the 1970s laying out a long-considered foreign policy view. Like other anti-Communist hawks at the time, he favored the restoration of what he called "strategic superiority" against contemporary trends of détente, arms control, and American cuts in defense. But he also revealed a specific perspective unusual among his fellow hawks. First, Reagan was appalled by the premise of mutual assured destruction between nuclear-armed superpowers. He despised nuclear weapons and over the long run looked to see them abolished. Second, Reagan was uncommonly opti-mistic that the Soviet system was doomed because of its fundamental in-ternal flaws—"a temporary aberration which will one day disappear from the earth." America's free-market economy would eventually outcompete the Soviet Union, he believed, so long as US economic weight was mili-tarily leveraged. Reagan's specific aim, laid out publicly before 1980, was to rebuild the US military, pressure Moscow into deep arms reductions on American terms, and lower the risk of nuclear warfare. As he suggested to his friend Richard Allen, the goal was "We win and they lose."[17]

Politically, Reagan's case was bolstered by the late 1970s through the rise of multiple forces on the right. The GOP's congressional caucus continued to drift in a more conservative, Sunbelt direction. Evangelical Protestants, leading business interests, taxpayers, and small property owners all began to mobilize and organize politically around a range of rightward-leaning domestic issues. So too did a variety of conservative foundations, think tanks, donors, and intellectuals. A set of anti-establishment lobbies known as the "New Right" used direct mail techniques to argue for a fresh combination of social populism and American nationalism, zeroing in on the Panama Canal treaty as an unwelcome indicator of erosion in the US position. Traditional and respected Cold War Democrats like Paul Nitze joined with leading Republicans and anti-Communist intellectuals in forming the Committee on the Present Danger, to make the case for a reinvigorated anti-Soviet foreign policy worldwide. And a new generation of intellectuals known as neoconservative, including authors such as Irving Kristol and Jeane Kirkpatrick, argued for supporting anti-Communist allies straightforwardly against radical insurgents, rather than retreating into flights of moralistic reform post-Vietnam. As Kirkpatrick put it, referring to cases such as Nicaragua and Iran:[18]

> Hurried efforts to force complex and unfamiliar political practices on societies lacking the requisite political culture . . . not only fail to produce the desired outcomes; if they are undertaken at a time when the traditional regime is under attack, they actually facilitate the job of the insurgents.[19]

Interestingly, Reagan assumed that a diverse range of social and economic conservatives would concur on an anti-Communist foreign policy, and on "maintaining a superior national defense, second to none." He deliberately looked to unite all of these forces, including working-class cultural conservatives, into a "new, lasting majority" whereby the GOP would shed its "country club-big business image."[20]

Reagan's successful run for the 1980 Republican presidential nomination confirmed the party's rightward, Sunbelt drift. Running on themes of national military and economic rejuvenation, traditional social values, and unabashed patriotism, Reagan reached out to GOP moderates while maintaining a variety of conservative policy positions. Many voters worried that a Reagan presidency would increase the chance of war with the

Soviet Union. But the increasingly widespread perception of Carter as a failed president, combined with Reagan's winning manner on the stump, helped to tilt the electoral outcome, and Reagan's promise to restore national defenses and respect for the United States resonated under the conditions of the time. In the end Reagan won in a landslide, securing the votes not only of GOP conservatives, moderate Republicans, and independents, but a full 41 percent of conservative Democrats. He ran especially well with white Southern Democrats, along with culturally traditionalist Catholics in the North.[21]

Reagan's foreign policy leadership style was considerably better than his contemporary critics alleged. To be sure, he had little interest in policing bureaucratic squabbles, and this sometimes led to failures of management or implementation. Yet he also possessed abundant leadership qualities. He offered a clear overall vision that inspired his supporters; was a capable negotiator, a persuasive public spokesman, politically canny, and calm in crisis situations. On the major foreign policy decisions of his administration, contrary to some impressions at the time, he was very much the person in charge.[22] He began from a sincere set of policy beliefs, but was unwilling to risk disaster in order to maintain ideological purity. The specific outlines of his foreign policy strategy in office emerged gradually and contained a number of key components:

1. An American defense buildup, to restore diplomatic leverage with the Soviet Union.[23]
2. Indirect military assistance, training, and weapons to anti-Communist insurgents in Afghanistan and Nicaragua.[24]
3. A reorientation on nuclear arms control negotiations, in the direction of restoring Western defenses before reaching any further agreements with Moscow.[25]
4. Disputation of Communist domination in Eastern Europe, especially via US support for the Polish union movement Solidarity in coordination with the Vatican.[26]
5. Economic warfare against the Soviet bloc, through attempted restrictions on Western trade, technology, and credit.[27]

6. A stinging public diplomacy challenge to the Soviet Communist model as fundamentally illegitimate, immoral, and doomed—an "evil empire," as Reagan described it, and a "bizarre chapter in human history whose last pages are even now being written."[28]

7. Energetic research and development into a national US missile defense system, or Strategic Defense Initiative (SDI).[29]

All these elements were part of a gradually developed, deliberate strategy through which Reagan looked to pressure the Soviet Union relentlessly, imposing costs upon its weak points through global diplomatic, military, ideological, economic, and technological competition. National Security Decision Directives such as NSDD-32 of May 1982 (US National Security Strategy) clarified that the administration sought to "contain and reverse the expansion of Soviet control and military presence throughout the world," to "weaken the Soviet alliance system by forcing the USSR to bear the brunt of its economic shortcomings, and to encourage long-term liberalizing and nationalist tendencies within the Soviet Union itself." The goal here was not simply parity or containment, but—wherever possible— rollback, reassertion, preponderance, and success.[30]

With regard to large-scale military interventions abroad Reagan tended to be cautious and self-restrained, in spite of his crusading language. Two cases from 1983—Grenada and Lebanon—provide telling illustrations. In relation to Grenada, fearing another Soviet ally astride Caribbean sea-lanes, Reagan decided to overthrow that island's leftist government through sudden and direct US intervention. The invasion was a "sloppy success" operationally, as described by General Colin Powell, and an unusually direct rollback of a Marxist regime. In relation to Lebanon, Reagan deployed American troops under multinational peacekeeping auspices to help counteract Syrian influence. But after a suicide bombing attack on Marine barracks, US forces were quietly withdrawn in early 1984. A better solution might have been not to deploy them under such unfavorable conditions in the first place. Nevertheless, Reagan demonstrated in both cases one key element of his overall strategy: namely, a preference that military interventions be brief, effective, small-scale, and popular within the United States—or terminated, with minimal domestic political fallout.[31]

Reagan's energetically anti-Communist policies and language during his first term in office left Soviet leaders alarmed. Renewed superpower tensions peaked in the fall of 1983, with the shooting of South Korean airliner KAL 007 over Soviet airspace, followed by NATO military exercises known as Able Archer. Leading Soviet officials feared that Able Archer might be used as cover for a nuclear first strike against the USSR. When Reagan learned of this fear, he was sufficiently appalled as to offer both private and public assurances that the United States had no such plans. While offering no substantive policy concessions, he supplemented continuing hardline policies with a certain shift in tone, emphasizing the need for "reducing the risk of war" through a "better working relationship." As he said, "the fact that neither of us likes the other system is no reason to refuse to talk." This emphasis on the common desire for peace was also wisely highlighted heading into the 1984 re-election campaign. Reagan's Democratic opponent, Walter Mondale, stressed the dangers of deepening US military involvement in Central America and even nuclear war, both issues of real popular concern. Yet in the end most voters viewed Reagan as better able to manage these pressing security challenges, combining peace with strength—and gave him credit for a considerable restoration of national pride. Domestic economic recovery and Reagan's own winning manner helped tilt the election outcome into a landslide victory for the incumbent, solidifying a new GOP coalition of evangelicals, white Southerners, working-class, and Catholic voters. Yet Reagan's hardline anti-Soviet foreign policies were in many ways quite controversial at the time. It was only successful, practical performance in government that gave his agenda broad appeal.[32]

The most significant global development early in Reagan's second term was Mikhail Gorbachev's takeover as General Secretary of the USSR's Communist Party. While initially committed—like Reagan—to a continuation of Cold War proxy competition, Gorbachev was simultaneously ready to experiment with bold new approaches internationally in order to buy time for domestic Soviet reforms. The two leaders met at Geneva in 1985 and established a productive personal rapport. The following year they met again, in Iceland, and came close to agreeing on mutual nuclear weapons abolition, an incredible proposal in every sense of the word. The main sticking point was Reagan's support for SDI, alongside Gorbachev's determination to see that program mothballed. Moving on to more solid ground, they proceeded at the Washington summit of 1987 to agree upon an Intermediate Nuclear Forces (INF) Treaty, whereby an entire class of intermediate and medium-range land-based nuclear weapons was verifiably eliminated. Since this agreement represented, in effect, Soviet acceptance of Reagan's arms control position dating back to 1981—and since it gave him something to show for years of hardline stands—Reagan was happy to say yes. By the time he visited Moscow during his last year in office, he was able to honestly say that the Cold War tensions of his first term represented "another time, another era."[33]

Reagan's tenure was often represented as the triumph of a neoconservative foreign policy approach, emphasizing a kind of muscular idealism with regard to democracy promotion overseas. And certainly, neoconservative intellectuals during the 1980s reached a new prominence and policy influence they had not earlier possessed. But of course the first generation of neoconservatives, such as Jeane Kirkpatrick, had emphasized an unapologetic defense of US interests, rather than global democratic transformations as such. In truth, Reagan presided over a broad political coalition within which intellectuals were a relatively minor component. Some neoconservative intellectuals, such as Norman Podhoretz, were actually disappointed that the president was not more aggressive in rolling back the Soviet bloc directly. Fortunately Reagan ignored such criticisms. The more practical question with regard to democracy promotion was exactly when to side with US allies, or against them—a question on which neoconservatives themselves disagreed. In any case, looked at overall, Reagan's approach toward democracy promotion overseas was subtle and effective. Certainly, he believed in the superiority of democratic forms of government. But he also believed that nothing could be worse for the democratic cause than for anti-American radicals to triumph worldwide.

Initially therefore, his instinct was to back non-Communist allies in developing countries rather than to hector them, even in cases such as South Africa when their actual practices were far from democratic. A significant shift came in 1986, once Reagan became convinced that pro-American autocrats such as Ferdinand Marcos of the Philippines could be pressured on human rights, or even overthrown, without risking something worse. The administration therefore switched to a somewhat more pointed approach in pressing authoritarian allies on issues of human rights, and this pressure—in combination with reassurances, assistance, and above all internal factors within each allied country—left significant regions in the East Asian littoral and Latin America more democratic than when Reagan first entered the White House.[34]

By the time Reagan left office Cold War tensions had faded dramatically, with Moscow conceding on a wide range of military issues and proxy conflicts. Gorbachev's choices here were certainly central, but Reagan did his share as well. He realized when few others did that the Soviet Union was vulnerable at critical points, and through a deliberate strategy of pressure, forced Moscow to make difficult choices. He began by forcing Soviet leaders back on the defensive. Then he improved relations with those same leaders, negotiating from strength to conclude a major arms control agreement on American terms. This was practical success, attained by alternating between diplomacy and intransigence as appropriate to the situation. Reagan's uplifting foreign policy speeches are also easily misunderstood. In reality, he was generally cautious and careful regarding any large-scale or protracted use of military force. Nor did he try to institute regime change within Eastern Europe through direct US intervention. In practice, his foreign policy involved greater circumspection than his speeches might have indicated. By refusing to overreach internationally, he helped to ensure both global and domestic political success for his foreign policy approach.[35]

Viewed in terms of foreign policy, the presidency of George H. W. Bush (1989–1993) was a kind of successful denouement to the Reagan years, managed with hands-on professionalism. The pedigreed son of a Connecticut US senator, Bush fought in the Pacific theater as a naval pilot during World War II before returning to make his personal and political fortune in Texas. Securing a series of high-ranking appointments during the Nixon-Ford era, gaining international along with executive experience in the process, Bush ran for the Republican presidential nomination in 1980 as the surprise favorite of GOP moderates. He then served as vice president, becoming Reagan's heir apparent and the party's own nominee by 1988. Framing the general election decision as a broad choice between liberal and conservative values, and under relatively favorable conditions of peace and prosperity, the Bush campaign had little difficulty in the end holding on to the Reagan coalition and defeating Democratic opponent Michael Dukakis that November—including on issues of national security. Bush then set out to consolidate the international gains from the previous eight years while placing US–Soviet relations on what he viewed as a more even keel. Unlike Reagan, Bush's conservatism was of the dispositional rather than ideological kind. He was skeptical of centralized solutions to social or economic problems, and did not seek radical policy departures in any direction. This sensibility also influenced his foreign policy. Drawing lessons from the 1930s, Bush very much believed in a leading role for America in the world, buttressed by international alliances, strong US armed forces, and free-trade arrangements. Yet by temperament and conviction he emphasized pragmatism, stability, caution, and prudence in nudging forward US interests on a case-by-case basis. In other words, rather than stressing grand designs, he applied the Hippocratic Oath to matters of foreign policy: "First, do no harm."[36]

After an initial pause to reassess America's Soviet policy, Bush put forward bold new proposals on arms control, looking for the "integration of the Soviet Union into the community of nations" with a Europe "whole and free." Events soon overtook even the most creative imaginings. Over the summer and fall of 1989, numerous Communist governments in Eastern Europe allowed for genuinely sweeping democratic reforms inside their own borders, and unlike past Soviet leaders, Gorbachev permitted these reforms peacefully to go forward, capped off by the destruction of the Berlin Wall. Like most Americans, Bush was pleasantly astonished at these events, but he refused to gloat over them. Indeed he worried that a violent collapse of the Soviet Union itself could be dangerous for nuclear stability. Partly for this reason—and in contradiction to strong bipartisan currents of American opinion—he was unenthusiastic about supporting Baltic or Ukrainian independence in 1990–1991. Instead he tried to use quiet diplomacy and the prospect of US economic aid to constrain any Soviet Baltic crackdown, while warning Ukrainians about the dangers of "suicidal nationalism." Bush did, however, press American advantages relentlessly against Moscow on numerous other issues, including the freedom of Soviet satellites in Eastern Europe. In relation to Germany, Bush and his foreign policy team—together with West German Chancellor Helmut Kohl—helped orchestrate a masterful diplomatic process resulting in the peaceful unification of East and West Germany as a sovereign member of NATO. In relation to superpower arms control and Third World proxy conflicts ranging from Angola to Nicaragua, the Bush administration pushed for and achieved a set of diplomatic successes and agreements very much on American terms. Of course, it was Gorbachev who repeatedly made the crucial decisions to concede. Yet overall, Bush presided over a series of astonishing and peaceful Cold War diplomatic victories. This was a vindication of not only his particular approach, but of American strategic engagement going back to the 1940s.[37]

Another defining moment for Bush came with Iraq's invasion of Kuwait in August 1990. The president deployed American troops to protect Saudi Arabia, secured UN sanctions against Iraq, and soon decided that Saddam Hussein's forces would be ejected from Kuwait one way or another. Working a knack for personal diplomacy, Bush assembled a broad international coalition of support, including not only US Arab and Western allies but the UN Security Council. With regard to his domestic American audience, the president built support for this approach by referring to hopeful post–Cold War prospects for a "new world order," a Wilsonian vision of "a world where the rule of law supplants the rule of the jungle." Bush's insistence on the forcible liberation of Kuwait was hardly uncontroversial; most Democrats initially opposed the resort to war, preferring to let sanctions operate. But the president secured a majority vote in Congress for an authorization of force, and on January 16, 1991, the United States began a series of punishing airstrikes against Iraqi forces. American and allied ground troops then moved in on February 24, liberating Kuwait and producing a cease-fire within a hundred hours. Bush mistakenly believed that Saddam would quickly be overthrown, encouraging Kurdish and Shiite civilians to rise up against the Iraqi dictator. Still, Bush saw little merit in trying to occupy Iraq itself. When no successful uprising occurred, the United States settled into a policy of no-fly zones, containment, deterrence, sanctions, inspections, and periodic airstrikes against Saddam's forces—a policy that would essentially continue under various administrations well into 2001.[38]

In other foreign policy arenas, as in Eastern Europe and the Persian Gulf, Bush acted as a conservative internationalist with a realist cast—committed to free trade, collective security, alliances, and the protection of vital US interests, but broadly skeptical regarding humanitarian intervention in the affairs of other countries. With regard to China—which he viewed as both a strategic and economic partner—Bush resisted strong bipartisan pressures for an aggressive US response after Beijing's Communist government cracked down violently on peaceful protestors in Tiananmen Square. With regard to trade, Bush held firmly against protectionist sentiment, favoring negotiations with Canada and Mexico on the NAFTA signed in 1992. And with regard to humanitarian outrages against civilians in Bosnia and Somalia, Bush's early instinct—against liberal, congressional, and human rights critics—was to avoid armed US intervention in cases of civil conflict unamenable to external military solutions. Only in the final weeks of his term did he finally authorize a limited American operation in Somalia to help deliver food supplies, and in Bosnia he never signed off on any major intervention. As Bush put it: "Before I'd commit American forces to battle, I want to know what's the beginning, what's the objective, how's the objective going to be achieved and what's the end."[39]

By 1992, Bush's foreign policy came in for criticism from two directions, left and right. On the right, conservative commentator Pat Buchanan decided to challenge Bush for his own party's presidential nomination.

Opposed to the 1991 Persian Gulf War, inspired by the support of paleo-conservative intellectuals, and finding the administration to be insufficiently hard line on a range of domestic issues, Buchanan ran a spirited campaign against the president, capturing over a third of the vote during the opening GOP primary in New Hampshire. The cheerful right-wing firebrand decried apparent job losses from free trade, and stressed the need to reorient both America and the Republican Party back toward a more detached US foreign policy stance. As he explained his position: "We call for a new patriotism, where Americans begin to put the needs of Americans first, for a new nationalism where in every negotiation, be it arms control or trade, the American side seeks advantage and victory for the United States. . . . He is a globalist and we are nationalists. He [Bush] believes in some Pax Universalis; we believe in the Old Republic. He would put America's wealth and power at the service of some vague New World Order; we will put America first." While he did not win a single state primary, Buchanan won almost three million votes against Bush, indicating considerable discontent at the base of the Republican Party as well as among independents. Buchanan's populist, nationalist, and paleo-conservative pitch still had limited appeal in 1992, and he himself was too far right to capture the nomination, but he offered one possible foreign policy direction for Republicans throughout the 1990s, and in retrospect key aspects of his campaign would turn out to be prophetic.[40]

The more immediate challenge to Bush's re-election, once Buchanan had been defeated, of course came from the Democratic nominee, Arkansas Governor Bill Clinton. On foreign policy, Clinton adopted the tone of a relatively hawkish liberal internationalist, critical of Bush on human rights, while at the same time making clear his primary focus on domestic economic revival. This center-left stance was probably about the best Clinton could do, since in truth Bush held a massive advantage over Clinton on national security and foreign policy issues. Fortunately for Clinton, foreign policy was simply not as salient as it had been for most American voters before the Soviet Union's collapse. The general public gave Bush high grades on foreign policy, but turned against him for other reasons, above all domestic economic. In fact the same thing had been true during the 1992 GOP primaries: most Republicans and independents preferred Bush to Buchanan on international issues. Bush's real weakness politically was popular dissatisfaction over the economy and the lack of a clearly communicated domestic agenda. In the November general election, independent candidate and Texas billionaire Ross Perot helped siphon off the votes of discontented independents and moderate Republicans, as Clinton won handily. Conservatives would go back into opposition, forced to grapple with new internal divisions over US foreign policy.[41]

During the 1990s, the collapse of the Soviet Union and the election of Bill Clinton left the GOP uncertain as to the proper direction for US foreign relations. Most Republicans agreed that Clinton was not a strong commander-in-chief, but beyond that there was considerable cross-cutting and intraparty debate over foreign policy matters between GOP nationalists and internationalists, realists and idealists, hardliners and noninterventionists. Realists like Henry Kissinger argued for the careful use of force and diplomacy to maintain balances of power overseas, rather than emphasizing domestic conditions inside other countries. Onetime Cold War hawks like Jeane Kirkpatrick largely agreed, suggesting that it was "not within the United States' power to democratize the world." Pat Buchanan and his paleo-conservative supporters went much further, arguing for the termination of many US international commitments, protection against foreign commercial competition, and rollback of open immigration laws. Libertarians such as Representative Ron Paul (R-TX) were more liberal than Buchanan on certain social issues, but positively dovish on foreign policy.[42]

At the other end of the foreign policy spectrum, a new generation of neoconservative intellectuals such as Robert Kagan and William Kristol argued for rogue state rollback, increased military spending, "the re-moralization of American foreign policy," and energetic intervention abroad in a range of cases to promote democracy and human rights as well as US interests. In the 1996 presidential primaries, Republican Party voters continued the pattern of nominating a relatively pragmatic conservative internationalist in Senator Bob Dole (R-KS), rejecting stark alternatives like Paul or Buchanan for president. But in Congress, as in the country, the predominant feeling among GOP conservatives throughout the Clinton era—as embodied by key figures like Senator Jesse Helms (R-NC), not to mention Newt Gingrich's 1994 Contract with America—was a kind of hawkish nationalism, attracted to US alliances and military strength, but deeply unenthusiastic about UN peacekeeping missions, humanitarian intervention, arms control agreements, foreign aid, and any cession of US national sovereignty. Neoconservatives were able to find common cause with Helms and Gingrich on a number of issues, but remained frustrated by the obvious lack of enthusiasm at the base of the party for Wilsonian interventions overseas—a sentiment that revealed itself most fully in the confused congressional responses to crises in Bosnia and Kosovo. Still, the new Republican idealists like Kagan had created a clear foreign policy alternative, one quite different from the original recommendations of first-generation neoconservatives like Jeane Kirkpatrick. What remained needed was the moment, and the leader.[43]

Texas Governor George W. Bush ran for the presidency in 2000 on a platform of "compassionate conservatism," strengthened military defenses, and skepticism toward nation-building overseas. No strict libertarian, this son of the forty-first president believed that government power could be used toward conservative and morally worthwhile purposes. At the same time, he was initially cautious regarding arguments for multiple military interventions overseas. Tutored by a team of senior and respected Republican foreign policy experts, the Texas governor settled on an early posture emphasizing increased military spending, free trade, bolstered missile defenses, support for US allies, and a hardline approach toward America's competitors overseas. At the same time, he criticized Bill Clinton for overextending the US military on nonessential missions, offered to be more careful regarding the use of force abroad, and questioned the value of key multilateral agreements such as the ABM Treaty, International Criminal Court, and Kyoto Protocol. This overall combination was sufficiently plausible so as to not harm Bush in his 2000 campaign efforts. In fact it helped rally Republican nationalists and internationalists around a common focal point, while differentiating Bush's position from the Clinton-Gore era in some significant ways. During the exceptionally close election that November against Vice President Al Gore, exit polls showed that voters favored Bush over Gore on issues of foreign policy and national defense. The opening months of 2001 saw no great shift toward US intervention overseas. On the contrary, Bush appeared focused on domestic policy matters, and disinclined to make any drastic shifts in US policy regarding either China, North Korea, or Iraq. To be sure, Bush moved forward with a more nationalist stance on key matters such as the International Criminal Court and missile defense. In reality however, the initial Bush policy toward Iraq was one of hardened containment, rather than rogue state rollback—arguably more realist than neoconservative.[44]

Al Qaeda's September 11, 2001 attack on the United States transformed the Bush administration's foreign policy. The president quickly became convinced not only that the United States would have to pursue jihadist militants far more energetically, but that the United States had a broader ideological mission bound up with counterterrorism. Bush began by demanding that the Afghan Taliban hand over Al Qaeda's leader Osama Bin Laden. When the Taliban refused, Bush launched a US-led war with broad international support, using special operations forces, American airpower, precision strikes, and regional allies to topple the fundamentalists from power. The failure to capture Osama Bin Laden permitted Al Qaeda to regroup inside Pakistan, but at the time America's strikingly rapid advances against the Taliban encouraged the administration to entertain further missions in the newly announced war on terror, and for Bush the next mission would be Iraq. Concerned that Saddam Hussein could not be indefinitely contained; anxious that the Iraqi dictator might build and hand over weapons of mass destruction to terrorists like Bin Laden; convinced that a democratized Iraq might act as a positive example for the Arab world; and determined to showcase American resolve in the wake of 9/11, Bush settled on a decision to confront Saddam. This decision was bound up with the announcement of a new US National Security Strategy in 2002, one placing fresh emphasis on America's prerogative to launch preventive military action against rogue state sponsors of terrorism like Iraq. More broadly, Bush declared with this ambitious new doctrine that the United States looked to press democratic freedoms worldwide, freedoms he described as "nonnegotiable demands" applicable "and unchanging for all people everywhere." In sum, the president responded to 9/11 by adopting a much more sweeping and even idealistic foreign policy approach than he had campaigned on the previous year.[45]

Politically, the prospect of invading Iraq was deeply controversial, though not in a way that harmed Bush at first. On the contrary, Democrats were initially more divided over it than were Republicans. Proponents of the war included not only the Bush administration, but for all practical purposes the great majority of Republicans, particularly in Congress, along with a crucial segment of liberal Democratic hawks convinced of the war's moral and strategic necessity. Opponents of the coming war as of winter 2002–2003 included roughly half the Senate's Democrats, certainly the left-liberal base of the Democratic Party, and a vocal minority of Republican conservatives—whether paleo-con, realist, or libertarian. Indeed a newly energized noninterventionist movement on the right organized around fresh venues, like the magazine *The American Conservative*. Many traditional conservatives were uneasy about the coming war in Iraq. Yet for the most part GOP conservatives at the time accepted Bush's argument for war, in part because it tapped into precisely those same nationalist sentiments that had long energized Republicans. In the wake of a violent attack on America itself, most grassroots conservatives were entirely ready to hit back hard in an unyielding war on terror, even in a case like Iraq where the links were tenuous. Bush thereby tapped into the uncompromising nationalism so dear to American conservatives, redirecting it toward a remarkably high-risk, assertive, idealistic, and even Wilsonian strategy within the Middle East. There is every indication that he was in earnest.

Internationally, Bush fixed on the issue of Iraqi weapons of mass destruction, and secured the passage of United Nations Resolution 1441 in September 2002, declaring that Iraq was already in violation of other UN resolutions from the previous decade. He was unable to secure a second resolution from the Security Council lending explicit support to a US-led invasion. Since Saddam would not fully cooperate with international weapons inspectors—and since Bush would accept nothing less—this diplomatic process could only end with armed conflict. In the end, America went to war in Iraq with some thirty allies, including roughly half the members of the European Union. The US-led invasion in March 2003 again showcased America's conventional military excellence, toppling Saddam's regime within a few weeks. But the United States had occupied Iraq with little effective preparation for what would come next, whether in the form of counterinsurgent operations, postwar reconstruction, or constabulary responsibilities. Instead, initial planning appears to have gone forward on the optimistic assumption that Iraq was a fine candidate for democratization, that it would welcome an outside occupying army, and that the country's reconstruction would be largely self-financing. Those who questioned Iraq's cultural suitability for democracy were dismissed as ethnocentrically biased. The chaotic situation following Saddam's collapse allowed for widespread violence, looting, and disorder. The United States toppled Saddam's autocracy but did not initially put anything viable in its place. Some of Saddam's former loyalists began a low-level insurgency against US forces. This insurgency then gathered support from Iraq's Sunni Arab minority, resentful of its loss of privileges. By the fall of 2003 it was clear that Bush's invasion had not gone as planned. Insurgent violence continued, Saddam's weapons of mass destruction were never found, Shiite militias proliferated, and foreign jihadists flooded into Iraq. Still, Bush was still able to make the case—quite plausibly—that a US withdrawal would only undermine America's reputation and leave the situation worse inside Iraq.[46]

The 2004 elections featured Iraq as a central issue, with Bush as a polarizing figure energizing both admiration and contempt in differing circles. The bulk of the Democratic Party had by this time turned entirely against the Iraq war, to the extent that Democratic primary voters flirted with antiwar candidate and former Vermont Governor Howard Dean before settling on the more staid Senator John Kerry of Massachusetts. Kerry and Bush engaged in a hard-fought autumn campaign, but the Massachusetts senator was never able to settle on an appealing persona and stance with regard to either domestic or international issues. In the end Bush defeated Kerry by a clear yet narrow margin, winning over not only the GOP's conservative base, but swing voters including Catholics, married women, and suburbanites. Those voters identifying Iraq as their leading concern cast their ballots for Kerry. On the whole however, broader issues of terrorism and presidential leadership clearly worked in Bush's favor, giving him a crucial and winning edge over his opponent. Indeed there is considerable evidence that in the absence of the stalemated and frustrating war in Iraq, Bush would have won re-election by an even greater margin. Political observers noted that Bush and the GOP appeared able to regularly carve out close but decisive political victories—and perpetuate the old Reagan coalition—by bundling together conservative social, economic, and national security concerns, together with selected cross-partisan policy appeals designed to win over political moderates and independents. Fred Barnes called this formula "big government conservatism," a striking combination of moral traditionalism, increased government spending, and interventionist foreign policy. Certainly Bush's clear position on national defense and counterterrorism played a central part in holding together and expanding his political coalition, at least during the president's first term in office. Some of his own supporters lauded his foreign policy approach as "revolutionary." But Bush had overreached in Iraq, and the tipping point was near.[47]

In his second inaugural address of January 2005, Bush highlighted his sweeping and ambitious international vision, centering on the "expansion of freedom in all the world." Declaring that America's "interests and beliefs are now one," he announced that "every nation and culture" ultimately welcomed the spread of democracy and human rights, as a universal truth. Iraq was now the main test case for this theory. Unfortunately the situation on the ground in that country over the course of 2005–2006 continued to deteriorate. Insurgents killed or wounded thousands of American troops; Iraq's central government proved painfully inadequate to the task at hand; Shiite militias began fighting back against Sunni jihadists; ethnic cleansing triggered massive refugee flows; and the multidirectional violence threatened to spiral into full-scale civil war along sectarian lines. By 2006 the American public had lost its patience with the war, as even an increasingly vocal minority of conservative Republicans called for reassessment and disengagement. The November 2006 congressional midterm elections led to dramatic losses for the GOP, and there is little doubt Iraq contributed to it.[48]

Basically, Bush had two options by the fall of 2006 with regard to the Iraq war: either disengage American forces under politically respectable cover, or double down through some form of reinforced commitment. The first choice was the one favored by much of the Washington foreign policy establishment, not to mention a clear majority of the general public. The second choice—to bolster US troop levels, emphasize population security, and adopt more effective operational techniques—was the option favored by a limited number of counterinsurgency experts both in and out of the career military. Another president might have chosen the first option. Determined to avoid a failed outcome, Bush chose the second. In the opening weeks of 2007, he announced that the United States would send a number of added Army brigades to Iraq, and that General David Petraeus would be placed in charge of the new overall effort—one that came to be known as the "surge." Buying time for the surge to work, Bush defied congressional Democrats to defund the Iraq war, while most Republicans rallied behind the president in this one last wartime effort. Petraeus—who had discovered earlier local success in northern Iraq using counterinsurgent methods—did not disappoint. Indeed Sunni Arab leaders in the province of Anbar had already begun to turn against the exceptionally brutal Al Qaeda affiliate in Iraq. With an assertive mixture of special operations, diplomatic effort, better intelligence, military force, and local payouts, the United States was able to roll back Al Qaeda in Iraq and eventually bring some reduction of violence in that war-torn country. Petraeus, while careful to note the possibility of reversal under fragile conditions, was able to inform Congress of significant progress by September 2007, a testimony that undermined the antiwar movement and permitted Bush to implement limited rather than wholesale American troop withdrawals.[49]

The 2008 election season was powerfully influenced by the issue of Iraq, both directly and indirectly. For the most part, Republican primary voters remained unconvinced by antiwar arguments, and impressed by the effectiveness of Bush's surge. Under these circumstances, the race for the GOP presidential nomination gravitated toward Senator John McCain (R-AZ), an independent-minded and longtime national security hawk widely respected for his wartime service in Vietnam. Representative Ron Paul (R-TX) continued to carve out his distinct niche among libertarians and noninterventionists, but that niche was as yet a distinct minority view among GOP voters. Former Arkansas Governor Mike Huckabee ran surprisingly well as a Christian populist, winning the Iowa caucus along with numerous Southern primaries. But McCain's eventual capture of the nomination confirmed that Reaganite orthodoxies still dominated within the Republican Party as of 2008. Outside of the GOP, the domestic political impact of Iraq was more damaging. To be sure, the Democratic nominee for president, Senator Barack Obama (D-IL), did not possess McCain's national security credentials, and numerous polls indicated that McCain held clear advantages over Obama on issues of terrorism and national defense. But for the general public, these issues were simply not as central as they had been right after 9/11. More to the point, America's multiyear frustrations within the Middle East had created a political opening for a new type of liberal Democrat to present an anti-war case on Iraq and carry the White House. By 2008 the American public broadly speaking was tired of the war, and prepared to cast a negative retrospective vote on the tenure of President Bush. Arguably this retrospective judgment—very much bound up with the issue of Iraq—was Obama's single greatest asset in the November election, and it certainly helped propel him into the White House.[50]

Bush's foreign policy was hardly the unmitigated disaster of hostile caricature. On the contrary, with regard to nuclear nonproliferation, counterterrorism, bilateral trade agreements, US foreign aid, Africa, India, China, and Japan, his administration had a number of achievements to its credit. His 2006 Iraq surge decision was characteristically courageous, and vindicated by events. But of course that decision would not have been necessary in the absence of earlier grave mistakes in 2003. It was above all on his fateful, central decision to invade Iraq that Bush asked to be judged. And here it must be said he made severe and fundamental errors. The United States invaded Iraq under unrealistic, rosy assumptions that were ultimately the president's responsibility to sense and correct. It took him far too long to do so. These mistakes were not dishonest or malicious in intent, but they were tragic in their consequences, and there would be a reckoning.

The Obama years saw a splintering of Republican foreign policy ideas back into three perennial tendencies: hardline unilateralist, conservative internationalist, and noninterventionist. All three tendencies or groups were largely conservative, while disagreeing on certain crucial aspects of US foreign policy. GOP noninterventionists argued for a profound retrenchment of American military and financial commitments abroad. GOP internationalists—a diverse group in its own right—continued to favor a forward US strategic presence, including diplomatic, economic, and military components. GOP hardliners supported robust US military and counterterrorist defenses, but grew increasingly skeptical of American nation-building or pro-democracy interventions within the Muslim world.

Conservative internationalists of various types remained a powerful force within the Republican Party during the Obama era, particularly at the elite level. Moreover, many of the specific policy preferences cherished by GOP internationalists—including free trade, international alliances, and robust military spending—continued to receive a certain degree of support from Republican voters and their congressional representatives. Yet there was also an unmistakable shift in mood among conservatives, over the course of the Obama years, with regard to foreign policy and security issues. Republicans continued to support aggressive counterterror measures. But particularly after the frustrations of the 2011 Arab Spring— notably in Libya—a great many conservatives began to suspect that US-led interventions inside the Arab world had only opened the door for radical

Islamists. Increasing war-weariness and skepticism regarding democracy promotion dovetailed with a new prioritization of domestic constitutional and fiscal concerns. The rise of the Tea Party during Obama's first term only confirmed these shifts on the right. And intense GOP opposition to Obama's agenda tended to reinforce opposition toward his foreign policy, especially when Republicans did not trust the president to carry it out effectively.[51]

Tea Party foreign policy preferences during the Obama era were commonly mischaracterized as "isolationist." It would be more accurate to say they were hardline nationalist. Multiple polls found Tea Party members to be more supportive of US military commitments abroad than the average American. At the same time, Tea Party supporters really were unenthusiastic about humanitarian intervention, the United Nations, foreign aid, and any cessions of US national sovereignty. Foreign policy was simply not their primary concern. On balance, Republicans remained relatively hawkish on national security issues during the Obama era, and more likely to support increased defense spending than either Democrats or independents. Overwhelming majorities of Republicans supported drone strikes against suspected terrorists; preemptive strikes against Iran if necessary to prevent that country from building nuclear weapons; and US airstrikes against ISIS starting in 2014. So the overall shift in the GOP foreign policy mood during the Obama era—while certainly less interested in any Middle Eastern "freedom agenda"—was not toward a dovish posture, but rather a hard-edged conservative nationalism.[52]

Republican noninterventionists and libertarians like Senator Rand Paul (R-KY), Ron Paul's son, had an impressive run prior to 2014 in making their case on a range of foreign policy issues. Indeed the Kentucky senator was initially considered by many to be a strong presidential candidate. But the rise of ISIS that same year confirmed a traditional truth regarding grassroots conservative and GOP voters: namely, their instinctive hawkishness with regard to evident national security threats. Noninterventionists like the Pauls tended to argue that the overly aggressive nature of US foreign policy created enemies like Al Qaeda. This argument, while common enough on the left, was not especially popular among Republican conservatives. Most GOP voters in 2014 affirmed that they favored counterterrorism policies more aggressive than Obama's— not less so. The rise of ISIS thereby reconfirmed a serious gap between libertarian foreign policy thinkers and grassroots Republicans on key national security issues.[53]

At the presidential level, conservative internationalists predominated within the GOP throughout the 2012 election cycle. Ron Paul ran for the party's presidential nomination one last time, making his case for a US posture of strict nonintervention. But while he received a respectful hearing, conservative voters were not yet prepared to embrace Paul's radical critique of US global responsibilities. Most GOP candidates articulated hawkish criticisms of Obama, on issues ranging from Iran, China, and defense spending, to counterterrorism. Interestingly, more nationalist candidates like Texas Governor Rick Perry and Representative Michele Bachmann (R-MN) also expressed some profound doubts regarding existing military missions in Afghanistan and Libya. But the winning intraparty theme was still an embrace of American international leadership, and in the end former Massachusetts Governor Mitt Romney won the nomination running on a traditional GOP foreign policy platform. The Obama White House, for its part, was unfazed by Republican criticisms. Having authorized a successfully deadly raid on the hidden compound of Osama Bin Laden—and confident that most American voters were not looking for additional US military commitments overseas—Obama parried Romney's foreign policy criticisms with aplomb. National security was, in effect, temporarily removed from the table as a typical GOP electoral strength, and Obama won re-election employing traditional incumbent advantages.[54]

At the congressional level, most GOP conservatives starting in 2009 critiqued Obama from a hardline posture over issues of arms control, missile defense, Iran sanctions, counterterrorism, and US policy toward Israel. But there was also a noticeable shift in priorities, as many congressional Republicans—especially Tea Party freshmen—now emphasized domestic economic concerns rather than military expenditures or US interventions inside the Middle East. Tensions with the White House over fiscal priorities led Republicans to accept the 2011 Budget Control Act, by which defense spending was cut significantly over a ten-year period in exchange for equivalent domestic cuts. Most congressional Republicans also refused to openly support either Obama's Libyan intervention, or US airstrikes against Syria's Assad. In the wake of the Arab Spring, the bulk of congressional Republicans proved to be quite skeptical regarding arguments for US military strikes in either Syria or Libya. Constituent opposition, mistrust of Obama, and the risk of empowering Islamist radicals combined to nudge GOP members against intervention in these cases. Even in the case of Afghanistan, where 9/11 had originated, a significant minority of GOP members were ready by the summer of 2011 to call for clear exit deadlines. Only with the rise of ISIS in 2014 did congressional Republicans once again find themselves largely united in calling for more energetic US military action within a Muslim country.[55]

On issues of trade, the GOP caucus generally lent its support whenever Obama submitted new agreements to Congress. Indeed on cases relating to Panama, Columbia, and South Korea, the president had to rely on majority votes from Republicans, since congressional Democrats tended to oppose such agreements. But there was already some splintering of Tea Party support for new trade agreements during the Obama era, and beneath the surface, underappreciated divisions existed over free trade and globalization at the base of the GOP. A 2014 Pew Research Center poll highlighted these divisions. Noting that Republicans remained largely conservative on a wide range of public policy issues, including national defense, the Pew Center nevertheless found some striking differences between what it called Business Conservatives and Steadfast Conservatives. Optimistic and upscale Business Conservatives tended to support free trade, foreign policy activism, and immigration reform. Older Steadfast Conservatives, on the other hand, described themselves as suspicious of big business, opposed to further immigration or free trade, and angry and pessimistic about the future of the country. In other words, perhaps half of Republican voters—contrary to GOP establishment preferences—had turned sour on the benefits of globalization. No Republican presidential candidate had quite captured that frustration in previous cycles.[56]

Perhaps even more fundamentally, profound social changes had already taken place within the United States among non–college educated and working-class white voters—increasingly a mainstay of the GOP—over a period of many years. Astute observers such as Charles Murray documented the disturbing splintering of white America into a new upper class and a new lower class, increasingly separated not only by zip code but by continuing adherence to traditional middle-class norms of marriage, religiosity, and work. This sense of cultural erosion, socioeconomic frustration, loss of relative social status, and political disconnection was preparing the way for a populist revolt against existing party establishments more class-based than checklist-oriented, and consequently more severe. This was the lay of the land in the summer of 2015, when Donald Trump descended his building's escalator to announce his run for president.[57]

4
—

National versus Global

The Trump Era

For most Americans prior to the summer of 2015, Donald Trump was best
known as a celebrity billionaire, real-estate developer, and reality TV star.
He had changed parties back and forth more than once, and was not especially conservative. Given that his comments on specific foreign policy
issues over the years had sometimes been disconnected or ambiguous, it
was easy for the press to dismiss to him as having no overall worldview.
But in fact, Trump's public statements during a period of roughly thirty
years revealed, if not a full elaborated ideology, then at least a broad perspective with a certain amount of continuity. And that perspective was
one of populist American nationalism.

Essentially, dating back to the 1980s, Trump's argument was that
US-allied trading partners had taken advantage of American security
guarantees and lopsided commercial arrangements to promote their own
economic interests while free-riding off the United States. Other countries had not only "ripped off" America economically, but lost respect
for it in the process—or as Trump liked to say, "They're laughing at us."
With regard to US military interventions overseas, Trump tended to support such interventions when they went well—including in Iraq—and
abandon them went they went badly. He had no objection to high levels of
American defense spending per se, describing himself as "very hawkish,"
and regularly called for a strong US military. But he did object to an overall

pattern of armed US interventions overseas that seemed to him endlessly frustrating, inconclusive, and financially unrewarding from an American point of view: "We don't win anymore," "Defending wealthy nations for nothing," "We can't be the policeman for the world." He placed special blame on US political leadership and the Washington, DC policy elite for failing to pursue American economic interests overseas aggressively and intelligently. For the most part, up until 2015 Trump's comments on US foreign policy were framed as complaints, rather than specific policy recommendations. Still, the particular pattern of his complaints revealed a populist-nationalist foreign policy worldview with some distinct consistency to it. As he put it as early as 1987, with reference to key US allies: "Why are these nations not paying the United States for the human lives and billions of dollars we are losing to protect their interests? Let America's economy grow unencumbered by the cost of defending those who can easily afford to pay us for the defense of their freedom."[1]

A common pattern in GOP presidential primaries prior to 2016 was their eventual devolution into a contest between a mainstream, center-right internationalist with establishment support (e.g., Mitt Romney, John McCain), and an "insurgent" social conservative with close ties to evangelical Christians (Rick Santorum, Mike Huckabee). The evangelical favorite would do well in parts of the South and interior West, but ultimately lose to the more moderate candidate for lack of organization or broad appeal.[2] International issues were typically not a major source of disagreement between these candidates; both would be relatively hawkish, and neither would question the fundamentals of Republican national security policy. Those who did, like Ron Paul, lost badly.

During the 2016 presidential primaries, Donald Trump rearranged and broke down this expected pattern by locating and emphasizing new sources of division within the Republican Party—including on foreign policy. He campaigned as neither a staunch evangelical conservative nor an establishment-friendly pragmatist. Instead he ran as a furiously populist and anti-establishment nationalist. In doing so Trump initially alienated many college-educated Republicans, most conservative opinion leaders, and virtually the entire GOP establishment. Due to intense doubts surrounding Trump's character and unorthodox policy stands, his opening campaign was highly controversial and polarizing inside the Republican Party. The extraordinary nature of his candidacy drove up voter turnout in the Republican primaries, both for and against him. Over 17 million people cast their votes for candidates other than the eventual nominee—an unprecedented number in a GOP primary. But Trump's platform and candidacy turned out to have surprising reach toward a range of Republican primary voters across the usual ideological and regional intraparty divisions, and of course his opponents were divided. Exit polls from multiple primaries revealed that Trump's supporters saw him as a strong, independent-minded and practical businessman, capable of bringing needed change to Washington. For these particular voters Trump's brash, combative style, his war on political correctness, his outsider status, and his scathing attacks on the elites of both parties were all assets—not liabilities.[3]

Trump ran equally well in Northeastern and Deep South primaries, and among GOP moderates along with conservatives. Indeed on multiple domestic policy issues, such as entitlement reform, the minimum wage, and Planned Parenthood, he took early positions that were moderate to liberal. This was partly why many staunch Republicans fought Trump so bitterly in the primaries: he really had no prior connection to the American conservative movement, nor to its preferred policy positions on numerous issues. Yet Trump's populist persona and issue positioning turned out to be appealing to one major, numerous constituency: working-class Republicans, and those without a college education. Among this core constituency Trump did very well throughout the Republican primary season, across regional and ideological lines. He also polled particularly well with older white men. In the end, Trump won on average about 40 percent of the popular vote until his last opponent dropped out. This was enough for him to win most of the contested party primaries and caucuses outside of the Great Plains.[4]

The New York businessman's unusual stance on numerous international and transnational issues was certainly divisive, even inside the GOP, but at the same time important to his nomination. Several of his most attention-getting proposals, considered unworkable by policy experts from both major parties, were in fact overwhelmingly popular with Republican primary voters. These included his notion of a temporary ban on all Muslim immigrants into the United States, as well as a full-blown security wall on America's southern border paid for by Mexico.[5] While establishment internationalists tended to favor immigration reform, by 2015–2016 over 60 percent of Republican voters had come to view mass immigration into the United States as a "critical threat."[6] Trump tapped into this sentiment and encouraged it by suggesting the possibility of identifying and deporting some eleven million illegal immigrants living in the United States. Trump's protectionist stance on numerous international trade agreements, past and present, was also highly unusual for a winning GOP candidate. But since roughly half of Republican voters shared vaguely protectionist views on international trade, as of 2015, Trump's position held considerable populist appeal.[7]

Trump won over many of the GOP's noninterventionist voters with full-throated critiques of the 2003 Iraq invasion, denunciations of "nation-building," and repeated declarations that multiple US interventions within the Muslim world had produced nothing of benefit to the United States.[8] Yet he did not really run a foreign policy dove. On the contrary, he called for the most brutal measures against jihadist terrorists—up to and including torture—and a more aggressive campaign against ISIS along with increases in US defense spending. Trump's hawkish language against jihadist terrorism was crucial to his nomination. He won precisely by *not* being a thoroughgoing anti-interventionist on national security issues. The majority of Republican voters, including hardline unilateralists, did not and do not hold strictly noninterventionist views with regard to ISIS and Al Qaeda.

Altogether, the image offered by Trump was of a kind of Fortress America, separated from transnational dangers of all kinds by a series of walls—tariff walls against foreign exports, security walls against Muslim terrorists, literal walls against Hispanic immigrants, and with the sense that somehow all these dangers might be interrelated under the rubric of the "the false song of globalism."[9] For longstanding and hardline nationalists like Pat Buchanan, this was music to their ears—vindication, after decades in the wilderness.[10] And even for many GOP voters less strict than Buchanan, yet feeling displaced by long-term trends toward cultural and economic globalization, the promise of the country's security, separation, and reassertion of control sounded both plausible and compelling. In the end, Trump carved out unique niche appeal in the 2016 Republican primaries by combining a colorful celebrity personality with working-class appeal, a fiercely anti-establishment persona, unapologetic American nationalism, hardline stands against both terrorism and illegal immigration, protectionism on trade, media savvy, and a withering critique of past military interventions by presidents from both parties. The combination was highly unorthodox, controversial, and divisive, but it was enough to win the nomination.

The striking thing about public opinion and international policy issues in 2015–2016, however, despite Trump's rise, is that Republican sentiment on these issues was broadly similar to Republican opinion in 2011–2012. Public opinion polls taken over the years by organizations including Gallup, the Pew Research Center, and the Chicago Council on Global Affairs confirm this rather surprising finding. In 2015–2016 a clear majority of Republicans supported increased defense spending, energetic counterterror measures, US alliances, NATO, Israel, and a leading role for the United States internationally. The most common Republican concern was hardly that President Obama had overreached in fighting ISIS and Al Qaeda, but that he had not gone far enough.[11] GOP opinion was more divided on issues of trade, foreign aid, and immigration, but even here many Republicans—sometimes a majority—supported select "internationalist" positions in 2015–2016. Public opinion polls taken in 2011–2012 painted a rather similar picture to 2015–2016.[12] Like most Americans, Republicans had mixed feelings about numerous US international engagements partway through the Obama years. They continued to have mixed feelings by the end of his administration. And yet Republicans nominated Mitt Romney in 2012, as opposed to Donald Trump in 2016. This would seem to suggest that the nomination of a straightforward internationalist in the earlier case, and something quite different four years later, had at least

something to do with the contingencies of the presidential primary process, as opposed to any truly radical shift in overall Republican voter foreign policy opinion.

Foreign policy played into the 2016 general election campaign
against Democratic nominee Hillary Clinton, not always in ways favorable to Trump. Indeed in the final November results, voters gave
Clinton a double-digit advantage as the candidate better able to handle
foreign policy. But a number of other issues closely related played to
Trump's advantage, and of course in the end the election was not primarily about foreign policy at all. Exit polls from election night revealed
that voters gave Trump a clear advantage over Clinton on the issues of
terrorism, trade, and immigration. There was also a common feeling by
2016 that Obama's second-term handling of US national security had
been a little weak, and in particular that the war against ISIS was not
going well—both issues that favored Trump. So while foreign policy
strictly speaking tended to favor Clinton in the end, the perception
of transnational challenges to the United States—including terrorism,
Islamist radicalism, illegal immigration, and globalization—tended to
favor Trump.[13]

Where Trump really matched up against Clinton most effectively was
in a cluster of issues and concerns that were national in orientation rather
than international. First of all, there was a widespread belief among voters
that the country was on the wrong track, and that established elites in both
parties had failed the country over a period of several years. The norm in
any case is to switch parties in the White House after eight years. Clinton
could hardly pretend to be anything other than a status quo candidate,
nor was she viewed by the general public any more favorably than Trump.
Most Republicans with misgivings about their candidate rallied to him
in the end, out of party loyalty and against Clinton, on traditional conservative issues such as religious liberty, Supreme Court appointments,
criminal policing, and domestic economics. Finally, even though Trump
did not receive as many votes as Clinton nationwide, his voters were dis-
tributed with unusual efficiency. Specifically, Trump's set of issues and appeal went over especially well with a critical percentage of non–college

educated rural and small-town white voters living in key swing states from Pennsylvania through the Midwest to Iowa and Wisconsin. In winning over these particular voters—some of whom had voted for Obama in 2008 and 2012—Trump overcame widespread doubts about his viability, assembled a solid majority in the Electoral College, and secured the presidency.[14]

Trump approached the responsibilities of the presidency with an unusual background, personality, and managerial style. Indeed it was difficult to recall an incoming president who produced such intensely divergent assessments among voters from day one. Critics, of which there were many, viewed him as erratic, grotesque, and ill-informed. Supporters, on the other hand, saw Trump as a bold, pragmatic, and independent-minded leader willing to shake up Beltway conventionalities—in foreign policy as elsewhere. Intelligent observers on both sides agreed that the new president possessed previously unappreciated talents on the campaign trail: a pronounced Machiavellian streak, a willingness to question or shatter existing norms, a remarkable talent for self-promotion, a penchant for unpredictability, and a determination to apply his business background to the task of leading the United States.

Trump's own statements over multiple decades provided significant clues as to his decision-making style, about which he was quite candid. As he said years ago:

I play it very loose . . . I prefer to come to work each day and just see what develops. . . . I like making deals. . . . That's how I get my kicks. . . . I just keep pushing and pushing and pushing to get what I'm after. . . . It does take a certain intelligence, but mostly it's about instincts. . . . I like thinking big. . . . I always go into the deal anticipating the worst. . . . I try never to leave myself too exposed. . . . I also protect myself by being flexible. I never get too attached to one deal or one approach. . . . I'm a great believer in asking everyone for an opinion before I make a decision. . . . The best thing you can do is deal from strength, and leverage is the biggest strength you have. Leverage is having something the other guy wants. Or better yet, needs.

He went on:

You need to generate interest, and you need to create excitement. . . . I don't mind controversy. . . . That's why a little hyperbole never hurts. . . . there are times when the only choice is confrontation. . . . my general attitude, all my life, has been to fight back very hard. . . . You can't con people, at least not for long. . . . if you don't deliver the goods, people will eventually catch on. . . . I don't spend a lot of time worrying about what I should have done differently, or what's going to happen next.[15]

The question of course was whether this particular combination of beliefs, inclinations, and decision-making techniques would be favorable to the conduct of an effective foreign policy over the course of a four-year term.[16]

In his January 2017 inaugural address, forcefully aimed against established elites in both parties, Trump reiterated core nationalist themes from his campaign: "For many decades, we've enriched foreign industry at the expense of American industry; subsidized the armies of other countries while allowing for the very sad depletion of our own military; we've defended other nation's borders while refusing to defend our own; and spent trillions of dollars overseas while America's infrastructure has fallen into disrepair and decay. We've made other countries rich while the wealth, strength, and confidence of our country has disappeared over the horizon. . . . From this moment on, it's going to be America First. Every decision on trade, on taxes, on immigration, on foreign affairs, will be made to benefit American workers and American families. . . . We will seek friendship and goodwill with the nations of the world—but we do so with the understanding that it is the right of all nations to put their own interests first."[17]

Trump proceeded to assemble a foreign policy team headed by Secretary of State Rex Tillerson, Secretary of Defense James Mattis, and

National Security Advisor Michael Flynn. Flynn was replaced within weeks by H. R. McMaster. Other important players on these issues included CIA Director Mike Pompeo, Vice President Mike Pence, Secretary of Homeland Security John Kelly, Secretary of the Treasury Steven Mnuchin, National Economic Council Director Gary Cohn, Secretary of Commerce Wilbur Ross, US Trade Representative Robert Lighthizer, UN Ambassador Nikki Haley, Director of National Intelligence Dan Coats, senior counselor Steve Bannon, Chief of Staff Reince Priebus, presidential speechwriter and senior advisor Stephen Miller, National Trade Council Director Peter Navarro, and the president's son-in-law Jared Kushner. Trump demonstrated a special interest in the views of career military and business leaders, rather than Beltway foreign policy experts per se. In the summer of 2017, Kelly replaced Priebus as Chief of Staff, and Bannon was let go as senior counselor. These changes led to a somewhat more conventional policymaking process.

Several of the key administration figures—such as Mattis, McMaster, Tillerson, Haley, Pence, Coats, and Pompeo—were longstanding proponents of a certain US forward presence overseas, and could have easily served in any Republican administration. Others, including Bannon, Miller, and Navarro, were staunch economic nationalists along the lines of Trump's 2016 campaign, and deeply involved with it along the way. Bannon in particular—the head of Breitbart News, and Trump's late 2016 campaign director—generated tremendous initial attention as a media-savvy ideological nationalist determined to realign the GOP in an anti-establishment direction, while disrupting existing foreign policy practices on trade, immigration, counterterrorism, China policy, and military intervention. His departure in August 2017 was certainly significant. So was the president's reshuffling of his national security team a few months later, replacing Tillerson with Mike Pompeo, and H. R. McMaster with John Bolton.[18] Trump's foreign policy advisers therefore included a range of perspectives, from the traditional and center-right to the hardline unilateralist. As always, there was ample room for bureaucratic politics and inertia to play a part, especially with regard to policy implementation and staffing challenges. Both pro-Trump and anti-Trump journalistic outlets wrote of globalists arrayed against nationalists. But in truth, while outside observers on all sides tended to fixate on differences among key advisers, and while some of these differences were very real, there were also more commonalities than acknowledged. More to the point, as in any administration, the president was ultimately the one in charge of key foreign policy decisions, and no potential cabinet member or leading adviser would have either accepted or been nominated for the position had they not grasped that fact.[19]

The Trump administration made border control a major theme related to its foreign policy approach. As a candidate, Trump had electrified core supporters by calling for a ban on entry from Muslim nations due to US counterterror concerns. Within days of the president's inauguration, therefore, his administration started off with a bang by issuing a prohibition on travel into the United States from a number of Muslim nations.[20] This travel ban, intended to fulfill Trump's campaign commitment on the subject, was immediately contested within lower US courts, and soon replaced by new executive orders more likely to withstand legal challenge. A revised version of the travel ban was eventually upheld by the Supreme Court.[21] At the same time, the administration pressed ahead with efforts to crack down on illegal immigration. Trump had great difficulty in 2017–2018 securing congressional funding for his desired border wall with Mexico, and that country showed little inclination to pay for it. Indeed the issue of funding for the proposed border wall triggered a protracted standoff between the White House and congressional Democrats, entailing a government shutdown. However, increased enforcement of US border control did move forward, often by executive action, and the administration sent a clear signal to would-be immigrants not to risk the journey unless arriving legally.[22] Both the executive-ordered travel ban and the administration's approach toward illegal immigration— while perhaps not foreign policy strictly speaking—certainly had foreign policy implications, and had to be considered part of an overall effort by the president to fulfill campaign promises relating to the security of US borders.[23]

A striking shift in US trade policy constituted one of the most distinctive and important foreign issue developments of the Trump era. As a
presidential candidate, and indeed for decades prior, Donald Trump had
made clear his disdain for existing multilateral trading arrangements.
Arguing that these arrangements had cost American workers more than
they gained, he promised a new approach. He placed a special emphasis on
the reduction of US trade deficits.[24] Trump's trade policy team was distinct
from his foreign policy and defense team in that the major players were
not only a different cast of characters, but more regularly in alignment
with the president's early campaign platform. Peter Navarro and Robert
Lighthizer, in particular, were fully on board with Trump's approach, as
was Wilbur Ross.[25] During his very first days in office, as promised, Trump
withdrew the United States from the Trans-Pacific Partnership (TPP). He
then began talks to renegotiate US commercial relationships with China,
Canada, Mexico, and other trading partners. At first these efforts began
slowly, and it looked as though Trump might accept minor adjustments in
existing arrangements. For example, the administration renegotiated the
Korea-United States Free Trade Agreement (KORUS) with allies in Seoul.
But by spring 2018 it became clear that Trump was in fact determined to
extract significant concessions in multiple directions. The resignation of
Gary Cohn as director of the National Economic Council in April 2018
signaled the beginning of a new US tariff campaign.[26]

   The exercise of presidential authority in setting new US tariffs was justified by the White House on the grounds of national security and re-
dress of discriminatory practices under Section 232 of the 1962 Trade
Act and Section 301 of the 1974 Trade Act, respectively. The president
pressed Canada and Mexico for major revisions to NAFTA. He imposed
new tariffs on $250 billion worth of Chinese goods. He set new US
tariffs on imports of steel and aluminum from Canada, Mexico, and the
European Union among others. And he threatened tariffs on automo-
bile imports across the board. Most trading partners retaliated against
the United States with targeted and proportionate tariffs of their own.[27]
Disagreements over tariffs, especially between Trump and Canadian
Prime Minister Justin Trudeau, triggered the breakup of the G-7 summit

in Quebec without the customary unanimous communique between allies. Presented with the requested affirmation of "rules-based international order" in relation to international trade policy, Trump refused to sign it.[28] Yet weeks later he agreed to a truce in ongoing trade disputes with the EU, avoiding any further escalation for the moment.[29] And during the autumn of 2018, Canadian, Mexican, and American trade representatives signed a renegotiated NAFTA agreement—also known as the United States-Mexico-Canada Agreement—for Congress to consider.[30] Trump frequently insisted that he did not oppose international trade as such, but was looking for more balanced or reciprocal trading arrangements with US partners through the application of bargaining leverage—and that he preferred bilateral agreements to multilateral ones.[31] Most congressional Republicans did not particularly like the new tariff campaign, but demurred from binding attempts to block it.[32] US markets, while generally positive toward President Trump's domestic economic policies, responded unfavorably to the prospect of protracted trade wars. For Trump's earliest supporters, however—those who had voted for him in the GOP primaries—the promise of a more hardline US trade policy was precisely part of his appeal.

In relation to East Asia, the incoming Trump administration soon clarified that it would not simply walk away from America's military commitments in the region. Indeed in some respects the already frenetic pace of US naval patrols within the region actually increased, both to create demonstration effects toward North Korea and to enforce freedom of navigation in the South China Sea.[33] Yet the president also emphasized the need for commercial reciprocity from US allies, as well as from the People's Republic of China, toward the United States. Trump withdrew the United States from the TPP, as promised, during his first days in office. He then secured a renegotiated bilateral trade agreement with South Korea, and indicated a willingness to pursue similar agreements with other US trading partners in the region. From time to time, Trump reiterated his complaint that South Korea could bear more of the burden of its own defense. But since both South Korea and Japan were making serious efforts to bolster their own military capabilities, there was no fundamental disagreement on this point. Japan remained, as always, the single most important US ally in the region, cultivating good relations with Washington wherever possible, though deeply concerned by American protectionism. Trump encouraged improved US relations with the Philippines, in part by emphasizing common counterterror interests rather than publicly criticizing its president Rodrigo Duterte on human rights concerns.[34] Meanwhile the Trump administration continued to have high hopes for the maintenance and improvement of diplomatic partnership with a rising India on a wide range of timely issues including Afghanistan, counterterrorism, bilateral trade, investment, and the Chinese challenge. Overall, the new administration described its vision for the region as one of a "free and open Indo-Pacific"—including India and South Asia more generally—characterized by sovereign nation-states trading peacefully and on equal terms with one another.[35] The two main challenges to this proposed order emanated from China and North Korea.

With regard to China, Trump emphasized cooperation where possible, and competition where he deemed it necessary—especially on economic grounds. The president worked to corral Beijing's cooperation on sanctions against Pyongyang. He authorized new arms sales to Taiwan while reiterating America's traditional "One China" policy. He met repeatedly with Chinese President Xi Jinping, stressed good personal relations, and downplayed any public criticism of China's human rights record. Meanwhile the administration's economic pressure campaign against Beijing got off to a slow start, hobbled in part by internal divisions.[36] Initially it looked as though the United States might accept only token concessions. But over the course of 2018 Trump initiated a far more sweeping American effort to force changes in Chinese trade practices. He authorized new US tariffs against $250 billion worth of Chinese products, and threatened further tariffs in the absence of major concessions. Beijing retaliated with tariffs of its own against the United States, and the two gigantic countries settled in for a possibly lengthy trade war.[37] Overall, the administration made clear that it viewed a rising China as both a strategic and economic great-power competitor. Trump placed particular emphasis on Beijing's predatory foreign economic practices, and the need to redress them.[38] In a speech at the Hudson Institute, Vice President Pence articulated the administration's hardline policy on this issue. By 2018 there was bipartisan support within Congress, if not for all of the president's related decisions, then at least for a toughened US approach toward Chinese economic practices—a remarkable shift from only two years before. Both Congress and the administration moved forward with various economic countermeasures against the People's Republic, while the United States and Beijing negotiated over tariffs.[39]

In relation to North Korea, the Trump administration introduced a campaign of "maximum pressure" designed to force the complete denuclearization of that totalitarian state.[40] This included gathering support from American allies, China, and the UN for strengthened international economic sanctions against Pyongyang. It also included massive demonstrations of US military power in the region, along with mutual exchanges of blood-curdling threats between the American president and Kim Jong-un. During his first year in office, in notable addresses to both the US Congress and the United Nations, Trump spoke out forcefully against North Korea's atrocious record on human rights.[41] He then pivoted in the following months toward a diplomatic charm offensive, with considerable nudging from South Korea's pro-engagement President Moon Jae-in. Trump agreed to meet the North Korean dictator one-on-one at a June 2018 summit held in Singapore. The results of the summit were ambiguous. Warlike tensions were indeed reduced. The two sides released a brief statement affirming the common goal of "the complete denuclearization of the Korean peninsula," with "President Trump committed to provide security guarantees to the DPRK."[42] Trump also agreed to halt US military exercises with South Korea; spoke warmly of Kim's intentions; and at least temporarily dropped all reference to human rights concerns. North Korea agreed to halt missile and nuclear weapons testing for the moment. What Kim gave up beyond this was not entirely clear. Secretary of State Pompeo confirmed the two sides would continue to negotiate on the central matter of North Korea's denuclearization.[43] But of course Pyongyang's definition of peninsular denuclearization had traditionally included major American security concessions unacceptable to previous

US presidents. Whether Trump would accept such concessions, or even view them as such, remained to be seen.[44]

With regard to Europe, Trump had initially spoken of NATO's obsolescence. But even before his inauguration, he put that claim in the past tense.[45] As president, Trump regularly voiced his frustration with European allies—especially Germany—for not spending more on their militaries. The president fixed on prior allied agreements to spend at least 2 percent of GDP on defense, noting that few had done so. At a May 2017 summit he spoke that frustration with particular bluntness, choosing not to mention America's Article 5 commitment to the collective security of NATO members. But within weeks, at a major address in Warsaw, Trump explicitly reaffirmed Article 5.[46] This combination of complaints over allied defense spending, together with explicit reaffirmations of NATO, was again repeated by the president in the following year.[47] And indeed a leading theme of the administration's language with regard to NATO from the beginning was US support for it, combined with a call for increased allied burden-sharing. Relations with prominent American allies in Europe were bumpy on key issues, due to major differences over trade, global warming, human rights, defense spending, the Paris climate accord, Iran's nuclear deal, Russia outreach, the Israeli–Palestinian peace process, G-7 summitry, and broader concepts of world order. Trump was hardly popular on the ground within Western Europe, and this created political challenges for some European leaders. Key Western figures such as Angela Merkel voiced a new awareness that American support could no longer be assumed. Observers on both sides of the Atlantic spoke of transatlantic crisis. Nor was there always a single European position on these issues; some of America's European allies adapted more successfully than others.[48] Yet in practical terms, NATO survived, transatlantic cooperation continued on a variety of matters such as counterterrorism, and allied leaders developed businesslike and sometimes even friendly personal relations with the Trump administration, including the American president, working to sort out their differences. Pragmatically speaking, Europe continued to need the United States, not least militarily, having limited options of its own.[49]

On the issue of US–Russia relations, Trump had long made clear his desire for better relations with Moscow. He was reluctant to admit that Russia had attempted to interfere in the 2016 US presidential election, and resentful of the implication that he had not legitimately won the election.[50] The running issue of any Trump campaign collusion with Russia generated a tremendous amount of controversy and attention, along with a special counsel investigation led by Robert Mueller. The US–Russia issue was therefore severely politicized. At a 2018 summit in Helsinki, Trump stood beside Vladimir Putin and stated that on the issue of election interference he had no more reason to believe US intelligence reports than Putin's own strong assurances—remarks that triggered bipartisan backlash within the United States.[51] In many ways, however—perhaps in part due to the political obstacles created by this very controversy—US policy toward Russia moved forward in a mostly hardline fashion on the ground. The United States continued to bolster its military presence in Poland; increased American sanctions against Russia; reaffirmed its security commitments to NATO members; introduced direct military aid to Ukraine; and made no diplomatic concessions to Russia in Europe.[52] The administration then followed up by indicating a planned American withdrawal from the INF Treaty, on the grounds of Russian noncompliance.[53] If Putin had expected any dramatic softening of the US position against Russia in a variety of places, then he had good reason to be disappointed. No doubt Trump's foreign policy and defense team advised the president in this direction. But the US government could not have mounted a hardline policy against Russia without the president's own support, or at least his acquiescence.

In the Middle East, the Trump administration rejected Barack Obama's diplomatic accord with Iran, as well as the freedom agenda of George W. Bush. Instead, the new American emphasis was on pushing back against certain US adversaries, and supporting regional allies regardless of their domestic practices.[54] Trump, for example, encouraged warm relations with Egypt's Abdel Fattah el-Sisi, viewing him as a bulwark against Islamic radicalism.[55] Saudi Arabia's rulers were similarly encouraged by a US president who emphasized counterterrorism, economic cooperation, and the common menace from Iran, rather than democracy promotion in

the Arab world. Arab allies were not happy with President Trump's decision to recognize Jerusalem as Israel's capital—a bold and unconventional
decision—but most Israelis certainly were. Indeed Trump cultivated close
relations with Israel's Benjamin Netanayahu government, on security cooperation as on other matters.[56] The October 2018 suspected killing of
journalist Jamal Khashoggi by Saudi agents in Istanbul triggered a fire-
storm of criticism against Riyadh's crown prince Mohammed bin Salman
along with America's Saudi policy. In Washington, Congress responded
by blocking US aid to Saudi military efforts in Yemen, and by critiquing
Riyadh on human rights. President Trump continued to favor American
support for the Saudi regime.[57]

Lifting use-of-force restrictions on US airstrikes and Special Operations
helped speed the rollback of ISIS as a state-like entity starting in 2017,
an effort that had begun more slowly three years earlier. The government
of Iraq experienced some modest progress in reasserting control over its
own territory and improving admittedly difficult living conditions amidst
new democratic elections. But it was clear that jihadist terrorist groups
in the region would remain active, in one form or another, including inside Syria, and the question was how to counter those groups while simultaneously meeting Trump's goal of avoiding US-led nation-building.
Meanwhile the United States adopted a noticeably more confrontational
approach toward Iran than it had under Obama, stressing economic
pressures in particular.[58] This shift was welcomed by American allies in
the Middle East, though not by allies in Europe. Partly to see if European
governments could be won over to a hardline position, Trump delayed the
big decision over the Joint Comprehensive Plan Of Action until May 2018,
when he finally announced the United States would withdraw from that
agreement and reinstate sanctions against Tehran. The president criticized
Iran's human rights record, and said he welcomed political changes in that
country, without using the phrase regime change.[59]

With regard to the seemingly endless civil war in Syria, no one pre-
tended to have easy answers, and anyone who did was mistaken. Trump's
instinct was clearly to avoid any massive US ground presence, and perhaps cooperate with the Russians in ending a war that Bashar al-Assad

was already winning. The US president twice authorized airstrikes against Syria in punishment for Assad's proven use of chemical weapons against his own people, and at those moments Trump seemed genuinely outraged by such atrocities. But with regard to a broader view of the region, he made plain his belief that the United States could not reliably engineer democratic regime change through military nation-building exercises, and that the previous fifteen years had proven as much. As he put it:

> We cannot purge the world of evil, or act everywhere there is tyr-anny. No amount of American blood or treasure can produce lasting peace and security in the Middle East . . . the fate of the region lies in the hands of its own people.[60]

In December 2018, Trump announced that US troops would withdraw from Syria. There was considerable subsequent uncertainty over when or how this would happen, and under what precise conditions.[61]

In relation to the Americas, Trump introduced some significant US policy changes. He rolled back the Obama-era loosening of trade and travel restrictions on Cuba, highlighting human rights abuses inside that country and demanding domestic political changes under the Castro re-gime before any further US concessions.[62] The administration likewise adopted a more hardline approach toward Venezuela's leftist government, both diplomatically and in terms of new US sanctions. As Trump put it at the UN, "we call for the full restoration of democracy and political freedoms in Venezuela. The problem in Venezuela is not that socialism has been poorly implemented, but that socialism has been faithfully implemented."[63] Most other members of the OAS joined in criticizing the autocratic direction of the Venezuelan regime. Trump's policies to-ward Mexico were more contentious. His staunch emphases on border control, illegal immigration, a US–Mexican security wall, and the sup-posed unfairness of NAFTA—together with earlier provocative comments regarding Mexican Americans—made it difficult for any government in Mexico to fully cooperate with Trump. Yet the newly elected government of left-wing populist nationalist Andres Manuel Lopez Obrador offered to work constructively with the United States while holding to certain Mexican core interests.[64] Trump's approach toward Canada was less of a sweeping challenge, but Justin Trudeau's government was placed under intense pressure to make trade concessions on NAFTA among other issues. Altogether, US two-way trade with the Americas amounted to more than US trade with either China or the European Union. Concerns over the possible breakdown of North American trading relationships were partly alleviated by the signing of a new NAFTA by the end of 2018.

Defense policy under Trump in 2017–2018 reflected distinct presidential priorities combined with the reassuring presence of Secretary Mattis. As a candidate, Trump had emphasized major increases in military spending and aggressive counterterrorism—naming radical Islam as the threat—alongside an end to nation-building and regime change. Upon taking office in 2017, he requested only modest increases in US defense spending. But the following year, planning for FY 2019, the administration proposed and Congress approved of significant increases in military expenditure.[65] The Trump administration's Nuclear Posture Review embraced the robust modernization and recapitalization of America's nuclear triad, already begun under President Obama, based upon the fresh premise of great-power competition together with a growing North Korean threat.[66] Meanwhile the new National Defense Strategy contained a striking shift in emphasis from a lengthy era of counterterrorism toward long-term strategic competition with revisionist authoritarian nation-states—above all, China.[67] The administration's National Security Strategy hit upon similar themes, emphasizing among other things an internationally competitive environment, the domestic economic bases of American power, allied burden-sharing, commercial reciprocity, great-power rivalry, border security, and US energy dominance.[68] In October 2018, President Trump proposed a 5 percent cut in defense. But he subsequently reconsidered proposed cuts, supporting $750 billion in US military spending for fiscal year 2020.[69]

In relation to Afghanistan, the administration conducted a serious 2017 review to consider various policy options. Trump's reluctant conclusion, which he announced that August, was that the United States could not

afford to immediately disengage from the country without empowering jihadist terrorists. He announced that the United States would send several
thousand additional troops to better mentor and support Afghan government forces; loosen rules of engagement on US troops; discard any fixed
timelines for American withdrawal; suspend US aid to Pakistan, in the
hopes of compelling a more cooperative approach on that front; and keep
open the eventual possibility of negotiations with the Taliban. As he put it:

> My original instinct was to pull out—and historically, I like fol-
> lowing my instincts. But all my life I've heard that decisions are
> much different when you sit behind the desk in the Oval Office. . . .
> the consequences of a rapid exit are both predictable and unaccept-
> able. . . . Conditions on the ground, not arbitrary timelines, will
> guide our strategy from now on. . . . strategically applied force aims
> to create the conditions for a political process to achieve a lasting
> peace.[70]

In December 2018, Trump announced that several thousand US troops
would depart from Afghanistan. As with Syria, the details were initially
characterized by uncertainty. Meanwhile the United States pursued
negotiations with the Taliban, talks headed on the American side by envoy
Zalmay Khalilzad.[71]

Trump's declared affection for the American armed forces did not always extend to other instruments and tools of US foreign policy. From
the beginning, he made clear his limited patience for some of the most
cherished aspects of contemporary liberal internationalism, including foreign assistance, global governance, diplomatic protocol, multilateralism,
climate change initiatives, "soft power," and democracy promotion as central to US foreign policy. Trump withdrew the United States from the Paris
climate accord, arguing it would "undermine our economy, hamstring our
workers, weaken our sovereignty, impose unacceptable legal risks, and put
us at a permanent disadvantage to the other countries of the world."[72] In
2017 and 2018, the White House proposed deep cuts of roughly one-third
to US spending on both foreign aid and the State Department. As OMB

director Mick Mulvaney put it, "The overriding message is fairly straight-forward: less money spent overseas means more money spent here."[73] Bipartisan majorities in Congress pushed back against these requests and insisted on maintaining international expenditures relatively constant.[74] The president's 2017 address to the United Nations placed a striking emphasis on national sovereignty, national self-determination, and national autonomy as appropriate organizing principles in world politics.[75] With regard to democracy promotion and human rights, Trump was at times very outspoken on human rights abuses inside nations such as Cuba, Iran, Syria, North Korea, and Venezuela, calling for changes in the practices of those countries. But he was relatively quiet on such abuses inside Russia or China, and similarly low-key in relation to US allies. His instinct, apparently, was not to criticize foreign leaders on their own internal practices if he believed other American interests could be secured.[76]

Insofar as there is a Trump doctrine in US foreign policy, it might be described as an attempt to squeeze out what the president views as relative gains for the United States through the applied escalation and de-escalation of American leverage. Trump typically believes in making threats at each point of escalation in order to ensure that target audiences—including foreign governments—understand he may be willing to go even further than they are. Sometimes he escalates tensions in sudden, unpredictable ways. He can also de-escalate very rapidly and unexpectedly. Indeed the president makes it clear in almost every case that he's ultimately looking for a negotiated settlement, but one he finds satisfactory, and that he's willing to walk away from the bargaining table if it isn't.[77]

For Trump, then, the purpose of escalation is most often to de-escalate on favorable terms. To describe his approach as zero-sum is not strictly accurate. On the contrary, he regularly refers to the possibility of mutual benefit between the United States and other countries. But he is attuned to the relative gains to be had from these various negotiations—or at least what he thinks of as gains—and insists that America's material interests be pushed more aggressively within those same diplomatic frameworks. Moreover, he does not instinctively insulate economic issues from security concerns, nor US allies from adversaries. All are subject to the application of leverage up and down the ladder.

The actual foreign policy practice of the Trump administration therefore appears to involve a sort of pressure campaign, on multiple fronts. These fronts can be pictured as follows:

1. Pressuring adversaries over security issues.
2. Pressuring adversaries over commercial issues.
3. Pressuring allies over security issues.
4. Pressuring allies over commercial issues.

Some key advantages and disadvantages of these various pressure campaigns can be summarized briefly.

PRESSURING ADVERSARIES OVER SECURITY ISSUES

On the first front, the administration pressures Iran and North Korea via sanctions and deterrence, asserts American naval patrols around waters claimed by China, strengthens the US military presence along NATO's eastern border, conducts efforts against the Taliban, and forcefully rolls back ISIS. At the same time, President Trump makes clear his willingness to sit down and negotiate with any of these competitors, apart of course from ISIS.

These efforts to counteract and impose costs upon numerous authoritarian adversaries are justified, and have already produced some positive results. Of course, any foreign policy approach carries risks, and so does this one. One risk commonly noted, and a valid concern, is that of accidental military escalation with a peacetime competitor. But an equally valid concern is the risk of premature de-escalation involving excessive American concessions.

Take the case of North Korea. The 2018 Singapore summit brought a reduction in warlike tensions, a reduction welcome to most Americans. At the same time, in order to succeed, the US-led maximum pressure campaign against Pyongyang should be maintained without any lop-sided American compromise on key issues. Otherwise, what was its pur-pose in the first place? All things considered, the main challenge on this front is to build up negotiating leverage without veering into accidental warfare—and to hold out the promise of diplomacy without offering one-sided accommodations. The same might be said with regard to US Russia policy, especially after President Trump's 2018 press conference along-side Vladimir Putin in Helsinki. Fortunately, the administration's policies on the ground are for the most part tougher toward Russia than were President Obama's.

PRESSURING ADVERSARIES OVER COMMERCIAL ISSUES

On the second front, the main target is China's foreign economic practices. Here, the president levies tariffs against Chinese goods, referencing dis-criminatory practices under Section 301 of the 1974 Trade Act, and threat-ening additional tariffs while holding out hopes for resolution.

Trump deserves credit for drawing attention to a longtime pattern of Chinese abuses against the United States and its allies. These abuses in-clude intellectual property theft, state-sponsored cybercrime, forced tech-nology transfer, and industrial espionage on a massive scale. A forceful US response is long overdue. Punitive tariffs are an admittedly blunt tool in America's toolkit against predatory Chinese practices. The United States also has multiple other economic tools to use, if it chooses to use them—and it should. The goal should be to extract concessions on these practices, rather than fixating on the trade deficit per se. A lengthy Sino–American trade dispute of course carries economic costs and risks for both sides. But these risks are worth taking if they force significant policy changes from Beijing. In fact one possible danger is that the administration might concede too easily in exchange for superficial Chinese concessions on the US trade deficit. Again, the risks of premature de-escalation are worth considering.

PRESSURING ALLIES OVER SECURITY ISSUES

On the third front, Trump presses allies to bolster their own armed forces. Given the existing range and balance of allied capabilities, this effort centers especially on Europe.

NATO is arguably the most successful peacetime alliance in history. In terms of pressuring US allies to spend more on their own defenses, the central request, however roughly expressed, is not unreasonable. In fact numerous allies agree with the basic direction, and are taking steps to adjust. This was in evidence again at the 2018 NATO summit, where members agreed to keep bolstering common military capabilities. Some of course find this American request to be mostly unwelcome, obnoxious, or unrealistic, given their own domestic politics. Germany, in particular, prefers focusing on reiterations of rules-based order, while simultaneously buying natural gas from Moscow and relying on American troops for protection. Trump isn't actually wrong about that.[78] Liberal internationalists respond, in effect, that the United States must adopt German political preferences. But why US foreign policy should be based upon the Merkel government's particular conception of international security is not exactly obvious. In any case, with the current administration, that specific danger is absent.

As always with Donald Trump, there is a great deal to critique and debate on specifics. But assuming the administration looks to counter US adversaries, then all three of these pressure fronts are basically justified. It is the fourth front—trade wars with US allies—that has been most problematic, in part because it complicates the other three.

PRESSURING ALLIES OVER COMMERCIAL ISSUES

On the fourth front, the president has levied tariffs against US allies— notably Canada, Mexico, and the European Union—on the grounds of national security, referencing Section 232 of the 1962 Trade Act. Again, he offers to negotiate, but on his own terms.

To be clear: Neither the United States nor its democratic trading partners are entirely innocent of selective commercial protectionism. Some of
the specific American complaints regarding allied tariffs are well-founded.
Still, lengthy US trade disputes with democratic allies carry all of the economic costs of a trade dispute with China, but with no possible strategic
benefit. China is a great-power rival, an authoritarian force, and a longtime
practitioner of deeply predatory commercial practices. In terms of this
unique combination it is unlike any other US trading partner, and most
Americans know it. Trade wars with US allies, on the other hand, cost all
sides economically, while rendering strategic cooperation on other matters
less likely. The United States should therefore de-escalate these commercial
disputes with its allies, and focus on forming a common front with them
against Beijing. To its credit, the Trump administration appeared to move
in this direction during the second half of 2018, signing a renegotiated
NAFTA along with a trade trace in relation to the European Union.

Trump's impact on allied perceptions of the United States—well beyond
issues of trade—is one of the most striking aspects of his presidency.
His election surprised US allies, forcing them to grapple with the possibility they might not be able to count on American support. Of course,
for many overseas, the impression of gradual US disengagement predated
Trump's election, referencing moments such as President Obama's
unenforced red lines over Syria in 2013. In a number of important ways,
the Trump administration immediately reaffirmed traditional American
security commitments, and has continued to do so. Allied leaders and
officials have generally been appreciative whenever President Trump or
other US officials reaffirm these commitments. But the president personally unnerves many foreign leaders. They notice even the slightest gaps,
inconsistencies, or contradictions between the president and his advisers,
between documents and actions, between tweets and policies, and wonder
if they can truly rely upon Trump down the road. Indeed they are often
unclear what the president's policy is on a given specific issue, given these
shifting parameters, and this makes negotiations difficult. They are never
quite certain what the president will say or do from one moment to the

next. In this sense, Trump has accomplished something he set out to do. He has been unpredictable.

Allies have a number of broad options in responding to Trump.[79] They can hedge their bets, and improve relations with other countries—whether friend or foe—circumventing the United States in case American support breaks down. They can lie low, and try to wait Trump out. They can cooperate with one another, with or without the United States. They can view Trump's approach as a crisis moment. They can view it as an opportunity. They can push back on specific matters such as US tariffs. They can accommodate new American demands, and try to keep working with the United States. They can reaffirm their own conceptions of international order. They can welcome US policy adjustments that they favor. Or they can pursue several of these options at the same time. Indeed the latter is what most allies have done, with important variations from one government to the next. Among Middle East allies, Trump's policies are generally viewed as an improvement over Obama's. Key East Asian allies such as the Japanese have the usual concerns, but work pragmatically to promote their own interests given Trump's predilections. For the most part, it is within allied countries in Western Europe and North America that his approach has generated the greatest political controversies.

As it turns out however, America's allies do need the United States, and want its continued support, both strategically and economically. For this reason, although a number of allies may not like Trump's approach, for the most part they attempt to keep working with the United States on matters of common interest. And this is consistent with past experience as well. During the presidency of George W. Bush, for example, critics often predicted that assertively unilateral US policies would trigger allied counterbalancing. But as a number of important studies have shown in investigating those years, Bush's policies did not actually lessen allied desire for security cooperation with the United States. US capabilities are such that Washington has the ability to exercise leverage without always paying a heavy price for it.[80]

The issue of President Trump's foreign policy management style is perhaps the thorniest question of all. Trump's fiercest critics seem reluctant to concede that he has any strengths in this regard, while his most enthusiastic supporters seem equally unwilling to admit that the president has any weaknesses.

Trump's strengths include a willingness to question conventional wisdom, and a determination to act on promises made when first running for president. He is far from unintelligent, pursuing his basic objectives with forceful tenacity. And on a number of important policy matters, he has shown a readiness to learn, listen, and adapt. Many of the grievances and complaints that Trump raises with regard to past policies and processes are reasonable enough. Business-minded experience and perspectives are not irrelevant here. There really was a case, as of 2015–2016, for toning down some of the distinctly Wilsonian assumptions dominant in US foreign policy since the end of the Cold War. Moreover, it is not so mistaken to think of international diplomacy as a form of bargaining, whereby the United States must receive something in exchange for what it gives. If critics call this transactional, then so be it. The primary responsibility of a US president is to look out for the safety, freedom, and prosperity of American citizens, not to act as a kind of progressive transnational pontiff.

Unfortunately, like numerous other presidents, Trump's strengths come packaged together with some serious weaknesses. Trump has often been withering in his critique of past practices. Yet it is still far from clear that he understands the basic uses of America's foreign policy and national security bureaucracy, and how to utilize them in pursuit of his own agenda. These policy tools have their own separate patterns distinct from running a family-run business, however extensive. Trump too often approaches major foreign policy issues, meetings, and decisions with an explicit disdain for the idea that he might need to master the details and prepare. But a lack of preparation or of accurate details on a personal level is no true asset to any foreign policy agenda, including a nationalist one. No president can literally manage the US foreign policy process alone, or purely on instinct. Nor is a lack of coordination and a constantly shifting set of mixed signals some kind of secret weapon. Very often, given the president's miscellaneous statements—including in relation to his own appointees—it is hard to know what exactly his policy is on a given specific matter. Naturally this complicates diplomatic negotiations of any kind, including those undertaken in pursuit of the US national interest. Like his predecessor Barack Obama, Trump may overestimate the transformative effect of his own personality in relation to America's seasoned adversaries overseas.

Trump's recognized unpredictability is an excellent example of both the pluses and minuses of his particular approach.[81] To be sure, projecting a kind of unforeseeable menace can be extremely useful in relation to international adversaries. And Trump has done that more than once. Indeed it could be argued that his threats to use force are more believable than those of Barack Obama, whose verbal warnings to various autocrats rang increasingly hollow after 2013.[82] In operational terms, militarily, unpredictability is an asset. Still, the overall conduct of foreign policy goes well beyond this. If a president signals mixed messages or unpredictability regarding core alliance commitments, as Trump sometimes does off the cuff, this may eventually tempt aggressors to press their advantage. Unpredictable menace is certainly better than predictable weakness, but in terms of preventing deterrence breakdown, predictable firmness is best of all. As Secretary of Defense Mattis noted in the 2018 *National Defense Strategy*, the United States should seek unpredictability in operational matters, together with predictable strength in strategic ones.[83]

In any case, one major revelation of the Trump presidency worth noting is that the president's major foreign policy priorities are *directional*. In other words, he believes that existing international military and commercial arrangements have been disproportionately costly for the United States, and must be reoriented or renegotiated in the opposite direction. This is not the same as seeking a complete dismantling of America's post-World War II commitments, and the distinction is crucial. There is no conclusive evidence from either his words or actions as president that Trump is utterly fixed upon dismantling rules-based liberal international order, any more than on upholding it. It is simply not his primary reference point one way or the other. Rather, he looks to pull existing arrangements in the direction of what he views as material US interests, and is open to either renegotiating or abandoning those arrangements case by case. Drawing on his experience in real estate, he lays out attention-getting positions, some-times extreme ones, and then states his readiness to negotiate. Needless to say, this process unnerves his negotiating partners overseas, his domestic critics, and even some of his own staff, who rarely know Trump's final res-ervation point in any given situation. He himself may not know. The pres-ident reserves the right to decide, case by case. But the implication of all this is that many or perhaps even most aspects of America's forward pres-ence may very well survive his tenure, and in certain cases be reinforced. In effect, Trump is undertaking a kind of reassessment of America's global commitment portfolio, and its outcome is not predetermined.

All things considered, this means that the actual foreign policy choices, perspectives, and outcomes of the Trump administration are in practice a hybrid or mixture of the nationalist with the conservative internationalist. And as we have already seen, this is hardly unusual for Republican presi-dents. Trump's specific way of striking that balance is certainly unique. But then this was true of past presidents as well. And as with every past presi-dent, the current one is the single leading player in his own administration's major foreign policy decisions. As Trump said himself: "I'm a nationalist and a globalist. I'm both. And I'm the only one who makes the decision."[84]

Populism, Foreign Policy, and the GOP

A new conservative nationalism began to form among Republican voters during Barack Obama's first term in the White House. At that time the median GOP voter remained supportive of aggressive counterterrorism and strong defense spending, while revealing increased ambivalence toward economic globalization and protracted US military interventions overseas. Internationalist candidate Mitt Romney won the 2012 GOP nomination in spite of this ambivalence. Four years later, Donald Trump tapped into and encouraged the new conservative nationalism in his own direction with distinct stands on foreign policy, trade, and immigration. Yet Republican voter opinion has remained surprisingly stable on foreign policy issues throughout this time. Even on the now highly politicized issue of US–Russia relations, most Republican voters retain a negative image of Vladimir Putin. And on free trade, the base of the party is not so much protectionist as divided.

Viewed over the longer term, however—say, by comparison with the New Deal era—there has indeed been a profound shift in the composition of the Republican Party toward political populism, cultural conservatism, and white working-class voters. And again Trump is not so much the cause of this trend, as an effect. What Trump has done, to an unusual extent, is to bring the policy preferences of his newly empowered populist supporters into tension with orthodox conservative economics on selected key issues. For now, he retains the support of the vast majority of Republican voters, whether traditionally conservative or populist. But because a number of internal party differences over foreign policy, trade, immigration, and certain domestic economic issues predate his candidacy, and have now been brought into the open, these divisions will likely outlast him as well.

The long-term future of Republican foreign policy will therefore involve and require striking the right balance between conservative internationalist, hardline nationalist, and noninterventionist concerns. The specific character and substance of how this is done will be up to future conservative leaders. Donald Trump has cracked existing orthodoxies and opened up previously latent foreign policy options. Yet his very ability to do so indicates that he acts upon structural forces bigger than he is, and therefore likely to outlast him. For this reason, in one form or another, conservative nationalism is here to stay.

The Trump presidency has produced a continual stream of sweeping yet misinformed analysis regarding the internal state of the Republican Party. Amongst journalistic, academic, and political commentators today, the condition of opinion within the GOP regarding foreign policy issues is regularly misunderstood.[1] Here are several prevalent and mistaken assumptions that have circulated since November 2016:

1. Among Republican voters, support for internationalism is dead.
2. Republicans are now pro-Putin.
3. The GOP base strongly opposes free trade.
4. Republicans are deeply divided over President Trump's foreign policy.
5. Trump's foreign policy views are not representative of the median voter.
6. Donald Trump has revolutionized Republican foreign policy opinion.

A closer look at public opinion polling results from organizations such as Gallup, the Pew Center, and the Chicago Council on Global Affairs over

the past few years reveals a far more nuanced picture, often directly contradictory to these myths. Let's consider each one in turn.

AMONG REPUBLICAN VOTERS, SUPPORT
FOR INTERNATIONALISM IS DEAD

Trump's 2016 campaign offered a withering critique of Wilsonian foreign
policy traditions. But if conservative internationalism is defined as favoring
a certain kind of US activism overseas, including the maintenance of
alliances, then there is still considerable support for it among Republican
voters. A 2017 Pew Center study found that "Core Conservatives"—the
single biggest group of Republicans and Trump supporters—are more
likely to say that "it's best for the US to be active in world affairs," rather
than simply "focus on problems at home."[2] A Chicago Council study, also
from 2017, shows a solid majority of Republicans—some 65 percent—
agreeing that's it's best for the United States to "take an active part in world
affairs."[3] On the maintenance of existing alliances, a clear majority of
Republicans including core Trump supporters agree that the preservation
of NATO is "still essential" to US security.[4] Indeed with regard to the US
military presence in Europe, the Middle East, or the Asia-Pacific, Trump
supporters and Republicans generally are *more* likely than Democrats
to support either the continuation or enhancement of current US troop
levels.[5] A 2018 Chicago Council report found similar results, including
that Republicans are still more likely than Democrats to support the use
of American troops overseas if US allies are invaded.[6]

     To be sure, these same studies show a significant percentage of
Republicans—like a significant percentage of other Americans—ready
to question existing US alliances and force commitments, along with the
underlying premise of US foreign policy activism. Conservative internationalist and noninterventionist impulses do compete within the heart of
the GOP today. But this has always been true, including with regard to the
American public as a whole. The notion that Republican voters no longer
support US foreign policy activism is an oversimplification.

REPUBLICANS ARE NOW PRO-PUTIN

This is one of the most commonly suggested findings of the Trump era: namely, that GOP voters are now supposedly "warm" toward Putin and Russia.[7] A widely discussed YouGov poll found a significant shift in Putin's favorable ratings among Republicans over the course of 2016.[8] The logical implication is that this shift was in response to Trump's unusual language regarding Putin over the course of the 2016 campaign.

Some polls do indeed suggest that Republicans are now less likely than Democrats to view Russia as a major threat.[9] And insofar as the Russia issue has become entangled in domestic political and legal controversies related to ongoing special counsel investigations, party opinion has certainly polarized. However, the fact that tends to go missing amidst the headlines is that according to these same polls the majority of Republicans retained a negative impression of Putin before, during, and after the 2016 campaign. Moreover, the year 2017 saw a dramatic rise in the percentage of Republicans inclined to view Putin's Russia as an adversary. According to YouGov, as of February 2018 some 83 percent of Republicans viewed Russia as either "unfriendly" or an "enemy." This was actually a higher percentage than among Democrats.[10] Other polling organizations, such as Gallup, never found a significant rise in GOP voter favorability toward Russia in the first place.[11] In sum, an overwhelming majority of Republicans had a negative impression of Putin before the 2016 campaign, and an overwhelming majority of Republicans now hold that same position. The big and lasting story since 2014 is not that GOP voters have shifted toward Russia, but that Democrats have shifted against it.

THE GOP BASE STRONGLY OPPOSES FREE TRADE

A significant portion of Republican voters are and have long been skeptical regarding the benefits of economic globalization and free-trade agreements. Donald Trump won the 2016 GOP primaries in part by appealing to this constituency.[12] Yet any blanket statement that the Republican base simply opposes free trade is misleading. It would be more accurate to say that the base of the party is divided on this issue.

The Pew Research Center found in 2017, for example, that over half of GOP voters believe US involvement in global economy is good for new markets and growth. At the same time, a large minority of Republican voters disagreed with this statement.[13] Republicans are also divided over the question of whether trade agreements benefit the United States along with other countries. Core Trump supporters are more likely to believe that such agreements mostly favor other countries, and that NAFTA in particular has been bad for the United States.[14] Most Republican voters today—like most Americans—believe that international trade has been on balance good for the American economy, but bad for the job security of American workers. Party leaders are far more likely to say that global- ization has been good across the board.[15] This gap between popular and elite conceptions over US trade policy has been wide for many years, and was fully revealed in 2016.

As a presidential candidate, Donald Trump took an unusually stark position against numerous free-trade agreements. Yet since his inaugu- ration, there is considerable evidence from multiple polling organizations including Pew, Gallup, and the Chicago Council to suggest that popular support for free-trade agreements within the Republican Party has actu- ally gone up.[16] Polling on trade policy has produced contradictory images since 2016, in part depending upon the precise questions asked. Yet that is precisely the point. The picture that emerges of Republican voters as a whole is one of mixed feelings, rather than unalterable opposition toward free trade.

REPUBLICANS ARE DEEPLY DIVIDED OVER PRESIDENT TRUMP'S FOREIGN POLICY

Although there are broad divisions among Republican voters on a number of substantive international issues, when it comes to the ques- tion of supporting President Trump's foreign policy, there is no such even division. On the contrary, when asked simply whether or not they support the president's foreign policy, the vast majority of Republicans say yes, and have said so ever since his inauguration. Representative polls find the level of GOP voter support for Trump's foreign policy to be roughly 80 percent, and remarkably steady at that level for over a year now.[17] This is in keeping with trends during recent presidencies such as Barack Obama's. The pattern in recent administrations has been that fellow partisans are much more likely to support a president of their own party, even when there is internal party disagreement over substantive issues. Interestingly, the reverse is also true: voters of the opposite party have been far more likely in recent years to say they oppose a given president's foreign policy, even when they themselves are divided on matters of substance. According to the polls, this is certainly true for Democrats in the Trump era. As with Republicans, Democratic voters today express some serious internal divisions over numerous foreign policy issues including free trade, US foreign policy activism, and military intervention. But when asked simply whether or not they support the president's foreign policy, an overwhelming majority of Democrats reply that they do not.[18] There is even some evidence that the very fact of Trump's taking a given issue position produces Democratic voter movement in the *opposite* direction. The result is paradoxical: both parties are internally divided right now over international issues, with some overlapping mixed opinion on matters of substance. Yet when framed as supporting the president, party opinion lines up very differently, strongly for or against.

TRUMP'S FOREIGN POLICY VIEWS ARE NOT REPRESENTATIVE OF THE MEDIAN VOTER

The Chicago Council released a widely discussed report in 2017 asking whether US public opinion is closer to Donald Trump or the infamous "Blob"—that is, the bipartisan American foreign policy establishment based in Washington, DC. For those who wanted a quick takeaway, the report's subtitle was: "Americans are generally closer to the Blob." Yet a closer look at the Council's own results in that poll showed a much more complex picture. According to the poll, compared to elites in either party, the general public is considerably more skeptical of the benefits of free trade and globalization; more focused on job protection as a key US foreign policy priority; significantly more concerned at large numbers of immigrants and refugees coming into the United States; less likely to say the United States should take an active part in world affairs; and considerably less likely to say that defending allies' security should be an important US foreign policy goal.[19] Obviously large portions of Trump's foreign policy are quite controversial. Over 50 percent of Americans typically say they do not approve of his foreign policy overall. Yet insofar as the president projects mixed feelings or ambivalence regarding any of the usual components of internationalism—free trade, traditional alliances, intervention, and US foreign policy activism—he may not be so far from the median American voter.

DONALD TRUMP HAS REVOLUTIONIZED REPUBLICAN FOREIGN POLICY OPINION

On some issues, such as free trade and US Russia policy, there was an observable bump in support over the course of the 2016 campaign among Republican voters in the direction of Donald Trump's own stated views. But this bump is dwarfed by three larger and observable trends.

First, movements in GOP popular opinion specifically over the course of 2015–2016 toward trade protection or warmer relations with Russia appear to have been temporary, and may have already evaporated.[20]

Second, any observed changes in opinion during 2015–2016 applied to only a minority of Republican voters. All of these polls reveal that a majority of GOP voters never changed their views on issues such as Russia or free trade, one way or another.

Third, and perhaps most important, intra-GOP divisions over questions of trade and military intervention—and a sense of hardline nationalist resurgence—predated Donald Trump's presidential candidacy.

Roughly half of Republican voters expressed skepticism toward free trade and economic globalization several years before Trump's candidacy began. And increased popular Republican skepticism regarding US military interventions, counterinsurgency operations, and nation-building exercises was already noticeable during Barack Obama's first term. Donald Trump did not create these trends; he tapped into them. For an outspoken hardline nationalist to win the Republican presidential nomination was indeed unusual. But internal GOP divisions over issues of trade and intervention existed well before 2015.[21] The broad configuration of Republican foreign policy opinion is therefore much the same as it was before Trump ran for president.

Part of the confusion surrounding current analyses regarding the GOP, public opinion, and US foreign policy lies in the common mistaken simplification that bipartisan support previously existed for an agreed-upon definition of Wilsonian internationalism, only recently destroyed by Donald Trump. In reality, liberal Democrats and conservative Republicans have held some significant differences over these matters going back many years. Liberals and conservatives disagree and have long disagreed over issues of multilateralism, global governance, the United Nations, the use of force, humanitarian intervention, foreign aid, defense spending, arms control, immigration, covert action, counterterrorism, civil liberties, and the need to address environmental challenges including climate change. These broad interparty differences go back decades, arguably to the domestic political fallout from the US war in Vietnam. Ever since the 1970s, liberal Democrats have tended to favor cooperative, multilateral, or accommodating forms of liberal internationalism.[22] Conservative Republicans have tended to be more hardline. So for Republicans, a hawkish American nationalism in itself is nothing new. The great question has always been whether specific Republican presidents are capable of combining that impulse with realistic, engaged, and successful foreign policies under ever-changing conditions. Some have done so quite effectively.

An objective look at public opinion polls over the past few years reveals the limitations of some common and current misconceptions regarding popular Republican attitudes toward US foreign policy. Support for multiple aspects of conservative internationalism among Republicans has never really been extinguished. But this support takes the form of some specific policy preferences that liberal Democrats are unlikely to favor, which is presumably why we have more than one political party competing for high office.

The great majority of Republican voters have no affection for Putin's Russia. Nor is the base of the GOP overwhelmingly hostile toward free trade. Rather, there is a deep and longstanding division among GOP voters over the relative merits of free-trade agreements. A certain ambivalence toward economic globalization, military intervention, alliance commitments, and US foreign policy activism is prevalent among American voters writ large, including Republicans, now as in the past. Trump's particular formulations in response to this are of course new. But neither internal GOP divisions over important foreign policy issues, nor the presence of an intense American nationalism, are truly anything novel when it comes to the Republican Party. At the end of the day, the president retains the support of the overwhelming majority of Republicans for his foreign policy overall. Whether Trump has revolutionized US foreign policy remains a matter of intense debate. Every US president has the ability to reshape America's foreign relations, and his own party's projected image, in profound sometimes unexpected ways. But on the question of whether Trump has radically reshaped Republican voter *opinion* on foreign policy issues, altogether the polls over the last few years tell an interesting and perhaps counterintuitive story: He has not.

The rise of conservative-leaning populist nationalism throughout much of the Western world in recent years has garnered tremendous attention. Discussion of this trend has been characterized by far more heat than light. The best evidence located by scholars such as Ronald Inglehart and Pippa Norris indicates that voters most drawn to populist-nationalist parties and candidates on both sides of the Atlantic are indeed concerned by issues of economic inequality and globalization. Profound structural changes transforming the workforce and society in postindustrial economies— including the rise of the knowledge economy, technological automation, global flows of labor, goods, people, and capital, the relative decline of traditional manufacturing, and migrant inflow—have encouraged a sense of economic insecurity. To some extent this places such voters, candidates, and parties at odds with free-market conservative economics. At the same time, according to Inglehart and Norris, an even greater motivation for voters drawn to populist-nationalist candidates, parties, and movements is a sense of cultural upheaval. The very same rise of postmaterialist cosmopolitan, multicultural issues and values that inspire liberals has also triggered a culturally conservative reaction from those segments of the public unpersuaded by the benefit of such changes. As Inglehart and Norris put it, whereas cosmopolitan liberals embrace progressive values, populist nationalists embrace traditional values. This is simply a different dimension of concerns from that of free-market conservatives.[23]

One striking feature of Donald Trump's 2016 presidential campaign was the way in which it rallied culturally conservative voters against cosmopolitan elites in both parties. Or to put it another way, that election represented a further step in the long-term transformation of US party alignments since the New Deal era to incorporate new sociocultural dimensions. The central finding of Alan Abramowitz on this matter is worth quoting at length:

The deep partisan divide that exists among the politically engaged segment of the American public as well as among political elites and activists is, fundamentally, a disagreement over the dramatic changes that have transformed American society and culture since the end of World War II, and that continue to have huge effects in the twenty-first century. The challenges posed by technological change, globalization, immigration, growing racial and ethnic diversity, and changes in family structure and gender roles have produced diverging responses from party elites and a growing alignment of partisan identities with deeper divisions in American society and culture. This "great alignment" has transformed the American party system and fundamentally altered American politics in the twenty-first century. On one side of this partisan divide are those who have benefitted from and welcome the new American society, including racial minorities, the LGBT community, religious moderates and skeptics, and more educated citizens who possess the skills to thrive in the economy of the twenty-first century. Those Americans voted overwhelmingly for Barack Obama in 2008 and 2012 and for Hillary Clinton in 2016. On the other side of the divide are those who find these changes deeply troubling and threatening, including religious conservatives and many less educated whites in small towns and rural areas. Those Americans voted overwhelmingly for John McCain in 2008, Mitt Romney in 2012, and Donald Trump in 2016.[24]

A couple of points are worth making regarding this finding. The first, as Abramowitz notes, is that most voters never actually changed party allegiance between 2012 and 2016. Those changes in voting that did take place were at the margin. Nevertheless these marginal changes were significant, and especially notable from the perspective of bipartisan opinion elites. This brings us to the second point. Most Republican political, economic, and intellectual leaders do not feel personally harmed or displaced by technological changes, globalization, immigration, or growing ethnic diversity. This leadership class possesses the skills to thrive in a twenty-first-century economy. Furthermore, some Republican political, economic, and intellectual leaders do not feel any particular objection to the social and cultural changes that have altered American life over the years. For such opinion leaders, the spectacle of a GOP verbally at odds with numerous post-1945 domestic and international changes is certainly disorienting. But strictly speaking, if we reread the description by Abramowitz of who now votes Republican and why, one word certainly applies to these voters' perspective: conservative. According to Abramowitz, many GOP voters are troubled by the broad changes that have swept American life over the past couple of generations, and prefer to either slow down or resist these changes. Consequently, the very meaning of the word conservative politically is being questioned and redefined in a more literal direction.

So has there been—or is there likely to be—a "populist" realignment within the GOP? And if so, what does this mean with regard to foreign policy issues?

In part, the answer depends upon our definition of populism. In American politics there is a tradition of using the word to describe nothing more than a folksy style or demeanor on the part of individual politicians—like breakfast served with a Southern accent. Current academic definitions of populism, however, tend toward the extremely sinister. Drawing on comparative historical analysis, scholars such as Jan-Werner Muller define populism as nothing less than authoritarian. According to this definition, populists by their very nature oppose political pluralism and minority rights; claim to represent the majority of a given nation's ordinary citizens against a small, privileged, and self-interested elite; regularly indulge in conspiracy theories; favor aggressive forms of identity politics; disparage political opponents including "the establishment" as downright illegitimate; erode constitutional norms; deliberately undercut civil society; press toward authoritarian forms of government; and thereby threaten the very bases of liberal democracy itself. Hugo Chavez, Benito Mussolini, Vladimir Putin, and Donald Trump are then commonly placed by concerned observers into the same category as real or potential populist authoritarian leaders, past and present. Indeed there is already a small cottage industry of prominent non-fiction books and articles categorizing recent populist trends in this way, and decrying the trend as fascistic.[25]

The trouble with this sweeping definition of populism as necessarily authoritarian, however, is that it fails to capture the historical reality of the matter within the United States. European and—increasingly—US scholars have imported European categories of analysis into the study of American populism that do not entirely apply. This has encouraged transatlantic analyses of American populism that both take it too seriously, and not seriously enough. They take it too seriously in claiming that it is a harbinger of fascism. Yet they do not take it seriously enough in terms of actually listening to any specific or valid complaints of populist voters. The American experience with populism is not identical to that of Venezuela or the Balkans. There are democratic as well as authoritarian forms of populism internationally, and within the United States at least, it is democratic versions—on both left and right—that have had much more lasting effect.

To say that populism is anti-establishment is clearly correct. Certainly, populism at its worst can and sometimes does tend toward conspiracy theory. But any built-in tendency toward authoritarianism is hardly inevitable. As Roger Kimball points out, populism may be an attempt to press the question of who rules. And for populists, the proper answer to that question is never the nation's managerial elite per se, but rather the people as a whole, through their elected representatives. In other words, populism is a periodic effort to reassert the core principle of popular sovereignty against established elites.[26] In this sense populism is precisely the opposite of authoritarian or undemocratic.

Apart from its anti-establishment premise, perhaps the single most striking feature of American populism historically is its sheer variety in terms of attitudes, platforms, and specific issues of concern.[27] The American experience is that populist movements on both left and right have periodically informed and reshaped one or both political parties, to refresh a sense of small-d democratic politics, however unwelcome to existing elites. Populists change the subject, in terms of issue specification, and attack elite privileges. For established elites to decry this tendency as morally outrageous is a bit hard to take seriously. Naturally, existing elites look to defend their own status, interests, values, privilege, influence, and sources of income. But within the United States, these power struggles take place—as America's founders believed they would—within the framework of a federal constitutional republic. For example, one defining wave of populism within the United States was the agrarian movement of the late nineteenth century, eventually capturing the presidential nomination of the Democratic Party in 1896 under the leadership of William Jennings

Bryan.[28] Bryan's agrarian radicalism remade the Democratic Party to some extent, picking up electoral support in the West while losing it east of the Mississippi.[29] Bryan never became president, but succeeding generations of Democrats from Woodrow Wilson to Harry Truman had to factor in Bryan's core constituency of Western agrarians in order to build politically winning coalitions nationwide. FDR's New Deal certainly had its own populist aspect, directed against the nation's wealthiest financial elites. GOP conservatives have rarely found any lasting political success since that time without a least a populist coalitional component. The great question has always been its specific content.

Over the past seventy years, the GOP has become a more populist party by realigning itself in a conservative direction on social and cultural issues. Realignment is a process whereby the axis of division between political parties rotates and shifts to include new issue dimensions. And while the pursuit of mathematical formulas for lasting majorities has proven to be chimerical,[30] there really are shifting bases of division between the two parties, and those bases are worth understanding. After the US Civil War, for example, the Republican Party's base of support was primarily sectional, in the North. In 1896, William McKinley ran on a platform of sound money, against the agrarian populism of William Jennings Bryan. This solidified GOP support in the industrial Northeast, and among economic conservatives. McKinley's successor Theodore Roosevelt straddled the divide between conservatives and populist progressives within the GOP, while trending toward the latter—especially after leaving office. But Republican opposition to FDR's New Deal during the 1930s cemented the GOP as clearly the more conservative of America's two major parties on economic issues. This gave Republicans some new source of electoral support, but on balance they lost more than they gained, especially among urban, progressive, and working-class voters. The GOP became a party based narrowly among conservative, native-born, rural, and small-town Protestants outside of the South. This left it homogeneous, but at a definite disadvantage in relation to the Democrats' dominant New Deal coalition.[31]

Over the long term, Republicans were only able to escape mid-twentieth-century minority status by emphasizing a second dimension of issues, the social or cultural, as opposed to simply the domestic economic. Most Americans never wanted a complete rollback of FDR's New Deal. There was, however, a latent center-right majority waiting around concerns related to religion, civil rights, law and order, national security, social transformation, moral tradition, and issues of national identity.[32] The social and political changes and upheavals of the 1960s, in particular, highlighted these new concerns, fracturing the old Democratic coalition.[33] Over time, as Democrats moved to the left on these issues, and Republicans moved to the right, the two parties rearranged their own bases of support. Socially liberal candidates and voters moved out of the GOP, into the Democratic Party. Socially conservative candidates and voters moved in the opposite direction.[34] It took decades for this process to work itself out. Barry Goldwater, Richard Nixon, and Ronald Reagan played especially important roles in marking out the basic direction. Goldwater reached out to white Southerners on the issue of civil rights. Nixon aimed at a new Republican majority based on a center-right populist platform. In the words of Republican strategist Kevin Phillips, the aim circa 1970 was to construct a center-right coalition based upon "middle-class realpolitik" against the "ambitious social programming" of LBJ's Great Society liberalism, with the South newly positioned as "the pillar of a national conservative party."[35] Ronald Reagan, for his part, made clear his desire for a new GOP coalition with blue-collar appeal uniting social and economic conservatives around his own sunny demeanor, and achieved more than any other Republican in doing so. By the late twentieth century the GOP was left as the more ideologically conservative party on both economic and social issues, with the Democrats taking up precisely the opposite position.[36] This left Republicans with increasingly strong support from white working-class voters—once the mainstay of the New Deal coalition—on the basis of numerous cultural concerns. The GOP was now an alliance between economic and social conservatives—enough to be highly competitive at the national level. Yet it also left the party with inevitable tensions between the two wings.[37]

The great majority of those who voted for Trump in the 2016 general election also voted for Romney in 2012. Similarly, the great majority of those who voted for Clinton in 2016 voted for Obama four years earlier. There was no massive voter defection on either side. For the most part, traditional party loyalties held firm.[38] Nevertheless, there were some significant shifts at the margins, and when these marginal shifts are enough to produce a surprising presidential win then they tend to be of interest. Some of the voters most likely to shift from Obama 2012 to Trump 2016—and to vote for Trump in the GOP primary that year— were white working-class, non–college educated voters in Rust Belt small-town counties. These voters tend to be center-left on economics but conservative on cultural issues: the classic populist position. These are also the voters who allowed the 2016 GOP nominee to win over a national electoral majority in key states such as Pennsylvania, Michigan, Wisconsin, and Ohio. They are to the right of the GOP donor class on immigration, but to the left of it on pocketbook issues such as Social Security and economic inequality. Viewed in aggregate, their politics are quite literally center-right. But the specific way in which they are center-right is the precise opposite of upper-income Republican elites, who tend to favor strict conservative economics combined with more open immigration. Naturally these substantive policy differences produce intraparty tensions, once brought out into the open. And so they have.[39]

Reports from both the Pew Research Center and the Democracy Fund Voter Study Group confirm there are now significant divisions between large groups of Republicans and Trump supporters over major policy issues, along the following lines. A plurality of Republican voters, typically described as staunch or core conservatives, favor conservative policies across the board on both social and economic matters, along with enhanced border security. They support President Trump. Another very large cluster of downscale Republican voters are suspicious of national elites, center-left on economics, less internationalist, often culturally conservative, protectionist-leaning, and anti-immigration. These were the voters most likely to rally around Trump early on.

Trump Republican Coalition (c. 2018–2019)

Issue	Core conservatives	Populist-nationalists
US global role	active	guarded
Use of force overseas	hawkish	less interventionist
View of US allies	assets	free-riders
Trade policy	free trade	more protectionist
Defense spending	support	support
Counterterrorism	hardline	hardline
Immigration	border security	border security
Economics	conservative	populist
Social issues	conservative	conservative
Demographic	college educated	non–college educated
2016 primary	other candidates	Trump
Support Trump?	yes	yes

A third, smaller group—perhaps a quarter of Republican voters—are libertarian-leaning, conservative economically, more moderate on social issues, pro–free trade, pro-immigration, and the least supportive of Trump.[40]

The 2016 presidential primary and general election, in effect, affirmed the long-term movement of the GOP toward white working-class voters, and toward cultural conservatism, at the expense of some orthodox conservative economic positions.[41] Moreover, the specific version of cultural conservatism endorsed in the Republican primaries was not a pious religiosity, but instead a right-leaning populist nationalism focused on questions of immigration, trade, criminal policing, citizenship, and national identity.[42] To an unusual extent, this brought the Trump campaign into tension with traditional economic conservatives. At various points in the 2016 campaign Trump broke with orthodox conservative economic positions and endorsed a more populist or center-left stance on a range of issues including the need for large-scale infrastructure spending, Social Security, taxes, and the minimum wage. At the same time he took a very hard line on illegal immigration. As it turned out, this exact combination was the preferred position of a great many Republican voters.[43] Yet these more populist voting groups still existed alongside traditional conservatives at all income levels who continued to prefer traditional Republican economics. Consequently the GOP could and can only be described as a big-tent coalition with some significant internal tensions and divisions over important policy questions. And of course this includes foreign policy along with related transnational matters. Trump's most distinct core supporters tend to favor trade protection, immigration restrictions, and a rather less interventionist foreign policy. They are also more willing to question America's traditional alliances. Traditional Republicans are more likely to support free trade, overseas alliances, and US foreign policy activism. In sum, there has indeed been a long-term trend or realignment toward a more populist cultural conservatism within the GOP, with significant implications for US foreign policy, and these pressures are unlikely to disappear anytime soon.

Having examined the past and present, what might be the future of Republican foreign policy?

It seems clear that most GOP voters will in all likelihood continue to support President Trump and his foreign policy efforts for as long as he is in office. This in turn will continue to influence congressional Republican responses. In every single administration, including this one, the most important person in shaping foreign policy is the president. For all of these reasons, both American and Republican foreign policy during the Trump administration will continue to be primarily determined by the president, though not necessarily in ways he initially expected.

A more interesting question may be the future of conservative foreign policy, after Trump. And here, there are now a wide range of possibilities. Three of them are sketched here, very briefly.

First, conservatives could embrace a foreign policy of strict nonintervention, slashing military spending, dismantling US alliances and bases overseas, and ending any concept of a war on terror once and for all.

Second, conservatives could double down on Donald Trump's most distinctive early 2015–2016 campaign suggestions, for example by raising tariffs comprehensively, deporting unprecedented numbers of illegal immigrants, banning all Muslims from entry into the United States, allowing key Asian allies such as South Korea and Japan to acquire nuclear weapons, and pronouncing NATO obsolete.

Third, conservatives could move to revive key priorities of George W. Bush, including multilateral free-trade agreements, pro–immigration reforms, regime change, preventive military action against rogue states, and additional large-scale, pro-democracy US military interventions in the Muslim world.

In the abstract all three are possible, and given the surprises of recent years, it would be unwise to rule anything out. Still, even to list those three possibilities is to immediately notice the massive domestic political, economic, and international obstacles to the strict implementation of any one of them. A more likely outcome, as even Donald Trump has discovered, is that future Republican leaders will have to strike balances between more purist versions of nonintervention, hardline unilateralism, and conservative internationalism. Coalition-building will be inevitable. But the specific way in which this is done—in terms of character, style, and substance—will be up to future presidents, just as it is now and has been in the past. Contingent events will no doubt provide new, currently unexpected opportunities for one or more faction. For conservatives of all varieties, the possibilities on foreign policy are now wide open.

Trump has shattered existing orthodoxies and opened up a previously latent debate over US foreign policy fundamentals. He and his supporters have made some valid criticisms of the elite liberal internationalist consensus, from both a nationalist and noninterventionist point of view. Establishmentarians in both parties will have to come to grips with this. The 2016 election result should have been a wakeup call, if one was needed, that Wilsonian platitudes are not as persuasive as they used to be. It was also a surprising indicator that a populist-conservative coalition can in fact win a national election. Trump himself has never really offered an entirely coherent agenda. He is among the least philosophical or ideological of presidents; indeed he never really claimed to be a conservative. But he is an instinctive American populist, and he did tap into and speak for a latent, specific, and current form of conservative nationalism that is very real. Moreover, it has deep roots in this country's history, and because it is bigger than Donald Trump, it will probably outlast him. Whether in one form or another, conservative nationalism is here to stay.

One issue area of particular significance will be the long-term direction of Republican foreign policy preferences on trade. The GOP was once the party of high tariffs, from Lincoln to Hoover. Then, under leaders like Eisenhower, it eventually shifted in a pro–free trade direction. This shift was caused by changes in international incentives, dominant ideas, coalitional interests, and political leadership. Numerous scholars have argued that changes in a political party's underlying economic interests can have a powerful impact on its orientation toward free trade. Pro-trade forces remain powerful inside the Republican Party not only among business interests, but more broadly with the managerial or white-collar wing of the party. Among congressional Republicans, these interests are well represented. But as the party has increasingly drawn its base of support from white working-class populist voters, especially in the nation's Rust Belt, an internal constituency now exists for more protectionist policies that was not previously recognized. Moreover, the fierce sense of nationalism at the heart of the GOP can be turned either for or against free trade, if Republican presidents so choose. Donald Trump sensed this, and through his campaign catalyzed a dramatic alteration on the issue. Since the base of the Democratic Party—including labor unions, progressives, and environmentalists—are no friendlier toward new multilateral free-trade agreements than is Donald Trump, it is entirely possible that the two major party presidential nominees will compete in 2020 to see who can be most protectionist.

In relation to China at least, there really is a case for US retaliatory measures, but they need to be conceived of and implemented in a way that is targeted, coordinated, and sensible. In relation to allied US trade partners, the case against free trade is much weaker. Yet the politics of this issue have plainly shifted. One distinct possibility is that the Republican Party has now begun a long-term realignment in a far more protectionist direction, catalyzed by underlying changes in international incentives, coalitional interests, and presidential leadership. This would amount to a reversal of Eisenhower's achievement. Another possibility is that while Trump has tapped into working-class concerns about globalization and free trade, having heard these concerns, future conservative leaders will try to strike responsible balances on trade policy without dismantling all the advantages of relatively open trading arrangements with US allies. Prudent Republicans should develop new ways of tackling trade policy that recognize existing frustrations and divisions; push back against China more effectively; and preserve the benefits of international trade for the United States. As with every other aspect of American foreign policy, factoring in domestic politics, there is more than one possibility here.

What the Trump phenomenon has clarified, above all, is that no version of liberal internationalism can be popularly sustained in the absence of an underlying nation-state felt by its own citizens to be prosperous, sovereign, and secure. And if the nation's leaders ever forget that again, the voters will be sure to remind them. In this sense, there is really no such thing as "Trumpism." There is only America.

Age of Iron

In his *Works and Days,* the ancient Greek poet Hesiod sketched an interpretation of history very different from the modern liberal one. He suggested that over time humanity had developed through a series of historic eras, beginning with a prehistoric golden age, then passing through silver, bronze, and heroic eras. Some earlier eras had been characterized by epic struggle on the part of preceding generations: "Their hearts were tough as steel." Only for Hesiod, the overall trajectory was not one of progressive improvement, but degeneration. The final era, his own, he described as an age of iron. He was hardly optimistic about this new era, in which "scoundrels will be honored . . . and shame will vanish." And he was quite realistic about describing its power dynamics. As he said of ordinary mortals in the new era: "Their lot will be a blend of the good and bad. . . . Only fools need suffer to learn." Nevertheless, he did not recommend the embrace of inequity. On the contrary, like the author of Ecclesiastes, Hesiod spoke out against abusive kings, and urged his readers to "follow justice," while keeping a keen eye on the new reality. The age of iron would require a close protection of those nearest and dearest: "Remember that neighbors come first." Above all, he recommended the cultivation of honest and effective labor toward constructive purposes: "Whatever your lot, nothing will be as good as work."[1]

The great fear of many observers today is that the United States is voluntarily abandoning a kind of seventy-year golden age of liberal internationalism. The months and years since Trump's election have seen an outpouring of concern that the United States is discarding what advocates call the rules-based liberal international order. According to its leading proponents, such as Princeton University's John Ikenberry, that order "is complex and sprawling, organized around economic openness, multilateral institutions, security cooperation, democratic solidarity, and internationalist ideals." It is "a strategic environment with rules, institutions, partners, and relationships," and the United States sustains it by providing "public goods" and agreeing to "restrain itself and operate within an array of regional and global institutions." In Ikenberry's view:

> Underpinning US global leadership has been the United States' support for multilateral rules and institutions. This is what has made US power so unique—and legitimate. . . . As a result, other countries realized that they could benefit from US ascendancy. Global institutions fostered cooperation and allowed Washington to attract allies, making its global presence more acceptable and durable. These institutions helped the international order solve common problems. . . . countries gravitated toward a global liberal internationalist system.

For Ikenberry, "a hostile revisionist power has indeed arrived on the scene, but it sits in the Oval Office, the beating heart of the free world. . . . Trump has abdicated responsibility for the world the United States built. . . . Liberal democracy itself appears fragile, vulnerable in particular to far-right populism" that "disdains the multicultural and open character of American society." His solution is to reiterate the benefits of liberal internationalism "with more conviction," reclaim "the master narrative," and encourage US allies such as Germany to "push back" against the United States: Angela "Merkel, as the leader of the country that perhaps most embodies the virtues and accomplishments of the postwar liberal order, is uniquely positioned to speak as the moral voice of the liberal democratic world."[2]

In outlining some of the many benefits of a US-led international order outside of the Soviet Union, Russia, and China since the end of World War II, Ikenberry is not wrong. The United States has indeed benefitted on the whole from a relatively open international trading order in which it is the leading guarantor. It is easy take the benefits of this order for granted. Both allies and the United States have gained from it. Strategically, the backbone of that order has been a network of US peacetime commitments, military bases, defensive alliances, and force deployments around the Eurasian perimeter. This US forward presence contains and deters competitors; upholds balances of power in regions of vital interest; protects global sea lanes and thereby peacetime trade; reassures American allies; dampens regional security competition; permits humanitarian relief when appropriate; and allows the United States to protect its citizens from an advanced posture. That basic strategic posture has been a keystone support for an international order relatively benign, prosperous and democratic by historic standards. The United States still stands at the center of a broad system of partnerships and alliances that help solidify peaceful relations between dozens of nations. No other power has a set of alliances like this; it is a major asset.[3]

Since the end of the Cold War, however, a number of weaknesses in both the theory and practice of the liberal international order have become increasingly apparent. These can be clustered into three broad categories: economic, national, and geopolitical.

The *economic* challenge to liberal order emanates from perceived domestic and international shifts over the years in the relative material advantage to be gained from open global trading arrangements. A certain percentage of Americans in both parties simply do not view globalization or free trade as materially beneficial to them. Of course US voters have always had mixed feelings about economic globalization, and by some measures support for it has not actually declined. According to one Chicago Council poll from 2017, a majority of US citizens still agree that globalization brings net economic benefits to American consumers, US companies, and the American economy as a whole. Yet according to that same poll there is also a majority feeling that globalization has been bad

for the job security of American workers.[4] Nor are these concerns entirely
without merit. The relatively open international commercial system led by
the United States since the 1940s has brought tremendous net economic
benefits to the United States as well as other countries. But these gains have
been uneven. There is considerable evidence that the greatest beneficiaries
of economic globalization in recent decades have been the rising middle
class in emerging economies such as China and India, along with the very
wealthy worldwide. Working-class and middle-class Americans, in particular, have not benefitted to the same extent.[5] Indeed the pattern for many
Americans in the twenty-first century has been stagnant wages and job
insecurity. This pattern is due to long-term technological changes, more
than to US trade policy. But insofar as free-trade agreements and economic globalization are viewed as part of a package that chiefly advantages
the wealthiest and most privileged of their fellow citizens, some voters
will continue to cast ballots for populist candidates, regardless of expert
admonitions to the contrary—and the notion of a liberal international economic order based upon free trade will continue to be buffeted.[6]

The *national* challenge to liberal order emanates from reassertions of
nation-state sovereignty against internationalist norms, institutions, ideas
and expectations. The pattern in recent years has been for commentators
to lump together the nationalism of authoritarian regimes (Russia, China)
with that of democratic ones (the United States, Great Britain) as part of
a worrisome overall trend.[7] Liberal internationalists clearly believe that
nationalism, in itself, is a threat. But this belief elides some very different versions of nationalism, while bypassing or ignoring the powerful
arguments in favor of popular self-government and democratic accountability at the global level. The United States was not founded as a sovereign nation only to see its independence submerged into a mishmash of
global governance. It is perfectly reasonable for Americans living in a free
polity to want to preserve their own particular national traditions, cus-
toms, and way of life. It is furthermore reasonable for Americans to insist that controversial domestic social issues be resolved by domestic and
democratic processes, rather than through the backdoor of international
jurisprudence. The fact that this is now viewed as controversial is in itself

astonishing, and revealing of the changes in liberal internationalism over time. For conservatives, of all people, local is better—and this applies to issues of global governance as well. International organizations should do only what national governments truly cannot.

In many cases of vital interest, multilateral organizations work at the edge of international power, not at its center, and their edicts are often un-enforceable. There is really no such thing as a general reputation for mul-tilateralism, and the greatest international challenges are not problems of legality. US foreign policy elites should have modest and realistic expec-tations for what these institutions can achieve, rather than treating their empowerment as an end in itself. Any sensible American leader will want to choose between unilateral, bilateral, and multilateral solutions and approaches to specific US foreign policy challenges, case by case. In fact this is what the most successful presidents have done, from both political parties. To declaim that multilateral approaches are inherently morally and practically superior, or to insist upon them as a kind of religion, is not convincing. It is unclear, to say the least, why multilateral organizations with unelected leaders and dictatorships among their members should be considered morally superior to national governments democratically elected.[8]

The *geopolitical* challenge to liberal order emanates from long-term structural changes, power shifts, and persistent weak points inherent within the internationalist project. To understand why this is so requires a little elaboration as to what can be gained from a geopolitical analysis.

Geopolitics refers to the study of the relationship between interna-tional politics and geographic facts. These facts on the ground can include human and political realities like trade networks, national boundaries, and constellations of military or economic power, along with persistent natural features such as rivers, oceans, or mountains.[9] Many of the key geopolitical insights were laid out by British parliamentarian Halford Mackinder and Dutch-American scholar Nicolas Spykman over the first half of the twen-tieth century. Broaching the subject in a 1904 *Geographical Journal* article, Mackinder suggested that the era of European maritime predominance established four hundred years earlier was coming to an end. Western

naval and colonial powers had previously been able to outflank and dominate the Asian landmass through superior technology. But the consolidation of great continental-sized land powers such as Russia and potentially
China—combined with changes in land transportation—meant that insular maritime democracies such as Great Britain would have a more difficult time maintaining their global position. Mackinder asked his readers
to envision continental Europe, continental Asia, and continental Africa
as a single "World Island," possessing most of the world's population and
industrial potential. The core of this world island he called the Heartland,
inaccessible to sea power—essentially, Russia, Mongolia, Tibet, and
Central Asia, including parts of China and Iran. If the world island were
ever united under a single political entity, with a base in the Heartland, it
would possess overwhelming economic and military advantages over the
outer crescent of geographically insular maritime powers such as Great
Britain, Japan, and the United States. Mackinder's recommendation was
for these maritime powers to encourage the creation of geopolitical buffer
zones, for example in Eastern Europe. He viewed the League of Nations as
well-intentioned but almost beside the point, if it did not embody a material determination on the part of the world's great seagoing democracies to
maintain favorable balances of power on the Eurasian continent.[10]

The League of Nations' failure to prevent a second world war
encouraged a new appreciation for geopolitics. Writing in the early 1940s,
Nicolas Spykman modified Mackinder's formulations by pointing to the
existence of what he called an amphibious Rimland—located in between
the Heartland and its great offshore islands—and stretching from Western
Europe around the Middle East, across India, ending in coastal China.
Spykman pointed out that most of the world's productive potential was in
the Rimland, not within the Heartland as such. Control of the Rimland
therefore meant control of the world—precisely what was at stake during
both world wars—and this would be determined by struggles between
mixed alliances, rather than by simply lining up sea powers versus land
powers straightforwardly. Spykman understood that Americans, as offshore islanders, are always tempted by an offshore strategic approach, but
he did not view such an approach as viable. If the United States failed to

maintain control over vital sea and airspace in the Atlantic and Pacific, then some other power eventually would. Even a predominant US influence in South America's southern cone could hardly be taken for granted, given the vast distances involved, and if that influence were lost then even a hemispheric defense would collapse into something more constrained and impoverished. Taken as a whole, the Rimland's economic and military weight pointed to no secure resting place for Americans in the absence of internal Old World balances, and these balances would have to be actively upheld by the United States. As he put it, America's "main political objective, both in peace and in war, must therefore be to prevent the unification of the Old World centers of power in a coalition hostile to her own interests." Spykman was more sanguine than Mackinder that this could actually be done, both through a forward US strategic presence and through technological developments in American airpower properly deployed and maintained in bases far away from the United States.[11]

What is the geopolitical situation in our own time? According to British scholar Barry Buzan, only superpowers have global military reach.[12] In geopolitical terms then, since the collapse of the Soviet Union—and even now—the United States remains the world's only superpower. In fact the United States has possessed more broadly based economic and military capabilities than any other major power since the end of World War II. This condition is sometimes called primacy, and it is indeed a condition, not a strategy in itself.[13] An objective net assessment of America's material advantages today reveals a nation with a range of capabilities still unmatched by any other country. These include a gigantic national economy, deep financial markets, a favorable geographic position, vast natural resources, revolutionary advances in the domestic production of shale oil and gas, robust demographics, a large population, high per capita income, a scientific and technological edge in innovation, a strong civil society, worldwide alliance networks, the leading military capabilities on the planet, a continuing lead in precision strike technology, and an underlying political-constitutional order of tenacious strength. Other major powers possess some of these advantages, but none of them possess all, apart from the United States.[14]

Having said that, since the 1990s there have clearly been some very significant shifts within the international balance of power, in broad alignment with Mackinder's predictions over a century ago. The single greatest gravitational shift in relative economic and military weight has been from the Atlantic toward the Pacific, and from Europe toward Asia. As Robert Kaplan argues, we appear in some ways to be returning to the premodern world of Marco Polo, in which Western Europe was only one portion of a vast Eurasian commercial network encompassing roughly equal civilizations, centered on China as much as on other imperial powers.[15] The Indo-Pacific, rather than Europe's Western half, is increasingly the focus of the world's greatest economies, militaries, and geopolitical ambitions. Obviously this long-term power shift has profound implications for America's interests, its allies, its primacy, and indeed the very idea of liberal world order.[16]

The power shift within the Eurasian Rimland, from west to east, has gone hand in hand with the stubborn persistence and even revival of authoritarian forms of government internationally, and this is probably not coincidental. Leading authoritarian regimes whose demise, reform, or transformation was confidently predicted during the heyday of post–Cold War optimism have managed to survive and adapt. The great "third wave" of democratization, stretching from the 1970s into the 1990s—and bringing Mediterranean Europe, much of Latin America, key portions of littoral Asia, and most of Central-Eastern Europe into the democratic fold—has long since ended. Now we live in an age in which autocratic regimes have discovered creative new techniques to extend their rule and push back on democratic opponents, worldwide and inside their own countries.[17]

Internationally, we see revisionist authoritarian forces pushing up against existing regional orders to assert alternative political-ideological visions, including their own increased influence, status, and external and internal security. Such forces take three main forms. First, there are the two great authoritarian continental-sized powers, namely Russia and China. Second, there are regional rogue states—primarily Iran and North Korea—with aggressive revisionist ambitions. Third, there are

salafi-jihadist terrorist groups such as ISIS and Al Qaeda, along with radical Islamist factions hostile to the West. These various autocratic forces
do not necessarily cooperate; sometimes they compete with or combat
one another. Moreover, their degree of enmity toward the United States
varies considerably. China, for example, is a powerful challenger that
benefits tremendously from open international economic arrangements
and does not actively seek violent conflict with the West. Al Qaeda, on the
other hand, is at perpetual war with the United States by its own choosing.
Still, it is useful to understand that none of these authoritarian powers are
actually genuine partners or friends of the United States.

In terms of sheer material capabilities, the weightiest of the authoritarian challengers is China. Over the past forty years, following
Deng Xiaoping's reforms, China has transformed itself from a Maoist,
impoverished Third World country into one of the two largest national
economies in the world. Indeed when measured by purchasing power
parity, China's gross domestic product surpassed that of the United States
in 2014. This material growth has gone hand in hand with a vast expansion of Chinese trade and investment on every inhabited continent, including Africa and South America. Under its Belt and Road Initiative,
the PRC funds large-scale infrastructure projects across Asia and beyond,
tying diverse regions together economically under enhanced Chinese influence. In terms of its commercial and financial reach, the PRC is now a
global power. Moreover, Beijing can and is using this newfound wealth to
fund impressive modernizations of its army, navy, and air force, so as to
lend itself better deterrent and coercive leverage in relation to any crisis
around the country's vast perimeter on land, air, and sea. Under President
Xi Jinping, the Chinese government has abandoned Deng's emphasis on
biding time, and has announced an ambitious "China dream" whereby the
nation reasserts itself as one of the truly great powers in the world. Beijing
may ultimately attempt to supplant the United States as the predominant
alliance leader within East Asia, a role it played for centuries before the
arrival of Western and Japanese imperial influence, and a role the Chinese
view as rightly theirs. Of course China also has serious weaknesses and
vulnerabilities, both demographic, domestic political, economic, military,

and international. It does not yet have a global military or strategic presence to match that of the United States. Nevertheless, China's continuing rise offers a serious challenge to US interests, to American allies, and to the very concept of liberal international order.[18]

Vladimir Putin's Russia offers another great-power challenge to US interests in Europe and beyond. Under Putin, Moscow aims to reconstitute lost spheres of influence from the Soviet era, push against the West, and reassert itself as a major power within (what it hopes to be) a multipolar system. The various instruments used include disinformation, covert action, oil and gas pressure, cyberattacks, realpolitik diplomacy, economic and military pacts, weapons sales, and direct armed intervention, as in Syria, Georgia, and Ukraine. Its re-entry as a major player within the Middle East has been especially striking, as was the 2014 seizure of Crimea. Putin looks to cut an imposing figure on the world stage, break up distinctly Western institutions, reassert Russia's status, secure its buffer zones, and maintain his own regime in power against any "color revolution" at home. The United States is viewed as a major obstacle to achieving these ends. Russia continues to suffer from some severe long-term economic, strategic, and demographic vulnerabilities limiting its international role. Nevertheless it uses what capabilities it has, aggressively, to promote its own stature while challenging broad notions of liberal international order.[19]

The conventional wisdom regarding Sino–Russian cooperation used to be that their relationship was nothing more than an axis of convenience.[20] Unfortunately, this is no longer true. To be sure, Moscow and Beijing still have many foreign policy differences, and their coordination falls well short of any formal military alliance. But Russia and China now have a working strategic partnership that reaches across multiple issue areas, including weapons sales, oil and gas supplies, security coordination, and defense against liberal norms.[21] The two authoritarian regimes see eye to eye in protesting supposed outside interference in their own affairs—and in creating or recreating regional spheres of influence as economic and security buffer zones. Both ultimately look to see a world free from unmatched American hegemony, and characterized instead by the internal and external security of their own authoritarian regimes. Moreover, both powers often have businesslike and mutually beneficial relationships with other leading autocracies such as Iran and North Korea. Altogether, the result is a Eurasian landmass dominated by a de facto Sino–Russian partnership and its attendant supporters, whether dictatorial or simply weak. This is something close to Halford Mackinder's geopolitical nightmare: an Old World increasingly dominated by an authoritarian Heartland, against an outer crescent of maritime democracies.

After these great-power competitors, the next category of actor to challenge anything resembling liberal conceptions of regional order are the rogue states of North Korea and Iran. Both regimes have already lasted longer than many post–Cold War observers expected. North Korea has been ruled as a brutally totalitarian system by the Kim family since the end of World War II. Iran is dominated by a repressive Shiite theocracy with elements of military dictatorship. Both regimes look to upend regional balances and expel American influence, whether in the form of existing alliances or otherwise. Iran uses proxy forces, covert action, mendacious diplomacy, and support for terrorism to promote its influence in Syria, Iraq, Lebanon, Yemen, and beyond. North Korea uses aggressive brinksmanship—including the threat of its existing nuclear arsenal—to pressure the United States and its allies with the stated long-term purpose of reunifying the Korean peninsula under the control of Pyongyang.[22] Both regimes are highly authoritarian, anti-American at a deep ideological level, and possessed of revisionist regional ambitions with longstanding WMD programs. Both regimes are also capable of considerable tactical flexibility, including negotiated arms control settlements, in pursuit of their long-term goals.

Finally, jihadist terrorists and radical Islamists pose a continuing security challenge. Transnational networks of salafi-jihadists such as ISIS, Al Qaeda, and affiliated and likeminded groups target regional US allies, American forces, and US civilians, including within the United States. Salafi-jihadist organizations operate in the form of many local groups and affiliates across large parts of Africa; South, Southeast, and Central Asia; and of course the Middle East. Sometimes these terrorist groups compete with one another; sometimes they coordinate; sometimes they fight internal disputes. But they are all bitterly hostile toward the United States in a fundamental sense, and wage perpetual war upon it by their own choice. Their declared goal going back several decades is to topple regional governments within the Muslim world, expel Western influence, recover previously Muslim territories, establish strict sharia law, and eventually restore the unity of the Islamic world culminating in a restored caliphate. To that end they utilize terrorist attacks, work with local tribal leaders when they can, look to bog down US forces, attempt to win over Muslim support both inside and outside the Western world, and wage something like a decentralized global insurgency campaign. These methods and objectives do not carry the support of most Muslims worldwide, but they do carry the support of a significant minority in many countries, and it would be delusional to deny it. The appeal of salafi-jihadist ideology to that minority will continue to bring these terrorist groupings a certain number of recruits, even when the United States successfully undermines specific organizations. In particular, the dismantling of ISIS as a state-like entity, while most welcome, does not indicate the end of either ISIS or jihadist terrorists more generally. Salafi-jihadist terrorist groups do not possess the material capabilities of even a single major nation-state. But their demonstrated willingness and ability to inflict mass civilian casualties, including through suicide bombing attacks, combined with their overall resilience and adaptability, necessarily makes them a persistent security concern for the United States and its allies.[23]

The challenge of politicized radical Islam is actually broader than that of these groups, even though neither is equivalent to the Muslim religion as a whole. Even political Islamists who do not support terrorist attacks on American civilians, and who work through parliamentary methods, often support attacks on US troops in the Muslim world, and take for granted the need to expel Western influence. Egypt's Muslim Brotherhood prior to the Arab Spring was one such group, which is what made its ascension to power in 2011–2012 such a disaster for US interests, not to mention for Egyptians.[24] Most Islamists, by definition, are not committed to liberal democracy, but instead use it as a means toward a very different end. They also frequently harbor a vicious anti-Semitism culminating in calls for the physical destruction of Israel.[25] Such groups have a degree of local support within the Muslim world beyond that of terrorist organizations. Factional disputes among politicized radical Islamists—and with terrorist groups like Al Qaeda—will certainly continue. As with salafi-jihadists, political Islamists are a very diverse group. Fortunately radical political Islam as a specific ideology is not equivalent to the Muslim religion as a whole, and it is unhelpful to pretend that it is.[26]

The US-led international order that has existed since the 1940s is a real achievement, not to be lightly dismissed. But it rests upon a power-political superstructure, and especially since the end of the Cold War too many liberal internationalists on both sides of the Atlantic have forgotten this. Even into the twenty-first century, the global political system remains in many ways an anarchy in which independent nation-states interact and compete for advantage. No multilateral organization—not even the United Nations—really has the power to enforce law and order at the international level. That leaves independent nation-states reliant on themselves to protect vital national interests. In this sense, some of the most enduring realities of international politics have never really changed that much from one century to the next. Although technologies have certainly advanced, numerous features of international power politics have not. Strategic competition between major powers is not historically abnormal—quite the contrary. Diplomacy must still be backed by material weight or force of some kind. Nations use carrots and sticks, or promises of reward and punishment, to secure their interests in relation to one another. And military instruments of power of national power are by no means outmoded in our time. These are the points made by foreign policy realists, past and present, and their caveats are worth taking seriously.[27]

Under these circumstances, what sort of foreign policy should the United States pursue?

A number of academic foreign policy realists advocate an alternative American strategy of offshore balancing.[28] This would involve deep reductions in US land forces, the forswearing of counterinsurgency operations, and the avoidance of international projects entailing the governance or occupation of other countries. Under a strategy of off-shore balancing, Washington would move toward disbanding inherited alliance commitments in Eurasia, cut US defense spending, abandon the pursuit of American hegemony, focus on limited air and sea capabilities, and for the most part avoid warfare overseas. The United States would station its armed forces over the horizon, and rely upon local state actors to balance one another. If these actors proved genuinely unable to protect regional balances of power, then and only then would US forces come ashore against the revealed threat to restore the balance and return home. Offshore realists suggest that such a strategy would undercut support for anti-American terrorism or weapons of mass destruction on the part of other nations. They further argue that it would curb the powers of the US national security state, rely on America's insular geographic position for security, and permit a much-needed focus on domestic priorities. Similar and overlapping strategic proposals go by the name of deep retrenchment, restraint, or noninter-vention.[29] Within the community of foreign policy commentary, these alternate strategies have particular support from libertarians at the CATO Institute, as well as from some venues on the right such as *The American Conservative*.[30]

Realists are right to suggest that any plausible foreign policy must begin with a specification of national interests. US vital interests begin with the defense of American territory from attacks of any kind, the preservation of the country's sovereign integrity and independence, and the protection of America's distinctive system of limited government. Internationally, the responsibility of the US government is to behave in such a way as to safe-guard these interests, protect the lives and property of American citizens, and enhance economic opportunities for the United States overseas. The preservation of regional balances of power within Europe and Asia is certainly in the American interest. So is the security of oil supplies flowing from the Persian Gulf. Past these basic interests, the United States has a vital stake in the maintenance of American primacy—defined as the re-tention of more broad-based material capabilities than any other major power—since the promotion of every other American interest will be easier if that primacy is conserved.[31]

The problem with a strategy of offshore balancing, however, is that it is hardly obvious it would secure these vital interests any better than a continued US forward presence. There are genuine risks to retrenchment, precisely from a realist perspective.[32] The costs of America's world role are visible and known. The potential risks and costs of dismantling that forward presence are less knowable, but potentially catastrophic. It is entirely possible that US strategic disengagement from Eurasia could invite greater nuclear proliferation, jihadist terror, authoritarian advances, and even major power warfare. Yet advocates of offshore balancing regularly operate on the unprovable assumption that no such destabilizing scenarios would materialize—or that they would be of no great interest to the United States. In all likelihood, as Americans were forced to rediscover during World War II, regional breakdowns coinciding with previous US disengagements would be of very great interest, requiring strategic re-entries far more costly than simply remaining forward committed.[33] Indeed this is why the United States has maintained a forward presence over the past seventy years in the first place. Conservatives, of all people, should beware the unintended consequences of dismantling strategic commitments that have served the United States tolerably well.

Instead of disengaging offshore, the United States should carefully safeguard its existing forward presence and pursue robust strategies of pressure against authoritarian competitors overseas, using a wide array of integrated policy tools. These mixed tools should include responsible foreign assistance, alliance relationships, economic sanctions, trade agreements, covert action, diplomatic capabilities, intelligence assets, forward bases, and a well-maintained armed forces.[34] Such an approach also requires coercive and deterrent threats that are serious, clear, and credible. The overarching goal should be to gain leverage, intensify pressure, and impose costs against challengers in differentiated fashion case by case. In some cases, such as China, this will certainly include continued economic and diplomatic engagement alongside a more disciplined competitive approach. But the overall shift in American strategy should be away from overly optimistic assumptions of the past, toward long-term strategies of pressure against US adversaries.

In relation to Putin's Russia, the United States should aim to deter, balance, and counter Russian assertions in credible fashion within the former Soviet Union and elsewhere. This can include tightened military coordination within NATO, with a fresh emphasis on eastward territorial defense; strengthened missile defense systems in that region; diplomatic, military, and technical assistance to the Ukrainian government; increased US oil and gas supplies to Europe; broadened economic sanctions against key Russian actors; new American ground and air forces deployed in Poland and the Baltic States; and enhanced US cyber defenses against election interference. The United States can still utilize businesslike diplomacy and work with Moscow on a range of dimensions, locations, and issue areas. But the United States should not assume that American accommodations in any of these issue areas will necessarily lead to broader cooperation from Moscow, because the record of the past twenty years suggests the opposite.[35]

With regard to China, the United States possesses a number of counterbalancing foreign policy tools, and it should make good use of them. The United States can bolster its military capabilities in the region; encourage strategic complementary and cooperation among US allies; develop ballistic missile defense systems against regional threats; consider entering a renegotiated TPP agreement; support regional security partners and allies consistently; increase controls on American technology exports useful to China militarily; explore additional US basing options within the Asia-Pacific region; support Japan's expansion of its own defenses; counter Chinese Communist Party influence operations; and help US allies better defend their own sea and air spaces. The United States will continue to engage with China both economically and diplomatically, as well it should. But Washington should simultaneously pursue focused, energetic, and credible policies of deterrence, pressure, and counterbalancing against Chinese regional assertions—as in the South and East China Seas—precisely in order to prevent any misunderstandings or mixed messages that might unintentionally lead to armed conflict.[36]

In the abstract, one option in relation to the current Sino–Russian part-nership would be for the United States to counterbalance Russia against China, by reaching out to Moscow diplomatically, in a kind of reversal of the Nixon-Kissinger outreach toward Mao during the early 1970s. Indeed this may be President Trump's preference.[37] The problem with this op-tion, however, is that Putin has demonstrated little interest in acting as a cat's paw for Washington against China. Moreover, the uses of an anti-American strategic position, together with common interests in continued Sino–Russian coordination, run too deep for the Chinese and Russian regimes.[38] Indeed President Barack Obama tried an accommodating ap-proach toward both Moscow and Beijing in 2009, only to discover its limitations. Certainly, the United States can avoid actions so foolish and precipitous that they unintentionally benefit Sino–Russian partnership. But under the circumstances, the United States really has no choice but to try to counteract aggressive and authoritarian pressures emanating out-ward from both Moscow and Beijing.

In relation to Iran, the United States can develop a comprehensive, in-tegrated strategy to pressure and frustrate the current regime from mul-tiple directions. This should include bolstered American deterrents in the region; US covert action; theater missile defenses in Europe; American foreign aid programs aimed at competing with Iran; strategic coordi-nation with US allies; intensified and fully enforced sanctions against Tehran; a more regular presence of an American carrier task force in the Mediterranean and Persian Gulf regions; and drawing attention to the issue of human rights inside Iran. Regional allies and adversaries both need to understand that the United States is not simply abandoning the region. The overall American goal should be to push back against Iranian aggressions, and retake the initiative from a hostile regime, by pressuring and imposing costs upon it well beyond the issue of nuclear weapons.[39]

With regard to North Korea, the United States must maintain a carefully focused pressure campaign to deter the North's aggression and set back its nuclear weapons capabilities while avoiding a second Korean war—a very delicate balancing act. This necessarily entails close security cooper-ation with Seoul and Tokyo; a strengthened US naval presence in nearby waters; intensified international sanctions; theater and national missile defenses; close diplomatic efforts with Beijing; and very clear US alliance commitments. There is no need for the United States to make either regime change or preventive warfare the centerpiece of its approach toward Pyongyang. But there is also no need to shy away from pointing out North Korea's outrageous human rights abuses, since the regime's totalitarian nature is ultimately the source of its own foreign policy. Over the long term, the only real solution to the peninsula's internal security tension is the reunification of Korea under a democratic government. In the meantime, the United States should avoid diplomatic concessions to the North that do not actually dismantle the regime's nuclear weapons arsenal—a common mistake of past arms control agreements with Pyongyang.[40]

Finally, in relation to jihadist terrorist groups such as ISIS, Al Qaeda, and their affiliates, the United States can pursue strategies of counterpressure involving training and advisory support to partner governments, special operations, drones, intelligence capabilities, detective work, technical assistance, counterterror cooperation with allies, financial sanctions, better homeland security, and direct military action when necessary. This includes cooperating with allied or partner governments in the Muslim world such as Egypt, Iraq, Afghanistan, and Saudi Arabia. It also includes supporting US intelligence agencies rather than undermining or castigating them. In the end, jihadist suicide bombers cannot be managed peacefully, but must be located, captured, turned, or killed before they are able to carry out deliberate attacks on innocent civilians. Of all the international competitors listed, jihadist terrorist groupings cannot really be contained, but must be forcibly preempted, rolled back, and destroyed.

The credible maintenance of US-backed pressure and deterrence against a number of authoritarian regimes overseas requires a certain level of American defense spending in order to keep the peace. US defense expenditures pegged at something like 4 percent of GDP would be necessary simply to meet existing commitments. There is certainly a strong case for reforming military payroll and benefits, along with weapons acquisitions practices, in order to economize on spending. But in terms of military research and development, procurement, modernization, major weapons systems, and the number of troops within each armed service, there is no current need for cuts. Quite the contrary.[41] The United States must maintain forces able to deter aggression in three separate theaters—Europe, the Middle East, and the Asia-Pacific—sufficient to win if deterrence fails. Without playing service favorites, this will especially require long-term commitment to an American naval buildup.[42]

In terms of the prospective use of force, over the past ten to fifteen years many Americans, including successive US presidents, have drawn powerful lessons from the 2003 invasion of Iraq. One lesson has been to avoid new large-scale counterinsurgency, nation-building, or stability operations overseas. In itself, that lesson is understandable. But there is another lesson that should be drawn as well: namely that if and when the United States intervenes militarily overseas, it should do so in a way that is serious, decisive, and fully considered, with prior and careful preparation for a wide range of contingencies. As former Secretary of Defense Robert Gates once wrote, the United States has never been particularly good at predicting future wars.[43] We cannot assume that "boots on the ground" are a future impossibility simply because the idea is unpopular. America's adversaries may not oblige these expectations. From time to time internationally the unexpected occurs, and the United States needs to prepare for it by maintaining a range of balanced capabilities. This includes military forces useful for great-power competition. It also includes not throwing away America's hard-earned capacities in counterinsurgency campaigns since 2001.

Is a conservative US foreign policy strategy of this type politically possible, or compatible with the recent surge of a more populist American nationalism? If we refer back to the last chapter's findings on public opinion, there is considerable evidence that it is. In reality, GOP voters have not turned altogether against free trade, American alliances, defense spending, aggressive counterterrorism, or a leading US foreign policy role in the world. However, many of these voters—like many Americans generally—have demonstrated increased skepticism or ambivalence toward certain aspects of economic globalization, along with large-scale US military interventions overseas. This skepticism should be respected, since it has some validity, and in any case carries political weight. But in truth, as we have seen throughout this book, most Republican voters will support the foreign policy decisions of a Republican president in most cases, so long as that president does not line up against issues of central concern to those voters. Presidents have considerable leeway on these matters, and future presidents will, as well.

To its credit, as we saw earlier, the Trump administration has adopted and pursued many of the policy directions recommended earlier, including a set of pressure campaigns against key US adversaries overseas. But there remain several areas of concern. They center especially on trade policy, alliance relationships, and presidential management style.

The first area of concern is US trade policy. One central premise of American foreign relations since the 1940s has been that freer trading arrangements help encourage an open international order more conducive to American interests. The pattern in the twenty-first century has been that multiple administrations from both parties pursue bilateral and regional trade deals with US partners and allies, independent of the WTO, since genuinely global trade talks have long since stalled. The politics of free trade are always difficult, since opposition to it from import-competing interest groups tends to be intense, vocal, and organized. The costs of free trade are sometimes dramatic and concentrated, while the long-term benefits are extensive but dispersed. Organized labor, environmentalists, and human rights groups on the progressive wing of the Democratic Party have long expressed deep skepticism toward both new and existing free-trade agreements.[44] Now they are joined by President Trump, along with some of his earliest supporters within the Republican Party, a shift that has upended the usual partisan divisions over trade.

For Americans as a whole, international trade promotes innovation, exports, and export-related jobs. It also produces strategic benefits in bolstering US allies against America's adversaries. For all of these reasons the Trump administration should seriously consider re-entering the TPP, revamped by US allies in 2018. American entry into this agreement would be one of the most effective ways to push back against Chinese economic influence within the Asia-Pacific. In general, trade with democratic allies should be distinguished from trade with authoritarian competitors who simply do not play by the same rules. China in particular has engaged in a massive campaign of intellectual property theft, forced technology transfer, cyber larceny, and trade-distorting state subsidies over the past generation. This predatory behavior has carried real costs for the United States. Consequently there truly is a case for developing a focused, targeted campaign against Chinese foreign economic practices. American tariffs or the threat of tariffs do constitute one tool in this effort, however blunt. But the main focus should not be trade deficits per se. Instead it should be on pressing for changes in the aforementioned Chinese practices, for example by zeroing in on those specific companies most guilty of offense. The United States has multiple economic tools at its disposal to use against China, if it decides to employ their full range. It should do so in concert with American allies, rather than fighting trade wars with them.[45]

The second area of concern is US alliance relationships. In any such relationship allies may fear being abandoned by their partner on the one hand, or entrapped in some unwanted conflict on the other.[46] During the Obama years, there was already a growing concern among numerous allies that the United States was edging away from a firm commitment toward some of its traditional alliances overseas.[47] Since President Trump made a withering critique of America's allies during his 2016 campaign, the question arises whether US long-term commitments will remain in force. Indeed the president has made it clear that he hopes to leverage that concern in new ways to press for allied concessions on both trade and military spending. But if taken too far, this will be neither healthy nor productive. If the United States were to give the impression of disengagement or intense ambivalence in relation to core alliance commitments, this could lead to dangerous misimpressions on the part of authoritarian aggressors. US allies afraid of abandonment might respond by accommodating American adversaries in ways contrary to US interests—or by lashing out in unwelcome ways.[48] The most reliable course is to demonstrate, concretely, that being an ally of the United States means something. If not, we can expect that these allies will ultimately explore other options less friendly to American interests.

The third area of concern is presidential management style. Within the American political system, presidents have considerable room to make foreign policy decisions. Trump's predecessor, President Obama, was sometimes criticized for a national security management style of excessive ambivalence, overconfidence, and ambiguity, combined with a strong aversion to being pinned down. One possibility is that the US political system increasingly produces politicians of this type. If so, it will be difficult to conduct cohesive foreign policy strategies of any kind. President Trump has no doubt shown a readiness to make bold foreign policy decisions. The question remains whether the execution of those decisions is typically characterized by clarity, steadiness, and adequate information as to the necessary specifics. There is definitely a case to be made that foreign policy strategy is inevitably emergent—that is to say, a successful adaptation to events, rather than a sort of preset rigid plan.[49] Flexibility and freedom from ideological blinders are indeed virtues in strategic affairs. But successful adaptation is in turn more likely with good information, attention to detail, serious preparation, and credibility at the presidential level. In the end, there is really no substitute for per- sistent and well-informed attention to foreign policy matters on the part of the commander-in-chief. When presidents do not impose a sensible overall order upon the US foreign policy process, certainly nobody else is empowered to do so.[50]

The Trump administration's foreign policy emphases appear utterly un- precedented only if earlier historical experience is ignored. To be sure, Trump is no liberal internationalist. But neither were most previous Republican presidents. Nor is doubling down on Wilsonian foreign policy assumptions the great necessity of our time. The liberal internationalist or Wilsonian tradition suggests that long-term global progress toward greater economic interdependence, democracy promotion, and multilat- eral organization ultimately combine to leave ancient patterns of power politics obsolete. Each post–Cold War president prior to Trump operated on some key premise within this tradition.[51] President Bill Clinton hoped that expanding the zone of market-oriented US allies through democratic enlargement would promote American values and interests at minimal cost. President George W. Bush hoped that preventive military action and a freedom agenda within the Middle East, combined with regime change in Iraq, would undermine support for jihadist terrorists inside the Muslim world. President Barack Obama hoped that international accommodations led by the United States would help to promote multilateral coordination around liberal policy goals. All three sets of hopes were sincere. All three had certain specific foreign policy successes. Yet in the end, all three were overly optimistic in some very significant ways. To be specific: history never ended. Historically normal patterns of strategic competition, international conflict, and great-power politics never entirely disappeared. Authoritarian powers both large and small discovered new ways to adapt and survive. And contrary to post–Cold War expectations, the major powers of the world did not all converge upon a single liberal democratic model or ideal. If anything, the twenty-first century has seen a resurgence of great-power competition. The conclusion of the Cold War did not bring an end to geopolitical realities. It only reconfigured them in new form.[52]

The realization that progress is not inevitable and history has not ended ought to lead to a certain shift in emphasis. Expanding international cooperation and human rights are both worthy goals, but neither one in itself can be the starting point for US foreign policy strategy. Greater weight must be placed on supporting America's allies, and pushing back against its rivals and adversaries, within an internationally competitive environment. The answer is not to disengage. Nor is to think that rivals can be lectured into accommodation—much less blasted away in a sudden burst of regime change. Rather, the answer is for the United States to prepare for steady, long-term, robust competition with a range of serious adversaries, so as to better protect existing democracies against a very real variety of threats. Diplomatic efforts should start with traditional alliances, rather than obvious competitors. There is little point being half-hearted while protecting American primacy. But there is also no need to prioritize strategies of preventive war or regime change as uppermost doctrinally, since unsuccessful interventions overseas only undermine broader US interests. The default preference should be regionally differentiated strategies of attrition, assertive containment, and peace through strength. Transformational global projects or promises from all directions must now be met with considerable skepticism. Today's great challenge is not to promote or transform any progressive world order, but simply to defend existing democracies. The United States is still much stronger than some believe. If it pursues tough-minded foreign policy approaches, tapping into its profound capabilities, it has the ability to outlast its challengers and prevail.

CHAPTER 1

1. For some leading contributions on these issues, see Benedict Anderson, *Imagined Communities: Reflections on the Origin and Spread of Nationalism* (London: Verso, 2016) ; Azar Gat, *Nations: The Long History and Deep Roots of Political Ethnicity and Nationalism* (New York: Cambridge University Press, 2012); Liah Greenfeld, *Nationalism: Five Roads to Modernity* (Cambridge, MA: Harvard University Press, 1992); Yoram Hazony, *The Virtue of Nationalism* (New York: Basic Books, 2018); Eric Hobsbawm and Terence Ranger, eds., *The Invention of Tradition* (New York: Cambridge University Press, 1983); Hans Kohn, *The Idea of Nationalism* (London: Routledge, 2005 edition); and Maurizio Viroli, *For Love of Country* (New York: Oxford University Press, 1997).

2. Samuel Huntington, *Who Are We? The Challenges to America's National Identity* (New York: Simon and Schuster, 2004), 37–62, 362–66.

3. Louis Hartz, *The Liberal Tradition in America* (New York: Harcourt, Brace, and World, 1955), 4–11; Samuel Huntington, *American Politics: The Promise of Disharmony* (Cambridge, MA: The Belknap Press of Harvard University Press, 1981), chapter 2; Russell Kirk, *The Roots of American Order* (Wilmington, DE: Intercollegiate Studies Institute, 2003); Seymour Lipset, *American Exceptionalism: A Double-Edged Sword* (New York: Norton, 1997), 31–52; Karl Marx and Frederick Engels, *Selected Correspondence, 1846–1895*, trans. Donna Torr (New York: International Publishers, 1942), 449, 467, 501.

4. Mlada Bukovansky, *Legitimacy and Power Politics: The American and French Revolutions in International Political Culture* (Princeton, NJ: Princeton University Press, 2010), chapter 4; Felix Gilbert, *To the Farewell Address* (Princeton, NJ: Princeton University Press, 1961), 16–17, 130–36; Michael Hunt, *Ideology and US Foreign Policy* (New Haven, CT: Yale University Press, 1987), 17–18; Walter McDougall, *Promised Land, Crusader State* (Boston: Houghton Mifflin, 1997), 36–75; Jeremy Rabkin, "American Founding Principles and American Foreign Policy," in *Modern America and the Legacy of the Founding*, ed. Ronald Pestritto and Thomas West (Lanham, MD: Lexington Books, 2006), 299–330; George Washington, "Farewell Address," September 19, 1796, in *The American Republic: Primary Sources*,

ed. Bruce Frohnen (Indianapolis: Liberty Fund, 2002), 72–78; and Gordon Wood, *The American Revolution* (New York: Modern Library Classics, 2002), 106–08.

5. On the previous paragraphs, see Henry Adams, *History of the United States of America During the Administrations of Thomas Jefferson* (New York: Library of America, 1986); Samuel Flagg Bemis, *A Diplomatic History of the United States* (New York: Holt, Rinehart and Winston, 1955 edition), chapters 7–20, 22; Carol Berkin, *A Sovereign People: The Crises of the 1790s and the Birth of American Nationalism* (New York: Basic Books, 2017); Daniel Boorstin, *The Americans: The National Experience* (New York: Vintage, 1967); Bernard DeVoto, *Across the Wide Missouri* (Boston: Mariner Books, 1998) and *The Year of Decision 1846* (New York: St. Martin's Griffin, 2000); Charles Edel, *Nation Builder: John Quincy Adams and the Grand Strategy of the Republic* (Cambridge, MA: Harvard University Press, 2014); John Lamberton Harper, *American Machiavelli: Alexander Hamilton and the Origins of US Foreign Policy* (New York: Cambridge University Press, 2007); Anders Stephenson, *Manifest Destiny: American Expansionism and the Empire of Right* (New York: Hill and Wang, 1996); Robert Tucker and David Hendrickson, *Empire of Liberty: The Statecraft of Thomas Jefferson* (New York: Oxford University Press, 1992); and William Earl Weeks, *The New Cambridge History of American Foreign Relations, Volume 1: Dimensions of the Early American Empire, 1754–1865* (New York: Cambridge University Press, 2015).

6. Kenneth Bourne, *Britain and the Balance of Power in North America, 1815–1908* (Berkeley: University of California Press, 1967); Gary Gallagher, *The Union War* (Cambridge, MA: Harvard University Press, 2012); John Gerring, *Party Ideologies in America, 1828–1996* (New York: Cambridge University Press, 1998), chapter 3; Abraham Lincoln, Second Inaugural Address, March 4, 1865, in *Lincoln: Speeches and Writings 1859–1865* (New York: Library of America, 1989), 686–87; James McPherson, *Abraham Lincoln and the Second American Revolution* (New York: Oxford University Press, 1992); Allan Nevins, *The War for the Union*, 4 vols. (New York: Scribner, 1959–1971).

7. Robert Bannister, ed., *On Liberty, Society, and Politics: The Essential Essays of William Graham Sumner* (Indianapolis: Liberty Fund, 1992), chapter 24.

8. Richard Hamilton, *President McKinley, War and Empire*, 2 vols. (New Brunswick, NJ: Transaction Publishers, 2006); Stephen Kinzer, *The True Flag: Theodore Roosevelt, Mark Twain, and the Birth of an American Empire* (New York: Henry Holt, 2017); Eric Love, *Race Over Empire: Racism and U.S. Imperialism, 1865–1900* (Chapel Hill: University of North Carolina Press, 2004); Ernest May, *American Imperialism* (New York: Atheneum, 1968); John Offner, *An Unwanted War: The Diplomacy of the United States over Spain and Cuba, 1895–1898* (Chapel Hill: University of North Carolina Press, 1992).

9. Immanuel Hsu, "Late Ch'ing Foreign Relations, 1866–1905," in *The Cambridge History of China, Volume 11: Late Ch'ing, 1800–1911, Part 2*, ed. John Fairbank (New York: Cambridge University Press, 1980), 70–141; George Kennan, *American Diplomacy* (Chicago: University of Chicago Press, 1985 edition), 46–47; Walter LaFeber, *The New Cambridge History of American Foreign Relations: Volume 2, The American Search for Opportunity, 1865–1913* (New York: Cambridge University

Press, 2015), chapter 8; William Appleman Williams, *The Tragedy of American Diplomacy* (New York: Norton, 2009 edition), chapter 1.

10. Michael Doyle, *Liberal Peace: Selected Essays* (Abingdon, UK: Routledge, 2011); John Ikenberry, *After Victory: Institutions, Strategic Restraint, and the Rebuilding of Order after Major Wars* (Princeton, NJ: Princeton University Press, 2000); Beate Jahn, *Liberal Internationalism: Theory, History, Practice* (Basingstoke, UK: Palgrave, 2013); Immanuel Kant, *Kant: Political Writings* (New York: Cambridge University Press, 1991 edition); Andrew Moravcsik, "Taking Preferences Seriously: A Liberal Theory of International Politics," *International Organization* 51, no. 4 (Autumn 1997), 513–53; Bruce Russett, *Triangulating Peace: Democracy, Interdependence, and International Organizations* (New York: Norton, 2000).

11. John Whiteclay Chambers, *The Eagle and the Dove: The American Peace Movement and U.S. Foreign Policy, 1900–1922* (Syracuse, NY: Syracuse University Press, 1991 edition), xxxiv–xliii; Emily Rosenberg, *Spreading the American Dream: American Economic and Cultural Expansion, 1890–1945* (New York: Hill and Wang, 1982), 7–13, 58–62; Tony Smith, *America's Mission: The United States and the Worldwide Struggle for Democracy* (Princeton, NJ: Princeton University Press, 2012 edition), chapter 2.

12. Woodrow Wilson, address to League to Enforce Peace, Washington, DC, May 27, 2016, in *Papers of Woodrow Wilson*, edited by Arthur Link, volume 37 (Princeton, NJ: Princeton University Press, 1981), 113.

13. Lloyd Ambrosius, *Woodrow Wilson and the American Diplomatic Tradition: The Treaty Fight in Perspective* (New York: Cambridge University Press, 1987); John Milton Cooper, *Breaking the Heart of the World: Woodrow Wilson and the Fight for the League of Nations* (New York: Cambridge University Press, 2001); Thomas Knock, *To End All Wars: Woodrow Wilson and the Quest for a New World Order* (New York: Oxford University Press, 1992); Arthur Link, *Woodrow Wilson: Revolution, War and Peace* (Arlington, IL: H. Davidson, 1979); Frank Ninkovich, *The Wilsonian Century* (Chicago: University of Chicago Press, 2001), chapter 2; Klaus Schwabe, *Woodrow Wilson: Revolutionary Germany and Peacemaking, 1918–1919* (Chapel Hill: University of North Carolina Press, 1985); Smith, *America's Mission*, chapter 4.

14. Warren Kimball, *The Juggler: Franklin Roosevelt as Wartime Statesman* (Princeton, NJ: Princeton University Press, 1991), 13, 18–19, 63–81, 95, 103–4, 107–57, 168–74, 182, 191; Robert Sherwood, *Roosevelt and Hopkins: An Intimate History* (New York: Harper, 1948), 266.

15. Robert Dallek, *Franklin D. Roosevelt and American Foreign Policy* (New York: Oxford University Press, 1995), 419, 481–84, 503–505; Robert Divine, *Second Chance: The Triumph of Internationalism in America During World War II* (New York: Atheneum, 1967), 70–71, 98–99, 105–107, 241–42; Brian Rathbun, *Trust in International Cooperation: International Security Institutions, Domestic Politics and American Multilateralism* (New York: Cambridge University Press, 2012), chapter 4.

16. Eduard Mark, "American Policy Toward Eastern Europe and the Origins of the Cold War: An Alternative Interpretation," *Journal of American History* 68, no. 2

(September 1981), 313–36; Dallek, *Roosevelt and American Foreign Policy*, 342, 389–90, 434, 524; Marc Trachtenberg, *A Constructed Peace: The Making of the European Settlement, 1945–1963* (Princeton, NJ: Princeton University Press, 1999), 4–33.

17. John Earl Haynes and Harvey Klehr, *Venona: Decoding Soviet Espionage in America* (New Haven, CT: Yale University Press, 2000), 8–22, 331–37, 352, 363; Robert Jervis, "Was the Cold War a Security Dilemma?" *Journal of Cold War Studies* 3, no. 1 (Winter 2001), 36–60; Stephen Kotkin, *Stalin: Waiting for Hitler, 1929–1941* (New York: Penguin, 2017); Vojtech Mastny, *The Cold War and Soviet Insecurity: The Stalin Years* (New York: Oxford University Press, 1998); Roy Medvedev, *Let History Judge*, trans. Colleen Taylor (New York: Knopf, 1971), 474–79; Vladmir Pechatnov, "The Big Three after World War Two: New Documents on Soviet Thinking about Post War Relations with the United States and Great Britain" (working paper, Cold War International History Project, Woodrow Wilson International Center for Scholars, July 13, 1995); Albert Weeks, *Stalin's Other War: Soviet Grand Strategy, 1939–1941* (Lanham, MD: Rowman and Littlefield, 2003); Vladislav Zubok and Constantine Pleshakov, *Inside the Kremlin's Cold War: From Stalin to Khrushchev* (Cambridge, MA: Harvard University Press, 1996), 9–35.

18. George Kennan to James Byrnes, February 22, 1946, *Foreign Relations of the United States, 1946*, 6 (Washington, DC: US Government Printing Office, 1969), 703–704; "Mr. X," [George Kennan], "The Sources of Soviet Conduct," *Foreign Affairs* 25 (July 1947), 566–82.

19. The definitive work remains Melvyn Leffler, *A Preponderance of Power: National Security, the Truman Administration, and the Cold War* (Stanford, CA: Stanford University Press, 1993). See also Aaron Friedberg, *In the Shadow of the Garrison State* (Princeton, NJ: Princeton University Press, 2000); John Gaddis, *The United States and the Origins of the Cold War, 1941–1947* (New York: Columbia University Press, 2000 edition), chapters 7–10, and *Strategies of Containment: A Critical Appraisal of American National Security Policy during the Cold War* (New York: Oxford University Press, 2005), chapters 1–4; Elizabeth Spalding, *The First Cold Warrior: Harry Truman, Containment, and the Remaking of Liberal Internationalism* (Lexington: University Press of Kentucky, 2006); and Trachtenberg, *A Constructed Peace*, chapters 2–4.

20. Robert Gilpin, *The Challenge of Global Capitalism* (Princeton, NJ: Princeton University Press, 2002), chapters 1–2; Judith Goldstein, *Ideas, Interests, and American Trade Policy* (Ithaca, NY: Cornell University Press, 1994), chapter 4; Charles Kindleberger, *The World in Depression, 1929–1939* (Berkeley: University of California Press, 2013 edition); Robert Pastor, *Congress and the Politics of US Foreign Economic Policy* (Berkeley: University of California Press, 1981), 4–5, 331; John Ruggie, "International Regimes, Transactions, and Change: Embedded Liberalism in the Postwar Economic Order," *International Organization* 36, no. 2 (Spring 1982), 379–415; Benn Steil, *The Battle of Bretton Woods: John Maynard Keynes, Harry Dexter White, and the Making of a New World Order* (Princeton, NJ: Princeton University Press, 2013); Mira Wilkins, *The Maturing of Multinational Enterprise: American Business Abroad from 1914 to 1970* (Cambridge, MA: Harvard University Press, 1974), 283–84, 301, 327–30.

21. Allen Weinstein and Alexander Vasilliev, *The Haunted Wood: Soviet Espionage in America—The Stalin Era* (New York: Modern Library, 2000), 283–85.

22. Andrew Busch, *Truman's Triumphs: The 1948 Election and the Making of Postwar America* (Lexington: University Press of Kentucky, 2012), 62; Alonzo Hamby, *Man of the People: A Life of Harry S. Truman* (New York: Oxford University Press, 1998), 356, 359, 454, 464–66; Lawrence Wittner, *Rebels Against War: The American Peace Movement, 1933–1983* (Philadelphia: Temple University Press, 1984), 187–88, 193, 196–97, 207–12. In spite of post–Cold War Soviet archival revelations, hagiographic portrayals of Henry Wallace continue to be written in the twenty-first century: e.g., John Culver and John Hyde, *American Dreamer: A Life of Henry A. Wallace* (New York: Norton, 2001).

23. John Fousek, *To Lead the Free World: American Nationalism and the Cultural Roots of the Cold War* (Chapel Hill: University of North Carolina Press, 2000), 2, 7–15; Friedberg, *In the Shadow of the Garrison State*; Hamby, *Man of the People*, 313, 421–22, 637–39; Leffler, *A Preponderance of Power*, 12–24, 499–504; Gregory Mitrovich, *Undermining the Kremlin: America's Strategy to Subvert the Soviet Bloc* (Ithaca, NY: Cornell University Press, 2009), chapters 1–2; Robert Osgood, *Ideals and Self-Interest in America's Foreign Relations* (Chicago: University of Chicago Press, 1953), 307, 416–25; Geoffrey Sloan, *Geopolitics in United States Strategic Policy, 1890–1987* (London: St. Martin's Press, 1988), 109–19, 125–44; Smith, *America's Mission*, chapter 6; Spalding, *The First Cold Warrior*, 2–8, 223–31.

24. Gaddis, *Strategies of Containment*, chapter 7–8; Patrick Lloyd Hatcher, *The Suicide of an Elite: American Internationalists and Vietnam* (Stanford, CA: Stanford University Press, 1990); Michael Latham, *The Right Kind of Revolution: Modernization, Development, and US Foreign Policy from the Cold War to the Present* (Ithaca, NY: Cornell University Press, 2010), chapter 5; Fredrik Logevall, *Choosing War: The Lost Chance for Peace and the Escalation of War in Vietnam* (Berkeley: University of California Press, 2001).

25. Ole Holsti and James Rosenau, *American Leadership in World Affairs: Vietnam and the Breakdown of Consensus* (Boston: Allen and Unwin, 1982), 108–33.

26. Robert David Johnson, *Congress and the Cold War* (New York: Cambridge University Press, 2005), chapters 4–6; Robert Kaufman, *Henry M. Jackson: A Life in Politics* (Seattle: University of Washington Press: 2000), chapters 9–20; Bruce Miroff, *The Liberals' Moment: The McGovern Insurgency and the Identity Crisis of the Democratic Party* (Lawrence: University Press of Kansas, 2007).

27. On Carter's foreign policy from various perspectives, see Betty Glad, *An Outsider in the White House: Jimmy Carter, His Advisors, and the Making of American Foreign Policy* (Ithaca, NY: Cornell University Press, 2009); Scott Kaufman, *Plans Unraveled: The Foreign Policy of the Carter Administration* (DeKalb: Northern Illinois University Press, 2008); Alexander Moens, *Foreign Policy Under Carter: Testing Multiple Advocacy Decision Making* (Abingdon, UK: Routledge, 1990); David Skidmore, *Reversing Course: Carter's Foreign Policy, Domestic Politics, and the Failure of Reform* (Nashville, TN: Vanderbilt University Press, 1996); Gaddis Smith, *Morality, Reason and Power: American Diplomacy in the Carter Years* (New York: Hill and Wang, 1987); Tony Smith, *America's Mission*,

chapter 9; Donald Spencer, *The Carter Implosion: Jimmy Carter and the Amateur Style of Diplomacy* (Santa Barbara, CA: Praeger, 1988); and Robert Strong, *Working in the World: Jimmy Carter and the Making of American Foreign Policy* (Baton Rouge: Louisiana State University Press, 2000).

28. James Boys, *Clinton's Grand Strategy* (London: Bloomsbury Academic, 2015); Douglas Brinkley, "Democratic Enlargement: The Clinton Doctrine," *Foreign Policy* 106 (Spring 1997), 110–27; John Dumbrell, *Clinton's Foreign Policy* (New York: Routledge, 2009); William Hyland, *Clinton's World* (Westport, CT: Praeger, 1999); Ikenberry, *After Victory*, 241–45; Tony Smith, *America's Mission*, chapter 12; Karin von Hippel, *Democracy by Force: US Military Intervention in the Post–Cold War World* (New York: Cambridge University Press, 2000).

29. For various perspectives on Obama's foreign policy, see Derek Chollet, *The Long Game* (New York: Public Affairs, 2016); Colin Dueck, *The Obama Doctrine* (New York: Oxford University Press, 2015); Martin Indyk, Kenneth Lieberthal, and Michael O'Hanlon, *Bending History: Barack Obama's Foreign Policy* (Washington, DC: Brookings Institution, 2012); Mark Landler, *Alter Egos: Hillary Clinton, Barack Obama, and the Twilight Struggle over American Power* (New York: Random House, 2016); Ryan Lizza, "The Consequentialist," *The New Yorker*, May 2, 2011; James Mann, *The Obamians* (New York: Penguin, 2012); Vali Nasr, *The Dispensable Nation: American Foreign Policy in Retreat* (New York: Doubleday, 2013); and David Sanger, *Confront and Conceal: Obama's Secret Wars and Surprising Use of American Power* (New York: Broadway Books, 2013).

30. Robert Keohane and Joseph Nye, *Power and Interdependence* (New York: Pearson, 2011 edition).

31. Robert Keohane, *After Hegemony: Cooperation and Discord in the World Political Economy* (Princeton, NJ: Princeton University Press, 2005 edition).

32. Francis Fukuyama, *The End of History and the Last Man* (New York: Free Press, 1992).

33. John Gerard Ruggie, *Winning the Peace* (New York: Columbia University Press, 1998), 4–5, 22, 25, 160.

34. John Ikenberry, "Institutions, Strategic Restraint, and the Persistence of American Postwar Order," *International Security* 23, no. 3 (Winter 1998/99), 43–78.

35. Joseph Nye, *The Paradox of American Power* (New York: Oxford University Press, 2003), 4–17, 39, 154–68, and *Soft Power* (New York: Public Affairs, 2005.)

36. "A Conversation with US Secretary of State Hillary Rodham Clinton," Council on Foreign Relations, July 15, 2009.

37. Carsten Holbraad, *Internationalism and Nationalism in European Political Thought* (London: Palgrave, 2003), chapter 4.

38. Edmund Burke, *Reflections on the Revolution in France* (New Haven, CT: Yale University Press, 2003 edition); Albert Hirschman, *The Rhetoric of Reaction* (Cambridge, MA: The Belknap Press of Harvard University Press, 1991), 6–13, 43–48, 81–83; John Kekes, *A Case for Conservatism* (Ithaca, NY: Cornell University Press, 2001), 5–13, 27–47, 72–79, 190–219; Robert Nisbet, *Conservatism* (Buckingham, UK: Open University Press, 1986), 21–74; Michael Oakeshott,

"On Being Conservative," in Oakeshott, *Rationalism in Politics and Other Essays* (Indianapolis: Liberty Fund, 1991), 407–37.

39. Ian Clark, *Reform and Resistance in the International Order* (New York: Cambridge University Press, 1980), 1–10; Samuel Huntington, *The Soldier and the State* (Cambridge, MA: The Belknap Press of Harvard University Press, 1981), chapters 1, 3, 17; Brian Rathbun, *Partisan Interventions* (Ithaca, NY: Cornell University Press, 2004), 2–3, 14–26.

40. The exact nature and mixture of these various premodern and classical liberal influences upon the American Revolution remains hotly debated to this day. Significant contributions on this question include Bernard Bailyn, *The Ideological Origins of the American Revolution* (Cambridge, MA: The Belknap Press of Harvard University Press, 1967); Peter Berkowitz, *Constitutional Conservatism* (Stanford, CA: Hoover Institution Press, 2013); Hartz, *Liberal Tradition in America*, 4–11, 47–50, 59–62, 147–58; Charles Kesler, "The Crisis of American National Identity," *Claremont Review of Books* (Fall 2005); Kirk, *Roots of American Order*, 301–44, 393–439; Clinton Rossiter, *Conservatism in America* (Cambridge, MA: Harvard University Press, 1982), 67–96, 198–201; Thomas West, *The Political Theory of the American Founding* (New York: Cambridge University Press, 2017); Gordon Wood, *The Creation of the American Republic* (Chapel Hill: University of North Carolina Press, 1969); and Michael Zuckert, *The Natural Rights Republic* (Notre Dame, IN: Notre Dame Press, 1996).

41. These categories are developed at greater length in *The Obama Doctrine*, chapter 4.

42. For competing definitions, see Knock, *To End All Wars*, 55–58; Charlie Laderman, "Conservative Internationalism: An Overview," *Orbis* 62, no. 1 (2018), 6–21; Paul Miller, *American Power and Liberal Order* (Washington, DC: Georgetown University Press, 2016); and Henry Nau, *Conservative Internationalism* (Princeton, NJ: Princeton University Press, 2013).

43. Among supporters of Trump in the GOP primaries, 64% said that "being a member of NATO is good for the US," while 30% disagreed. Support for NATO was even higher among other Republicans. Pew Research Center, "Public Uncertain, Divided over America's Place in the World," (April 2016), 47–48.

44. The Brookings Institution, "2013 American Values Survey: In Search of Libertarians in America" (Washington, DC: Brookings Institution, 2013).

45. Walter Russell Mead, *Special Providence: American Foreign Policy and How it Changed the World* (New York: Knopf, 2001), chapter 7.

46. Ibid., chapters 4, 6.

47. For a history of Republican foreign policy tendencies since 1940, see Colin Dueck, *Hard Line: The Republican Party and US Foreign Policy since World War II* (Princeton, NJ: Princeton University Press, 2010).

48. Helen Milner, *Resisting Protectionism: Global Industries and the Politics of International Trade* (Princeton, NJ: Princeton University Press, 1989), 28–33, 45–102.

49. Peter Trubowitz, *Defining the National Interest* (Chicago: University of Chicago Press, 1998), chapters 3–4.

50. Leroy Rieselbach, *The Roots of Isolationism: Congressional Voting and Presidential Leadership* (Indianapolis: Bobbs-Merrill, 1966), 21, 141–64.

51. Ole Holsti, *Public Opinion and American Foreign Policy* (Ann Arbor: University of Michigan Press, 2004 edition), chapter 3; Eugene Wittkopf, *Faces of Internationalism* (Durham, NC: Duke University Press, 1990).

52. For useful insights on these differences, see Peter Liberman, "An Eye for an Eye," *International Organization* 60, no. 3 (Summer 2006), 687–722; and Brian Rathbun, "Does One Right Make a Realist?" *Political Science Quarterly* 123, no. 2 (Summer 2008), 271–99.

CHAPTER 2

1. On TR's years in the Badlands, see William Hazelgrove, *Forging a President: How the Wild West Created Theodore Roosevelt* (Washington, DC: Regnery History, 2017).

2. John Morton Blum, *The Republican Roosevelt* (Cambridge, MA: Harvard University Press, 1977), 5–6. But see also Jean Yarbrough, *Theodore Roosevelt and the American Political Tradition* (Lawrence: University Press of Kansas, 2014).

3. Ernest May, *Imperial Democracy: The Emergence of America as a Great Power* (New York: Harper and Row, 1973), 214–23; Emily Rosenberg, *Spreading the American Dream: American Economic and Cultural Expansion, 1890–1945* (New York: Hill and Wang, 1982), 57–58; Cyrus Veeser, "Inventing Dollar Diplomacy: The Gilded Age Origins of the Roosevelt Corollary to the Monroe Doctrine," *Diplomatic History* (June 2003), 301–26; Mira Wilkins, *The Emergence of Multinational Enterprise: American Business Abroad from the Colonial Era to 1914* (Cambridge, MA: Harvard University Press, 1970), 70–110, 149–72.

4. Howard Beale, *Theodore Roosevelt and the Rise of America to World Power* (Baltimore: Johns Hopkins University Press, 1984), 47, 51, 65, 84, 101, 290–96; Richard Collin, *Theodore Roosevelt's Caribbean* (Baton Rouge: Louisiana State University Press, 1990), 99, 167–69, 193, 242–43, 274, 311, 400–401, 547; James Holmes, *Theodore Roosevelt and World Order: Police Power in International Relations* (Washington, DC: Potomac Books, 2005); Frederick Marks, *Velvet on Iron: the Diplomacy of Theodore Roosevelt* (Lincoln: University of Nebraska Press, 1982), 6–9; Nancy Mitchell, "The Height of the German Challenge: The Venezuela Blockade, 1902–3," *Diplomatic History* (April 1996), 185–210; Frank Ninkovich, "Theodore Roosevelt: Civilization as Ideology," *Diplomatic History* 10, no. 3 (Summer 1986), 221–45.

5. Roosevelt's first public reference to this saying seems to have been at the Minnesota state fair, on September 2, 1901. See Roosevelt, in *Works of Theodore Roosevelt*, ed. Hermann Hagedorn (New York: Charles Scribner's Sons, 1926), 13: 474.

6. Marks, *Velvet on Iron*, 134–42, 155–57.

7. Cited in Blum, *Republican Roosevelt*, 137.

8. Gordon Carpenter O'Gara, *Theodore Roosevelt and the Rise of the Modern Navy* (Westport, CT: Praeger, 1970), 109–12; Theodore Roosevelt, *Autobiography* (New York: Charles Scribner's Sons, 1924), 564–65.

9. Beale, *Rise of America*, 52, 304; H. W. Brands, *TR: The Last Romantic* (New York: Basic Books, 1997), 573–74; TR to Theodore Burton, February 23, 1904,

in *Letters of Theodore Roosevelt*, ed. Elting Morison (Cambridge, MA: Harvard University Press, 1954), 4:737.

10. Barton Bernstein and Franklin Leib, "Progressive Republican Senators and American Imperialism, 1898–1916: A Reappraisal," in *To Advise and Consent: The United States Congress and Foreign Policy in the Twentieth Century*, vol. 1, ed. Joel Silbey (Brooklyn, NY: Carlson, 1991), 1–44.

11. Robert David Johnson, *The Peace Progressives and American Foreign Policy* (Cambridge, MA: Harvard University Press, 1995), 44–45, 54–58; Robert James Maddox, *William E. Borah and American Foreign Policy* (Baton Rouge: Louisiana State University Press, 1969), 9–16; William Widenor, *Henry Cabot Lodge and the Search for an American Foreign Policy* (Berkeley: University of California Press, 1980), 175–217.

12. Lewis Gould, *The First Modern Clash over Federal Power: Wilson versus Hughes in the Presidential Election of 1916* (Lawrence: University Press of Kansas, 2016); Arthur Link, *Wilson: Campaigns for Progressivism and Peace, 1916–1917* (Princeton, NJ: Princeton University Press, 1965), chapters 1–4.

13. Johnson, *Peace Progressives*, 68; Maddox, *Borah*, 20–22.

14. On the Treaty debate, see Lloyd Ambrosius, *Woodrow Wilson and the American Diplomatic Tradition: The Treaty Fight in Perspective* (New York: Cambridge University Press, 1987); John Milton Cooper, *Breaking the Heart of the World: Woodrow Wilson and the Fight for the League of Nations* (New York: Cambridge University Press, 2001); Thomas Knock, *To End All Wars: Woodrow Wilson and the Quest for a New World Order* (New York: Oxford University Press, 1992), chapters 11–14; Ralph Stone, *The Irreconcilables: The Fight Against the League of Nations* (Lexington: University Press of Kentucky, 1970); and Widenor, *Lodge*, chapter 8.

15. Stone, *Irreconcilables*, 43.

16. Widenor, *Lodge*, 331.

17. Ambrosius, *Treaty Fight*, 99–102, 263.

18. Ibid., 282.

19. On Republican foreign policies from 1921 to 1933, see Warren Cohen, *Empire Without Tears: America's Foreign Relations, 1921–1933* (Philadelphia: Temple University Press, 1987); Frank Costigliola, *Awkward Dominion: American Political, Economic, and Cultural Relations with Europe, 1919–1933* (Ithaca, NY: Cornell University Press, 1984); Michael Hogan, *Informal Entente: The Private Structure of Cooperation in Anglo-American Economic Diplomacy, 1918–1928* (Columbia, MO: University of Missouri Press, 1977); Melvyn Leffler, *The Elusive Quest: America's Pursuit of European Stability and French Security, 1919–1933* (Chapel Hill: University of North Carolina Press, 1979); Margot Louria, *Triumph and Downfall: America's Pursuit of Peace and Prosperity, 1921–1933* (Westport, CT: Greenwood Press, 2001); and Benjamin Rhodes, *United States Foreign Policy in the Interwar Period, 1918–1941* (Westport, CT: Praeger, 2001), chapters 3–5.

20. Joan Hoff Wilson, *Herbert Hoover: Forgotten Progressive* (Prospect Heights, IL: Waveland Press, 1992), 3–64.

21. Herbert Hoover, *Memoirs, volume II: The Cabinet and the Presidency, 1920–1933* (London: Hollis and Carter, 1952), 28; Wilson, *Forgotten Progressive*, 79–121, 168,

175–84, 208; John R. M. Wilson, "The Quaker and the Sword: Herbert Hoover's Relations with the Military," *Military Affairs* 38, no. 2 (April 1974), 41–47.

22. Joseph Brandes, *Herbert Hoover and Economic Diplomacy* (Pittsburgh: University of Pittsburgh Press, 1962), 45, 155, 167, 170–96, 216; Hoover, *Memoirs, II*, 81–82.

23. Thomas Guinsburg, *The Pursuit of Isolationism in the United States Senate from Versailles to Pearl Harbor* (New York: Garland Pub., 1982), 275–93; Johnson, *Peace Progressives*, 149–52, 200–35; Leffler, *The Elusive Quest*, 170–80; Karen Miller, *Populist Nationalism: Republican Insurgency and American Foreign Policy Making* (Westport, CT: Greenwood Press, 1999), 97–117.

24. Brandes, *Economic Diplomacy*, 45; Costigliola, *Awkward Dominion*, 62, 170–80; Leffler, *The Elusive Quest*, 42, 79; Carl Parrini, *Heir to Empire: United States Economic Diplomacy, 1916–1923* (Pittsburgh: University of Pittsburgh, 1969), 234, 265–66; Joan Hoff Wilson, *American Business and Foreign Policy, 1920–1933* (Lexington: University Press of Kentucky, 1971), xi–xiii, 3–9, 20, 36–41, 75–76, 124–25, 155–56.

25. Cohen, *Empire Without Tears*, 31–32, 35, 47–48; Charles DeBenedetti, *The Peace Reform in American History* (Bloomington: Indiana University Press, 1980), 108–21.

26. John Donald Hicks, *Republican Ascendancy, 1921–1933* (New York: Harper and Row, 1963), 91–92; Johnson, *Peace Progressives*, 236–68; Robert Murray, *The Politics of Normalcy: Governmental Theory and Practice in the Harding-Coolidge Era* (New York: Norton, 1973), 59–61.

27. Roger Dingman, *Power in the Pacific: The Origins of Naval Arms Limitations, 1914–1922* (Chicago: University of Chicago Press, 1977), 140; Chalmers Vinson, *The Parchment Peace: The United States Senate and the Washington Conference, 1921–1922* (Athens: University of Georgia Press, 1955), 73–74, 90–91, 108–109.

28. Costigliola, *Awkward Dominion*, 56, 64–65, 176–80; Leffler, *Elusive Quest*, 32–42, 48, 81, 100, 170.

29. Cohen, *Empire Without Tears*, 68–75; Dana Munro, *The United States and the Caribbean Republics, 1921–1933* (Princeton, NJ: Princeton University Press, 1974), 12–70, 157–254.

30. Vinson, *Parchment Peace*, 116, 137–39, 177–80, 191–92.

31. Martin Fausold, *The Presidency of Herbert C. Hoover* (Lawrence: University Press of Kansas, 1985), 190–91; Hoover, *Memoirs, II*, v, 330–32, 377.

32. Alexander DeConde, *Herbert Hoover's Latin American Policy* (New York: Octagon Books, 1970), 18; Fausold, *Presidency of Hoover*, 32–33, 183–86; Munro, *Caribbean Republics*, 255–94, 309–41, 351–83.

33. Hoover, *Memoirs, II*, 70; Leffler, *The Elusive Quest*, 198, 219; Henry Stimson and McGeorge Bundy, *On Active Service in Peace and War* (New York: Harper, 1948), 276; and Wilson, *Forgotten Progressive*, 186.

34. Hoover, *Memoirs, II*, 366.

35. Elting Morison, *Turmoil and Tradition: A Study in the Life and Times of Henry L. Stimson* (Boston: Houghton Mifflin, 1960), 373–74; Armin Rappaport, *Henry L. Stimson and Japan, 1931–1933* (Chicago: University of Chicago Press, 1963), 148–49; Stimson, *On Active Service*, 222–24, 233–35.

36. Justus Doenecke, *Diplomacy of Frustration: The Manchurian Crisis of 1931–1933 as Revealed in the Papers of Stanley K. Hornbeck* (Stanford, CA: Hoover Institution Press, 1981), 46; Hoover, *Memoirs, II*, 377; Morison, *Turmoil and Tradition*, 313, 397–98; Stimson, *On Active Service*, 235–36, 259; Christopher Thorne, *The Limits of Foreign Policy: The West, the League, and the Far Eastern Crisis of 1931–1933* (New York: Putnam, 1973), 404–21.

37. Geoffrey Matthews, "Robert A. Taft, the Constitution and American Foreign Policy, 1939–1953," *Journal of Contemporary History* 17 (July 1982), 507–22; James Patterson, *Mr. Republican: A Biography of Robert A. Taft* (Boston: Houghton Mifflin, 1972), 95, 131, 166–67, 176, 192, 204, 213–16; Robert Taft, "The New Deal: Recovery, Reform, and Revolution," April 9, 1935, in *The Papers of Robert A. Taft*, ed. Clarence Wunderlin (Kent, OH: Kent State University Press, 1997), 1: 483; Robert Taft, "Shall the President Make War without the Approval of Congress?" in *We Testify*, ed. N. Schoonemaker and D. Reid (New York: Smith and Durrell, 1941), 215; and Clarence Wunderlin, *Robert A. Taft: Ideas, Tradition, and Party in US Foreign Policy* (Lanham, MD: Rowman and Littlefield, 2005), 2–6, 9–31, 36–38.

38. Wayne Cole, *America First: The Battle Against Intervention, 1940–1941* (Madison: University of Wisconsin Press, 1952), 10–30, 35–36, 118, 122–39; and *Roosevelt and the Isolationists, 1932–1945* (Lincoln: University of Nebraska Press, 1983), 397, 400, 411–13, 430–31; Justus Doenecke, "Power, Markets and Ideology: The Isolationist Response to Roosevelt Policy, 1940–1941," in *Watershed of Empire: Essays on New Deal Foreign Policy*, eds. Leonard Liggio and James Martin (Colorado Springs, CO: Ralph Myles, 1976), 132–61; Leroy Rieselbach, *The Roots of Isolationism: Congressional Voting and Presidential Leadership in Foreign Policy* (Indianapolis: Bobbs-Merrill, 1966), 35–49, 62–67, 80, 106–26, 143–50; Hendrik Meijer, *Arthur Vandenberg* (Chicago: University of Chicago Press, 2017), chapter 12; Roland Stromberg, "American Business and the Approach of War, 1935–1941," *Journal of Economic History* 13 (Winter 1953), 58–78.

39. Robert Jenner, *FDR's Republicans: Domestic Political Realignment and American Foreign Policy* (Lanham, MD: Lexington Books, 2010), 133–79, 191–200; Hadley Cantril, "America Faces the War," *Public Opinion Quarterly* 4 (July 1940), 387–407; Mark Lincoln Chadwin, *The Hawks of World War II* (Chapel Hill: University of North Carolina Press, 1968), 16–22, 44–45, 66–72, 159–66, 271–77; Stromberg, "American Business and the Approach of War," 72–75.

40. Robert Divine, *Foreign Policy and US Presidential Elections, 1940–1948* (New York: New Viewpoints, 1974), 33–35, 54–59, 81–83; Meijer, *Vandenberg*, chapter 13; Steve Neal, *Dark Horse: A Biography of Wendell Willkie* (Lawrence: University Press of Kansas, 1989), 12, 38–42, 57, 66–121, 159, 167–68, 176–79; Patterson, *Mr. Republican*, 213–18; C. David Tompkins, *Senator Arthur Vandenberg: The Evolution of a Modern Republican, 1884–1945* (East Lansing: Michigan State University Press, 1970), 45–46, 170–85.

41. Cole, *Roosevelt and the Isolationists*, 346–58, 411–13, 488–507; William Langer and S. Everett Gleason, *The Undeclared War, 1940–1941* (New York: Harper and Brothers, 1953), 520, 577, 748–58; Meijer, *Vandenberg*, chapter 14; Arthur Vandenberg, *The Private Papers of Senator Vandenberg* (Boston: Houghton Mifflin, 1952), 18.

42. Robert Divine, *Second Chance: The Triumph of Internationalism in America During World War II* (New York: Atheneum, 1967), 55–60, 70–71, 74, 78, 98–99, 120–22; H. Schuyler Foster, *Activism Replaces Isolationism: US Public Attitudes, 1940–1975* (Washington, DC: Foxhall Press, 1983), 20–22; Henry Luce, "The American Century," *Life* (February 17, 1941), 61–65; Neal, *Dark Horse*, 231–66, 277–92; Patterson, *Mr. Republican*, 248–91; address by Robert Taft at Grove City College, Taft to James H. Crummey, and address by Taft, "Peace or Politics," May 22, July 22, and August 26, 1943, in *Papers of RAT*, 2: 385, 446–49, 468, 476–80; Wendell Willkie, *One World* (New York: Simon and Schuster, 1943), 2, 69–102, 133–77, 192–203; Wunderlin, *Taft*, 77–90.

43. Richard Darilek, *A Loyal Opposition in Time of War: The Republican Party and the Politics of Foreign Policy from Pearl Harbor to Yalta* (Westport, CT: Greenwood Press, 1976), 59–74, 120–27, 139–40, 144–49; Divine, *Second Chance*, 186–89, 209–210, 216–17, 241–42, 270–71, 313; Meijer, *Vandenberg*, chapters 15–18, 20–21; Patterson, *Mr. Republican*, 296–97; Richard Norton Smith, *Thomas E. Dewey and His Times* (New York: Simon and Schuster, 1982), 263–65, 334, 338, 344–45, 382–438; Tompkins, *Vandenberg*, 191–218; Vandenberg, *Papers*, 30, 53–60, 69, 95–96, 200.

44. Smith, *Dewey*, 439–42; address by Taft, "What Foreign Policy Will Promote Peace?" June 8, 1944, *Papers of RAT*, 2:557; Tompkins, *Vandenberg*, 196–97.

45. Aaron Friedberg, *In the Shadow of the Garrison State* (Princeton, NJ: Princeton University Press, 2000), 40–61, 83–97, 155–75; Michael Hogan, *A Cross of Iron: Harry S. Truman and the Origins of the National Security State* (New York: Cambridge University Press, 1998), 20–21, 70–71, 115–18, 120–21, 157–58; Meijer, *Vandenberg*, chapters 19, 22–27; Robert Taft, "Inflation and the Marshall Plan," in *Papers of RAT*, 3: 355–59; Smith, *Dewey*, 469–70, 479–539; Vandenberg, *Papers*, 225–51, 373–412; Wunderlin, *Taft*, 112–32.

46. John Earl Haynes and Harvey Klehr, *Venona: Decoding Soviet Espionage in America* (New Haven, CT: Yale Nota Bene, 2000), 8–22, 331–37, 353, 363; David Kepley, *Collapse of the Middle Way: Senate Republicans and the Bipartisan Foreign Policy, 1948–1952* (New York: Greenwood Press, 1988), 53–61; Meijer, *Vandenberg*, chapters 28–29; David Oshinsky, *A Conspiracy So Immense: The World of Joe McCarthy* (New York: Oxford University Press, 2005 edition), 53–84, 95–138, 163–65; Patterson, *Mr. Republican*, 313, 425, 437–46; Richard Gid Powers, *Not Without Honor: The History of American Anti-Communism* (New York: Free Press, 1995), 272.

47. Ronald Caridi, *The Korean War and American Politics* (Philadelphia: University of Pennsylvania Press, 1968), 33–38, 75, 84, 93–102, 116–19, 131–37; Herbert Hoover, "Our National Policies in This Crisis," December 20, 1950, in Herbert Hoover, *Addresses Upon the American Road, 1950–1955* (Stanford, CA: Stanford University Press, 1955), 8–9; Robert Taft, *A Foreign Policy for Americans* (Garden City, NY: Doubleday, 1951), 11–23, 39, 47–66, 73–87, 100–120.

48. Stephen Ambrose, *Eisenhower: Soldier and President* (New York: Simon and Schuster, 1990), 245–87; Friedberg, *In the Shadow of the Garrison State*, 115–25; Hogan, *A Cross of Iron*, 266, 313, 335–44, 364–65; Patterson, *Mr. Republican*, 499–516, 560; Wunderlin, *Taft*, 177–205.

49. Ambrose, *Eisenhower*, chapters 1–10; Robert Divine, *Foreign Policy and US Presidential Elections, 1952–1960* (New York: New Viewpoints, 1974), 25–36, 50–56, 82–85.

50. Gary Reichard, *The Reaffirmation of Republicanism: Eisenhower and the Eighty-Third Congress* (Knoxville: University of Tennessee Press, 1975), 9–14; Steven Wagner, *Eisenhower Republicanism: Pursuing the Middle Way* (DeKalb: Northern Illinois University Press, 2006), 7.

51. Robert Bowie and Richard Immerman, *Waging Peace: How Eisenhower Shaped an Enduring Cold War Strategy* (New York: Oxford University Press, 1998), 43–48, 249–52; Eisenhower inaugural address, January 20, 1953, *Public Papers of the Presidents of the United States: Dwight D. Eisenhower [hereafter EPP], 1953* (Washington, DC: US Government Printing Office, 1960), 1: 1–8; Caroline Pruden, *Conditional Partners: Eisenhower, the United Nations, and the Search for a Permanent Peace* (Baton Rouge: Louisiana State University Press, 1998), 306, 310.

52. Bowie and Immerman, *Waging Peace*, 47, 96–108, 139–46; Friedberg, *In the Shadow of the Garrison State*, 130–33; NSC 162/2, October 30, 1953, *FRUS: 1952–1954* (Washington, DC: US Government Printing Office, 1983) 2: 593; William Stueck, *The Korean War: An International History* (Princeton, NJ: Princeton University Press, 1995), 326–30.

53. Eisenhower to Alfred Gruenther, December 2, 1955, *The Papers of Dwight David Eisenhower* (Baltimore: Johns Hopkins University Press, 1996), 16: 1919–20; NSC 162/2, *FRUS: 1952–1954*, 2: 583, 585; Marc Trachtenberg, *A Constructed Peace: The Making of the European Settlement, 1945–1963* (Princeton, NJ: Princeton University Press, 1999), 122–200.

54. Eisenhower speech to American Society of Newspaper Editors, April 16, 1953, *EPP: 1953*, 179–88; Andrew Erdmann, "War No Longer Has Any Logic Whatever," Dwight D. Eisenhower and the Thermonuclear Revolution," in *Cold War Statesmen Confront the Bomb: Nuclear Diplomacy since 1945*, eds. John Gaddis, Philip Gordon, Ernest May, and Jonathan Rosenberg (New York: Oxford University Press, 1999), 101–9.

55. Memorandum, Eisenhower conversation with Sherman Adams and Herbert Hoover Jr., November 5, 1956, *FRUS 1955–1957*, 26: 1000–1001; Johanna Granville, "Caught with Jam on our Fingers: Radio Free Europe and the Hungarian Revolution of 1956," *Diplomatic History* 29, no. 5 (November 2005), 811–39; Gregory Mitrovich, *Undermining the Kremlin: America's Strategy to Subvert the Soviet Bloc, 1947–1956* (Ithaca, NY: Cornell University Press, 2000), 158–65, 175–76.

56. Justus Doenecke, *Not to the Swift*, 232–37; Greenstein, *The Hidden-Hand Presidency*, 155–227; Hulsey, *Everett Dirksen*, 4–5, 82–83; Anna K. Nelson, "John Foster Dulles and the Bipartisan Congress," *Political Science Quarterly* 102, no. 1 (Spring 1987), 43–64; Reichard, *The Reaffirmation of Republicanism*, 28–68, 87–96, 227–28; Rieselbach, *Roots of Isolationism*, 44, 49, 51–53, 56, 108–9, 150; Duane Tananbaum, "The Bricker Amendment Controversy: Its Origins and Eisenhower's Role," *Diplomatic History* 9, no. 1 (Winter 1985), 73–93.

57. Raymond Bauer, Ithiel de Sola Pool, and Lewis Dexter, *American Business and Public Policy* (New York: Atheneum, 1964), 23–73, 152–53, 465–90; Dwight

Eisenhower, *Mandate for Change*, 194–95, 292–94; Douglas Irwin and Randall Kroszner, "Interests, Institutions, and Ideology in Securing Policy Change: The Republican Conversion to Trade Liberalization after Smoot-Hawley," *Journal of Law and Economics* 42, no. 2 (October 1999), 643–73; Burton Kaufman, *Trade and Aid: Eisenhower's Foreign Economic Policy, 1953–1961* (Baltimore: Johns Hopkins University Press, 1982), 7–9; Reichard, *The Reaffirmation of Republicanism*, 71–84.

58. Michael Doran, *Ike's Gamble: America's Rise to Dominance in the Middle East* (New York: Free Press, 2016); Mark Gasiorowski, "The 1953 Coup d'Etat in Iran," *International Journal of Middle East Studies* 19, no. 3 (August 1987), 261–86; Richard Immerman, *The CIA in Guatemala: The Foreign Policy of Intervention* (Austin: University of Texas Press, 1982), 14–19, 155–58, 161–86, 194–98; Stephen Rabe, *Eisenhower and Latin America: The Foreign Policy of Anti-Communism* (Chapel Hill: University of North Carolina Press, 1988), 33–42, 84–92, 177; Ray Takeyh, "What Really Happened in Iran," *Foreign Affairs* 93, no. 4 (July/August 2014), 2-14.

59. Memorandum of discussion at the 179th meeting of the National Security Council, January 8, 1954, *FRUS 1952–1954*, vol. 13, *Indochina*, pt. 1, 949; Melanie Billings-Yun, *Decision against War: Eisenhower and Dien Bien Phu, 1954* (New York: Columbia University Press, 1988), 92, 109, 132, 159–60.

60. Jeff Broadwater, *Eisenhower and the Anti-Communist Crusade* (Chapel Hill: University of North Carolina Press, 1992), 207; Divine, *Elections, 1952–1960*, 98–99, 136–39, 160; John Sloan, *Eisenhower and the Management of Prosperity* (Lawrence: University Press of Kansas, 1991), 10.

61. William Burr, "Avoiding the Slippery Slope: the Eisenhower Administration and the Berlin Crisis, November 1958–January 1959," *Diplomatic History* 18, no. 2 (Spring 1994), 177–205; Rabe, *Eisenhower and Latin America*, 100, 124–30, 157, 175; Peter Roman, *Eisenhower and the Missile Gap* (Ithaca, NY: Cornell University Press, 1996), 30–62, 104, 118–21, 175–93, 207.

62. Divine, *Elections, 1952–1960*, 286–87; John Gaddis, *Strategies of Containment*, 163, 175, 181–82, 197–234; Michael Latham, "Ideology, Social Science, and Destiny: Modernization and the Kennedy-Era Alliance for Progress," *Diplomatic History* 22, no. 2 (Spring 1998), 199–229; Iwan Morgan, *Eisenhower versus "The Spenders"* (New York: St. Martin's Press, 1990), 34–35.

CHAPTER 3

1. The Editors, "The Magazine's Credenda," *National Review*, November 19, 1955; Daniel Kelly, *James Burnham and the Struggle for the World* (Wilmington, DE: ISI Books, 2002), 115–237; George Nash, *The Conservative Intellectual Movement in America Since 1945* (Wilmington, DE: ISI Books, 2006 edition), chapters 1–6.

2. Robert Goldberg, *Barry Goldwater* (New Haven, CT: Yale University Press, 1995), 3–139, 154; Barry Goldwater, *The Conscience of a Conservative* (Princeton, NJ: Princeton University Press, 2007 edition), 6–19, 27–31, 37, 53–65.

3. Goldwater, *Conscience of a Conservative*, 82–84, 89–90, 105–20; and *Why Not Victory?* (New York: McGraw Hill, 1962), 29–30, 44–45, 84–89, 162–63.

4. Hulsey, *Dirksen*, 4–5, 82–82; Lisa McGirr, *Suburban Warriors: The Origins of the New American Right* (Princeton, NJ: Princeton University Press, 2001), 4–5, 8–10; Nicol Rae, *The Decline and Fall of Liberal Republicans* (New York: Oxford University Press, 1999), 163–67; Kirkpatrick Sale, *Power Shift: The Rise of the Southern Rim and its Challenges to the Eastern Establishment* (New York: Vintage, 1976), 17–53; Richard Norton Smith, *On His Own Terms: A Life of Nelson Rockefeller* (New York: Random House, 2014), 310–12, 344–45, 357, 373, 394, 402, 413–14.

5. Earle Black and Merle Black, *The Rise of Southern Republicans* (Cambridge, MA: The Belknap Press of Harvard University Press, 2002), 28–29, 150; Mary Brennan, *Turning Right in the Sixties: The Conservative Capture of the GOP* (Chapel Hill: University of North Carolina Press, 1995), 50–55, 75–81; Goldberg, *Goldwater*, 149–237; Kirk Porter and Donald Bruce Johnson, eds., *National Party Platforms, 1840–1968* (Urbana: University of Illinois Press, 1972), 683–89; Rae, *Liberal Republicans*, 53–70, 75; F. Clifton White, *Suite 3505: The Story of the Draft Goldwater Movement* (New Rochelle, NY: Arlington House, 1967), 11–98, 121–22, 199–213, 377–408.

6. Brennan, *Turning Right in the Sixties,* 104–16; Dan Carter, *The Politics of Rage: George Wallace, the Origins of the New Conservatism, and the Transformation of American Politics* (New York: Simon and Schuster, 1995), 324–70; James Sundquist, *Dynamics of the Party System* (Washington, DC: Brookings Institution Press, 1983), 376–77, 382–85.

7. Philip Converse, Warren Miller, Jerrold Rusk, and Arthur Wolfe, "Continuity and Change in American Politics: Parties and Issues in the 1968 Election," *American Political Science Review* 63, no. 4 (December 1969), 1083–105; Joan Hoff, *Nixon Reconsidered* (New York: Basic Books, 1994), 19–49, 115–44; Robert Mason, *Richard Nixon and the Quest for a New Majority* (Chapel Hill: University of North Carolina Press, 2004), 26–28; Richard Nixon, *RN: The Memoirs of Richard Nixon* (New York: Simon and Schuster, 1990), 264, 304–5, 354, 414; Kevin Phillips, *The Emerging Republican Majority* (New Rochelle, NY: Arlington House, 1969), 166–75, 181, 274–78, 462.

8. H. R. Haldeman, *The Ends of Power* (New York: Times Books, 1978), 81; Hoff, *Nixon Reconsidered*, 153; Kissinger, *White House Years* (Boston: Little, Brown, 1979), 9–48, 55–61, 69, 195; Richard Nixon, "Asia after Vietnam," *Foreign Affairs* (October 1967), 111–25; and *Memoirs*, 51, 340–41, 344–50; Melvin Small, *The Presidency of Richard Nixon* (Lawrence: University Press of Kansas, 1999), 28, 35, 52, 65–67, 98–99.

9. Ole Holsti and James Rosenau, *American Leadership in World Affairs: Vietnam and the Breakdown of Consensus* (Boston: Allen and Unwin, 1982), 108–33; John Mueller, *War, Presidents and Public Opinion* (New York: Wiley, 1973), 92, 119, 164–65; Nixon, *Memoirs*, 350–51; Rae, *Decline and Fall of Liberal Republicans*, 106; Eugene Wittkopf, *Faces of Internationalism: Public Opinion and Foreign Policy* (Durham, NC: Duke University Press, 1990), 23–26, 34–49, 118–19, 125.

10. Annual foreign policy report, February 9, 1972, *Public Papers of the Presidents: Richard Nixon: 1972*, 204–7, 211; Pierre Asselin, *A Bitter Peace: Washington, Hanoi, and the Making of the Paris Agreement* (Chapel Hill: University of North Carolina Press, 2002), 13–180; Gaddis, *Strategies of Containment*, 287–92, 295, 305; Kissinger,

White House Years, 116–19, 127–30, 265–69, 535, 765, 1089, 1132–34, 1250–55; Robert Litwak, *Détente and the Nixon Doctrine* (New York: Cambridge University Press, 1984), 2, 120; Nixon, *Memoirs,* 393–94, 551–80, 618, 697, 701–2, 725–26, 743.

11. Allen Matusow, *Nixon's Economy: Booms, Busts, Dollars, and Votes* (Lawrence: University Press of Kansas, 1998), 84, 87–106, 126–55; Nixon, *Memoirs,* 497, 515–22.

12. Black and Black, *Southern Republicans,* 25, 211, 230; Carter, *Politics of Rage,* 415–50; Mason, *New Majority,* 137–91; Arthur Miller, Warren Miller, Alden Raine, and Thad Brown, "A Majority Party in Disarray: Policy Polarization in the 1972 Election," *American Political Science Review* 70, no. 3 (September 1976), 753–78; Nash, *Conservative Intellectual Movement,* 513.

13. Robert Kaufman, *Henry M. Jackson: A Life in Politics* (Seattle: University of Washington Press, 2000), 266–81; Kissinger, *White House Years,* 653–83; and *Years of Upheaval* (Boston: Little, Brown, 1982), 324–27, 374–413, 615–38, 777–86, 985–98, 1052–110; Noam Kochavi, "Insights Abandoned, Flexibility Lost: Kissinger, Soviet Jewish Emigration, and the Demise of Détente," *Diplomatic History* 29, no. 3 (June 2005), 503–30; Peter Kornbluh, *The Pinochet File: A Declassified Dossier on Atrocity and Accountability* (New York: New Press, 2003), 3–18, 22–29, 36–78, 97–120, 146–60, 242–44.

14. Gerald Ford, *A Time to Heal* (New York: Harper and Row, 1979), 129, 133, 183, 218–19, 253–54, 263–64, 298–306; John Robert Greene, *The Presidency of Gerald R. Ford* (Lawrence: University Press of Kansas, 1995), 11–13, 67–72, 102–15, 124–26, 161; Christopher Jespersen, "Kissinger, Ford, and Congress: The Very Bitter End in Vietnam," *Pacific Historical Review* 71, no. 3 (August 2003), 439–73; 288–89; Henry Kissinger, *Years of Renewal* (New York: Simon and Schuster, 1999), 169–191, 243–55, 286–302, 463–95, 520–46, 635–64, 791–833; Daniel Thomas, *The Helsinki Effect: International Norms, Human Rights, and the Demise of Communism* (Princeton, NJ: Princeton University Press, 2001), 91–121, 285–86.

15. *The Gallup Poll: Public Opinion, 1972–1977* (Wilmington, DE: Scholarly Resources, 1978), 2: 881–82, 887–88, 902–11.

16. Adam Clymer, *Drawing the Line at the Big Ditch: The Panama Canal Treaties and the Rise of the Right* (Lawrence: University Press of Kansas, 2008), 25–39; Thomas Evans, *The Education of Ronald Reagan* (New York: Columbia University Press, 2006), 57–80, 111–53; Ronald Reagan, *An American Life* (New York: Simon and Schuster, 1990), 19–143, 178; Stephen Vaughn, *Ronald Reagan in Hollywood: Movies and Politics* (New York: Cambridge University Press, 1994), 37, 63–66, 124–26.

17. Paul Lettow, *Ronald Reagan and His Quest to Abolish Nuclear Weapons* (New York: Random House, 2005), 16, 22–27; Kiron Skinner, Annelise Anderson, and Martin Anderson, eds., *Reagan: In His Own Hand* (New York: Free Press, 2001), 10–12, 33–35, 60–63, 84–85, 99–102, 109–13, 118, 147–50, 480–87.

18. Thomas Edsall, *Chain Reaction: The Impact of Race, Rights, and Taxes on American Politics* (New York: Norton, 1991), 129–31; John Ehrman, *The Rise of Neoconservatism* (New Haven, CT: Yale University Press, 1995), 97–135; Rae, *Decline and Fall of Liberal Republicans,* 114, 118–21, 136–37, 158–62, 168; Charles Tyroler, ed., *Alerting America: The Papers of the Committee on the Present Danger*

(Washington, DC: Pergamom-Brassey's, 1984), 3–15, 42, 162, 179; Richard Viguerie, *The New Right—We're Ready to Lead* (Falls Church, VA: Viguerie Co., 1980), 19–81, 87, 123–26.

19. Jeane Kirkpatrick, "Dictatorships and Double Standards," *Commentary* (November 1979), 35–45.

20. Ronald Reagan, "Address to the Conservative Political Action Conference," Washington, DC, February 6, 1977, in *A City Upon a Hill: Speeches by Ronald Reagan Before the Conservative Political Action Conference*, ed. James Roberts (Washington, DC: American Studies Center, 1989), 31–37. For more on Reagan's reformulation of GOP conservative politics, see Henry Olsen, *Working-Class Republican: Ronald Reagan and the Return of Blue Collar Conservatism* (New York: Broadside Books, 2017).

21. Andrew Busch, *Reagan's Victory: The Presidential Election of 1980 and the Rise of the Right* (Lawrence: University Press of Kansas, 2005), 121, 130–44.

22. Lou Cannon, *President Reagan* (New York: Public Affairs, 2000), 153, 172–81, 263–65, 293–95, 375–76, 630.

23. Christopher Simpson, *National Security Directives of the Reagan and Bush Administrations* (Boulder, CO: Westview Press, 1995), 46–49.

24. Mark Lagon, *The Reagan Doctrine* (Westport, CT: Praeger, 1994), 78–82; James Scott, *Deciding to Intervene* (Durham, NC: Duke University Press, 1996), 25–27, 34–35.

25. See Adam Garfinkle, *The Politics of the Nuclear Freeze* (Philadelphia: Foreign Policy Research Institute, 1984), 234–38.

26. Carl Bernstein and Marco Politi, *His Holiness: John Paul II and the Hidden History of Our Time* (New York: Doubleday, 1996), 12, 260–69, 357.

27. NSDD-24 and NSDD-41, February 9 and June 2, 1982, Ronald Reagan Library [hereafter RRL], Simi Valley, CA; Alan Dobson, "The Reagan Administration, Economic Warfare, and Starting to Close Down the Cold War," *Diplomatic History* 29, no. 3 (June 2005), 531–56.

28. Reagan address at Notre Dame University, address to members of the British Parliament, and remarks to the National Association of Evangelicals, May 17, 1981, June 18, 1982, and March 8, 1983, *Public Papers of the Presidents: Ronald Reagan* [hereafter RPP]: *1981*, 434, *RPP: 1982*, 743–47, and *RPP: 1983*, 359–64.

29. Lettow, *Reagan and His Quest to Abolish Nuclear Weapons*, 61–72, 75–82.

30. NSDD-32, "US National Security Strategy," May 20, 1982, RRL. See also John Arquilla, *The Reagan Imprint* (Chicago: Ivan R. Dee, 2006), 38–43, 51–53, 227–35; Gaddis, *Strategies of Containment*, 353–56, 369–77; Lettow, *Reagan and His Quest to Abolish Nuclear Weapons*, 61–72, 75–82; Richard Pipes, *Vixi: Memoirs of a Non-Belonger* (New Haven, CT: Yale University Press, 2003), 188–202.

31. Robert Beck, *The Grenada Invasion* (Boulder, CO: Westview Press, 1993), 57–58, 106–13, 138; Ralph Hallenbeck, *Military Force as an Instrument of US Foreign Policy: Intervention in Lebanon, August 1982—February 1984* (New York: Praeger, 1991), 8–10, 131, 138–53; Colin Powell, *My American Journey* (New York: Random House, 1995), 292; Shultz, *Turmoil and Triumph*, 101–14, 220–32, 323–45; Weinberger, *Fighting for Peace*, 101–74.

32. Paul Abramson, John Aldrich, and David Rohde, *Change and Continuity in the 1984 Elections* (Washington, DC: Congressional Quarterly Press, 1986), 50–63, 70–79, 134–42, 163–204; Douglas Brinkley, ed., *The Reagan Diaries* (New York: Harper Perennial, 2007), 199; Reagan, *An American Life*, 584–89, 595, 602; Reagan, "Address to the Nation and Other Countries," January 16, 1984, *RPP: 1984*, 40–45; William Schneider, "The November 6 Vote for President: What Did It Mean?" in *The American Elections of 1984*, ed. Austin Ranney (Durham, NC: Duke University Press, 1985), 203–44.

33. Raymond Garthoff, *The Great Transition* (Washington, DC: Brookings Institution Press, 1994), 291–99, 307–38, 351–58; Mikhail Gorbachev, *Memoirs* (New York: Doubleday, 1996), 165–68, 405–8, 419, 444; Jack Matlock, *Reagan and Gorbachev* (New York: Random House, 2004), 215–37; Reagan address at Moscow State University, May 31, 1988, *RPP: 1988*, 684; Reagan, *An American Life*, 11–14, 567, 611–15, 628, 634–39, 675–91, 698–701, 707–8, 711; Shultz, *Turmoil and Triumph*, 531–33, 599–607, 699–702, 718–27, 751–80, 863–86, 989–1014, 1101–6, 1131.

34. Jeane Kirkpatrick, *The Reagan Phenomenon* (Washington, DC: American Enterprise Institute, 1983), 54, 61; William Kline and James Worthen, "The Philippines, 1983–1986: Arranging a Divorce," in *Dealing with Dictators*, ed. Ernest May and Philip Zelikow (Cambridge, MA: MIT Press, 2006), 137–65; Norman Podhoretz, "Appeasement by Any Other Name," *Commentary* (July 1983), 25–38; Shultz, *Turmoil and Triumph*, 636, 970; Tony Smith, *America's Mission* (Princeton, NJ: Princeton University Press, 1994), 268–71, 287–95, 300, 303–4.

35. Arquilla, *The Reagan Imprint*, 227–35; Melvyn Leffler, *For the Soul of Mankind* (New York: Hill and Wang, 2007), 448, 462–65; Peter Rodman, *More Precious than Peace* (New York: Charles Scribner's Sons, 1994), 197, 317–23, 477.

36. James Baker, *The Politics of Diplomacy* (New York: GP Putnam's Sons, 1995), 19–20, 32; Ryan Barilleaux and Mark Rozell, *Power and Prudence* (College Station: Texas A&M University Press, 2004), 5–12, 117–22; George Bush and Brent Scowcroft, *A World Transformed* (New York: Vintage, 1998), 18–19, 60; Jeffrey Engel, *When the World Seemed New: George H. W. Bush and the End of the Cold War* (Boston: Houghton Mifflin Harcourt, 2017), chapter 2; John Robert Greene, *The Presidency of George Bush* (Lawrence: University Press of Kansas, 2000), 45, 91, 99–100, 144; Steven Hurst, *The Foreign Policy of the Bush Administration* (London: Paul Cassell, 1999), 2–14; Paul Quirk, "The Election," in *The Elections of 1988*, ed. Michael Nelson (Washington, DC: Congressional Quarterly Press, 1989), 63–92.

37. Bush, "Remarks at the Texas A&M University Commencement Ceremony," May 12, 1989, in *Public Papers of the President: George H. W. Bush* [hereafter BPP], *1989*, 540–43, and "Remarks to the Supreme Soviet of the Republic of the Ukraine in Kiev, Soviet Union," August 1, 1991, *BPP: 1991*; Baker, *Politics of Diplomacy*, 45, 67–72, 149–71, 234–43, 250–52, 257–59, 472–75, 525–28; Bush and Scowcroft, *A World Transformed*, 7–16, 40–45, 79–85, 114–17, 141–43, 148–50, 162–74, 182–203, 279–89, 494–505, 510–20, 536–40; Engel, *When the World Seemed New*, chapters 4–5, 7, 11–18, 22–23; Garthoff, *The Great Transition*, 375–89, 404–18, 424–28, 432–37, 446–49, 461–72, 487–99; Celeste Wallander, "Western Policy and the Demise of the Soviet Union," *Journal of Cold War Studies* 5, no. 4 (Fall 2003), 137–77; Philip Zelikow and

Condoleezza Rice, *Germany Unified and Europe Transformed: A Study in Statecraft* (Cambridge, MA: Harvard University Press, 1997), 26–28, 93–98, 167–68, 182–84, 204–7, 215–17, 266, 341–42.

38. Bush, "Address Before a Joint Session of Congress on the Crisis in the Persian Gulf and the Federal Budget Deficit," September 11, 1990, *BPP: 1990*; Baker, *Politics of Diplomacy*, 1–16, 268, 276–77, 336, 362; Bush and Scowcroft, *A World Transformed*, 306–82, 441–43, 460–61, 486; Engel, *When the World Seemed New*, chapters 19–21; Lawrence Freedman and Efraim Karsh, *The Gulf Conflict* (Princeton, NJ: Princeton University Press, 1993), 25–27, 35–39, 206–208, 216–21, 266–73, 409; Powell, *My American Journey*, 446–517; and Steve Yetiv, *Explaining US Foreign Policy: US Decision-Making and the Persian Gulf War* (Baltimore: Johns Hopkins University Press, 2004), 61–81, 154–84.

39. Baker, *Politics of Diplomacy*, 104–5, 109–12, 308–9, 589–94, 606–11, 636–40, 648–50; Bush and Scowcroft, *A World Transformed*, 89, 97–110, 156–58, 174–78; Engel, *When the World Seemed New*, chapters 6, 8–10; Hurst, *Foreign Policy of the Bush Administration*, 170–93; Jessica Lee, "Bush Defends Gulf War Decisions," *USA Today*, August 5, 1992; Powell, *My American Journey*, 562; Jon Western, "Sources of Humanitarian Intervention: Beliefs, Information, and Advocacy in the US Decisions on Somalia and Bosnia," *International Security* 26, no. 4 (Spring 2002), 112–42.

40. Ross Baker, "Sorting Out and Suiting Up: The Presidential Nominations," in *The Election of 1992*, eds. Gerald Pomper et al (Chatham, NJ: Chatham House, 1993), 48; Timothy Stanley, *The Crusader: The Life and Tumultuous Times of Pat Buchanan* (New York: St Martin's Press, 2012), 157.

41. Paul Abramson, John Aldrich, and David Rohde, *Change and Continuity in the 1992 Elections* (Washington, DC: Congressional Quarterly Press, 1994), 26–30, 43–44, 131–220, 247; Barilleaux and Rozell, *Power and Prudence*, 40–41; Greene, *Presidency of George Bush*, 74–78, 151–55, 161–79.

42. Patrick Buchanan, "America First—and Second, and Third," *The National Interest* 19 (Spring 1990), 77–82; David Frum, *Dead Right* (New York: Basic Books, 1994), 124–58; Jeane Kirkpatrick, "A Normal Country in a Normal Time," *The National Interest* 21 (Fall 1990), 40–45; Henry Kissinger, *Diplomacy* (New York: Simon and Schuster, 1994), 808–36.

43. Derek Chollet and James Goldgeier, *America Between the Wars: From 11/9 to 9/11* (New York: Public Affairs, 2008), 20–21, 110–11, 140, 143–45, 172–74, 187–204; Terry Deibel, *Clinton and Congress: The Politics of Foreign Policy* (New York: Foreign Policy Association, 2000), 17–20, 36–56, 59–62, 64, 73; Francis Fukuyama, *America at the Crossroads: Democracy, Power, and the Neoconservative Legacy* (New Haven, CT: Yale University Press, 2006), 40–43, 48–49, 56; William Kristol and Robert Kagan, "Toward a Neo-Reaganite Foreign Policy," *Foreign Affairs* (July–August 1996), 18–32; William Link, *Righteous Warrior: Jesse Helms and the Rise of Modern Conservatism* (New York: St Martin's Press, 2008), 421–35, 444–58; Peter Spiro, "The New Sovereigntists," *Foreign Affairs* (November–December 2000), 9–15.

44. George W. Bush, "A Distinctly American Internationalism" and "A Period of Consequences," in *The George W. Bush Foreign Policy Reader*, ed. John Dietrich

(Armonk, NY: M. E. Sharpe, 2005), 22–31; Daniel Casse, "Is Bush a Conservative?" *Commentary* (February 2004), 19–26; James Mann, *Rise of the Vulcans: The History of Bush's War Cabinet* (New York: Viking, 2004), 244–60; Alexander Moens, *The Foreign Policy of George W. Bush* (Burlington, VT: Ashgate, 2004), 60–68, 87–117; Gerald Pomper, "The 2000 Presidential Election: Why Gore Lost," *Political Science Quarterly* 116, no. 2 (Summer 2001), 201–23.

45. Peter Baker, *Days of Fire: Bush and Cheney in the White House* (New York: Doubleday, 2013), chapters 7–13; George W. Bush, *National Security Strategy of the United States* (Washington, DC: Government Printing Office, 2002); Ivo Daalder and James Lindsay, *America Unbound: The Bush Revolution in Foreign Policy* (Washington, DC: Brookings Institution Press, 2003), 15–16, 46–49, 62–71; Douglas Feith, *War and Decision* (New Harper: Harper, 2008), 514–15; Richard Haass, *War of Necessity, War of Choice* (New York: Simon and Schuster, 2009), 192–246; Steven Metz, *Iraq and the Evolution of American Strategy* (Washington, DC: Potomac Books, 2008), 76–84, 102–3; Bob Woodward, *Plan of Attack* (New York: Simon and Schuster, 2004), 1–9, 29–66, 72–136.

46. Anthony Cordesman, *The Iraq War: Strategy, Tactics, and Military Lessons* (Washington, DC: Center for Strategic and International Studies Press, 2003), 497–557; James Fallows, *Blind Into Baghdad* (New York: Vintage, 2006), 43–106; Frederick Kagan, *Finding the Target* (San Francisco, CA: Encounter Books, 2006), 287–310; Jeane Kirkpatrick, *Making War to Keep Peace* (New York: Harper Perennial, 2007), 272, 279–83, 290–93, 300; Michael O'Hanlon, "Iraq Without a Plan," *Policy Review* 128 (January 2005); Thomas Ricks, *Fiasco* (New York: Penguin, 2006), chapters 4–16.

47. Fred Barnes, "A Big Government Conservatism," *Wall Street Journal*, August 15, 2003; James Ceaser and Andrew Busch, *Red Over Blue: The 2004 Elections and American Politics* (Lanham, MD: Rowman and Littlefield, 2005), 2–30, 97–99, 107–140; James Campbell, "Why Bush Won the Presidential Election of 2004," *Political Science Quarterly* 120, no. 2 (Summer 2005); Philip Klinkner, "Mr. Bush's War: Foreign Policy in the 2004 Election," *Presidential Studies Quarterly* 36, no. 2 (June 2006), 281–96; John Micklethwait and Adrian Wooldridge, *The Right Nation: Conservative Power in America* (New York: Penguin, 2005).

48. Gary Jacobson, "Referendum: The 2006 Congressional Elections," *Political Science Quarterly* 122, no. 1 (Spring 2007), 1–24; Metz, *Iraq*, 169–181; John Mueller, "The Iraq Syndrome," *Foreign Affairs* (November–December 2005), 44–54; Ricks, *Fiasco*, 398–433; Bob Woodward, *State of Denial* (New York: Simon and Schuster, 2006), 367–491.

49. Michael Gordon and Bernard Trainor, *The Endgame* (New York: Pantheon, 2012), part 2; Peter Mansoor, *Surge* (New Haven, CT: Yale University Press, 2013); Metz, *Iraq*, 182–90; Thomas Ricks, *The Gamble: General David Petraeus and the American Military Adventure in Iraq, 2006–2008* (New York: Penguin, 2009); and Linda Robinson, *Tell Me How This Ends* (New York: PublicAffairs, 2008).

50. James Ceaser, Andrew Busch, and John Pitney, *Epic Journey: The 2008 Elections and American Politics* (Lanham, MD: Rowman and Littlefield, 2009), 53–88, 131–62; Gary Jacobson, "The 2008 Presidential and Congressional Elections," *Political Science Quarterly* 124, no. 1 (Spring 2009), 1–30.

51. Stanley Kurtz, "Libya, War Powers, and Hawkish Conservatives," *National Review*, June 15, 2011; Pew Research Center, *2012 American Values Survey* (Washington, DC: Pew Research Center for the People and the Press, 2012), 79.

52. Rebecca Ballhaus, "WSJ/NBC Poll: Drone Attacks Have Broad Support," *Wall Street Journal*, June 5, 2013; Jeffrey Jones, "Americans Divided in Views of US Defense Spending," *Gallup*, February 21, 2013; Jeff Mason, "Most Americans Would Back US Strike Over Iran Nuclear Weapon: Poll," *Reuters*, March 13, 2012; Brian Rathbun, "Steeped in International Affairs? The Foreign Policy Views of the Tea Party," *Foreign Policy Analysis* 9, no. 1 (January 2013), 21–37.

53. Brookings Institution, *2013 American Values Survey: In Search of Libertarians in America* (Washington, DC: Brookings Institution, 2013); Sebastian Payne and Robert Costa, "Islamic State Prompts GOP to Strike More Hawkish Tone," *Washington Post*, September 4, 2014; Sam Tanenhaus and Jim Rutenberg, "Rand Paul's Mixed Inheritance," *New York Times*, January 25, 2014.

54. The Institute of Politics, John F. Kennedy School of Government, *Campaign for President: The Managers Look at 2012* (Lanham, MD: Rowman and Littlefield, 2013), 234–35; Gary Jacobson, "How the Economy and Partisanship Shaped the 2012 Presidential and Congressional Elections," *Political Science Quarterly* 128, no. 1 (Spring 2013), 15; James Lindsay, "Campaign 2012 Roundup: Is Foreign Policy a Problem for Ron Paul?" Council on Foreign Relations, November 28, 2011; John Sides and Lynn Vavreck, *The Gamble: Choice and Chance in the 2012 Presidential Election* (Princeton, NJ: Princeton University Press, 2013), 148–50, 163–64, 224–25.

55. Chris Cillizza and Aaron Blake, "Majority of House Leaning 'No' on Syria Resolution," *Washington Post*, September 6, 2013; Stephen Dinan, "Bipartisan Congress Rebuffs Obama on Libya Mission," *Washington Times*, June 3, 2011; Bob Woodward, *The Price of Politics* (New York: Simon and Schuster, 2012), 127–28, 203–4, 222–23, 348–56, 378–80.

56. Pew Research Center, "Beyond Red and Blue: The Political Typology," June 2014.

57. Charles Murray, *Coming Apart: The State of White America, 1960–2010* (New York: Crown Forum, 2013). See also Justin Gest, *The New Minority: White Working Class Politics in an Age of Immigration and Inequality* (New York: Oxford University Press, 2016); and Joel Kotkin, *The New Class Conflict* (Candor, NY: Telos Press, 2014).

CHAPTER 4

1. The last lines are from an open letter by Trump to *The Washington Post*, *Boston Globe*, and *New York Times*, published September 2, 1987. From that year through 2014, most of his public comments on foreign policy were either in a series of autobiographical books, or in TV interviews with CNN, Fox News, ABC, and NBC. For useful surveys of Trump's foreign policy statements and views prior to 2015, see John Haines, "Divining a Trump Doctrine," *Orbis* 61, no. 1 (Winter 2017) 125–36; Charlie Laderman and Brendan Simms, *Donald Trump: The Making of a World View* (London: I. B. Tauris, 2017); Reinhard Wolf, "Donald Trump's Status-Driven Foreign Policy," *Survival* 59, no. 5 (September 2017), 99–116; and Thomas Wright, "Trump's 19th Century Foreign Policy," *Politico*, January 20, 2016.

2. Henry Olsen, "A GOP Dark Horse?" *National Affairs* 8 (Summer 2011), 106–20.

3. James Ceaser and Andrew Busch, *Defying the Odds: The 2016 Elections and American Politics* (Lanham, MD: Rowman and Littlefield, 2017), chapter 3.

4. Ronald Rapaport and Walter Stone, "The Sources of Trump's Support," in *Trumped: The 2016 Election That Broke All The Rules*, ed. Larry Sabato (Lanham, MD: Rowman and Littlefield, 2017), 136–47.

5. Gregory Holyk, "Foreign Policy in the 2016 Presidential Primaries Based on the Exit Polls," Chicago Council on Global Affairs, April 7, 2016.

6. Chicago Council on Global Affairs, "America Divided: Political Partisanship and US Foreign Policy," (September 15, 2015), 31–32.

7. By 2015, Republicans were less supportive of foreign trade than the average voter. Justin McCarthy, "Majority in US Still See Opportunity in Foreign Trade," *Gallup*, March 9, 2015.

8. There is no evidence that Trump opposed the invasion of Iraq before it began. In fact his only public statement on the subject prior to March 2003 was in favor of the invasion. He later turned against the war over the course of 2003–2004. For Trump's recorded statements at the time, see Christopher Massie, Megan Apper, and Andrew Kaczynski, "A Guide to Donald Trump's Shifting Position on the Iraq War," *BuzzFeed*, February 20, 2016.

9. Donald Trump, "Trump on Foreign Policy," *The National Interest*, April 27, 2016.

10. Chris Cillizza, "Pat Buchanan says Donald Trump is the future of the Republican Party," *Washington Post*, January 12, 2016.

11. Pew Research Center, "Public Uncertain, Divided over America's Place in the World," (May 5, 2016), 1–2, 7–8, 16–17, 28–48.

12. Chicago Council on Global Affairs, "Foreign Policy in the New Millennium," (2012); Jeffrey Jones, "Americans Shift to More Negative View of Libya Military Action," *Gallup*, June 24, 2011; Pew Research Center, "In Shift from Bush Era, More Conservatives say 'Come Home, America,'" June 16, 2012.

13. Larry Sabato, "The 2016 Election That Broke All, or At Least Most, of the Rules," in Sabato, *Trumped*, 14–27.

14. David Byler, "Demographic Coalitions: How Trump Picked the Democratic Lock and Won the Presidency," in Sabato, *Trumped*, 30–51; Ceaser and Busch, *Defying the Odds*, chapter 4; Lee Drutman, "Political Divisions in 2016 and Beyond," Democracy Fund Voter Study Group (June 2017); and Gary Jacobson, "The Triumph of Polarized Partisanship in 2016: Donald Trump's Improbable Victory," *Political Science Quarterly* 132, no. 1 (2017), 9–41.

15. Donald Trump with Tony Schwartz, *Trump: The Art of the Deal* (New York: Random House, 1987), 3–44.

16. For useful discussion of Trump's background and decision-making style, from various perspectives, see Michael D'Antonio, *Never Enough: Donald Trump and the Pursuit of Success* (New York: Thomas Dunne Books, 2015), 322–46; Conrad Black, *Donald J. Trump: A President Like No Other* (Washington, DC: Regnery, 2018); Marc Fisher, "Trump's huge transition will start with his tight inner circle," *Washington Post*, November 10, 2016; Michael Genovese, *How Trump Governs: An Assessment and a Prognosis* (New York: Cambria Press, 2017); Newt Gingrich, *Understanding*

Trump (New York: Center Street, 2017), 3–57; Haines, "Divining a Trump Doctrine,"; Michael Kranish and Marc Fisher, *Trump Revealed* (New York: Scribner, 2016), especially chapter 4; Michael Kruse, "The Executive Mr. Trump," *Politico*, July/August 2016; Laderman and Simms, *Making of a World View*, 102–5; Walter McDougall, "Art of the Doge," *Foreign Policy Research Institute*, January 6, 2017; Bert Mizusawa, "Trump's Clear-Eyed Approach to Foreign Policy," *USA Today*, October 25, 2016; Michael Nelson, *Trump's First Year* (Charlottesville: University of Virginia Press, 2018) chapters 2–3; and James Pfiffner, "The Unusual Presidency of Donald Trump," *Political Insight* (September 2017).

17. Donald Trump, Inaugural Address, Washington, DC, January 20, 2017.

18. Michael Bender, "Last Piece of the Puzzle: Pompeo Completes Trump's New Foreign Policy Team," *Wall Street Journal*, April 27, 2018.

19. Thomas Wright, "Trump's Team of Rivals," *Foreign Policy*, December 14, 2016. On Bannon, see Max Fisher, "Stephen K. Bannon's CPAC Comments," *New York Times*, February 24, 2017; Joshua Green, *Devil's Bargain: Steve Bannon, Donald Trump, and the Storming of the Presidency* (New York: Penguin, 2017); Keith Koffler, *Bannon: Always the Rebel* (Washington, DC: Regnery, 2017); Donald McClarey, "Remarks of Stephen Bannon at a Conference at the Vatican," *The American Catholic*, November 18, 2016; and PBS Frontline, "Bannon's War," May 23, 2017.

20. Frontline, "Bannon's War."

21. Brent Kendall and Jess Bravin, "Supreme Court Upholds Trump Travel Ban," *Wall Street Journal*, June 26, 2018.

22. Annie Karni and Nicholas Fandos, "Trump Threatens to Close Border If Congress Won't Fund Wall," *New York Times*, December 28, 2018; Maria Sacchetti and Nick Miroff, "How Trump is Building a Border Wall that No One Can See," *Washington Post*, November 21, 2017.

23. Nelson, *Trump's First Year*, 61–63, 72–73; Ramesh Ponnuru, "How Trump Moved the Needle on Immigration Limits," *Bloomberg*, February 5, 2018.

24. Binyamin Appelbaum, "Struggles in a Steel Town Highlighted By Donald Trump," *New York Times*, July 4, 2016.

25. Peter Navarro, *Death by China* (Indianapolis: Pearson FT Press, 2011); Wilbur Ross, "Free Trade Is a Two-Way Street," *Wall Street Journal*, July 31, 2017.

26. Michael Bender, "Inside Trump's Trade War: How Tariff Backers Beat Free Traders," *Wall Street Journal*, March 9, 2018.

27. William Mauldin, "US tariffs Prompt Anger, Retaliation from Trade Allies," *Wall Street Journal*, May 31, 2018.

28. Michael Shear and Catherine Porter, "Trump Refuses to Sign G-7 Statement and Calls Trudeau 'Weak'," *New York Times*, June 9, 2018.

29. *The Economist*, "Donald Trump agrees to cease fire in the trade war with the EU," July 28, 2018.

30. Robert Fife and Adrian Morrow, "Canada, US Reach Tentative NAFTA Deal; Trump Approves Pact," *Globe and Mail*, October 1, 2018.

31. Remarks by President Trump to the World Economic Forum, Davos, Switzerland, January 26, 2018.

32. Sheryl Gay Stolberg, "As Ties With Allies Fray Over Trade, Congressional Republicans Back Trump," *New York Times*, June 11, 2018.

33. On the administration's early approach toward East Asia, see Daniel Blumenthal, "The Outlines of Trump's Asia Strategy," *The American Interest*, November 17, 2017; and Patrick Cronin, "Trump's Post-Pivot Strategy," *The Diplomat*, November 11, 2017.

34. Jessica Trisko Darden, "Did Trump's Charm Offensive Work in the Philippines?" *The Conversation*, November 13, 2017.

35. Remarks by President Trump on His Trip to Asia, The White House, November 15, 2017; The White House, *National Security Strategy of the United States of America* (December 2017), 46.

36. Bob Davis and Lingling Wei, "For China, the American Team of Trade Rivals Won't Be Easy to Please," *Wall Street Journal*, April 29, 2018; Hilton Root, "Who Controls America's China Policy?" *Real Clear World*, October 19, 2017.

37. Ana Swanson, "US and China Expand Trade War as Beijing Matches Trump's Tariffs," *New York Times*, June 15, 2018.

38. Michael Allen, "Combatting Chinese Economic Coercion in the NSS," *Foreign Policy*, December 15, 2017.

39. Jane Perlez, "Pence's China Speech Seen as Portent of 'New Cold War,'" *New York Times*, October 5, 2018.

40. Patrick Cronin, "Maximum Pressure: A Clarifying Signal in the Noise of North Korea Policy," *Texas National Security Review*, February 9, 2018.

41. Remarks by President Trump to the 72nd Session of the United Nations General Assembly, New York, September 19, 2017; and President Donald J. Trump's State of the Union Address, Washington, DC, January 20, 2018.

42. Joint Statement of President Donald J. Trump of the United States of America and Chairman Kim Jong-un of the Democratic People's Republic of Korea at the Singapore Summit, The White House, June 12, 2018.

43. Michael Gordon, "US Seeks Major Disarmament of North Korea During Trump's Term," *Wall Street Journal*, June 14, 2018.

44. On the Singapore summit, see David Adesnik, "At Summit, North Korea Offers Vague Denuclearization Pledge," *FDD Policy Brief*, June 13, 2018; Victor Cha, "Trump and Kim Have Just Walked Us Back from the Brink of War," *New York Times*, June 12, 2018; Nicholas Eberstadt, "Kim Wins in Singapore," *National Review*, June 21, 2018; Michael Rubin, "Trump Doesn't Realize How Hard It Will Be to Normalize North Korea," *New York Post*, June 13, 2018; and Daniel Sneider, "Mind the Gap: The Singapore Summit and US Alliances," *National Bureau of Asian Research*, June 14, 2018.

45. Michael Gove and Kai Diekmann, "Full Transcript of Interview with Donald Trump," *The London Times*, January 16, 2017.

46. Remarks by President Trump to the People of Poland, Warsaw, Poland, July 6, 2017.

47. Valentina Pop, Laurence Norman and Robert Wall, "Trump Unsettles NATO Allies with Demands As He Backs Alliance," *Wall Street Journal*, July 12, 2018.

48. See for example Paul Zajac, "Why France Feels (Relatively) Comfortable with Trump's America," *The American Interest*, April 24, 2018.

49. Richard Fontaine and Vance Serchuk, "The West Will Survive Trump," *The Atlantic*, July 11, 2018; James Kirchick, "An Independent Pole Isn't Plausible," *Washington Post*, May 22, 2018.

50. Greg Miller, Greg Jaffe and Philip Rucker, "Doubting the Intelligence, Trump Pursues Putin and Leaves a Russian Threat Unchecked," *Washington Post*, December 14, 2017. For useful and unconventional perspectives on this controversy, see Masha Gessen, "Russia, Trump, and Flawed Intelligence," *New York Review of Books*, January 9, 2017; and Jackson Lears, "What We Don't Talk About When We Talk About Russian Hacking," *London Review of Books*, January 4, 2018.

51. Rebecca Ballhaus, "Trump Questions Finding of Russia's 2016 Meddling As He Appears With Putin," *Wall Street Journal,* July 16, 2018. For a hard assessment, see Will Inboden, "How Much Damage Did Trump Cause in Helsinki?" *Foreign Policy*, July 19, 2018.

52. Andrew Kramer, "Ruble Tumbles as US Sets Out New Sanctions on Russia," *New York Times*, August 9, 2018; Daniel Vajdich, "Trump's Russia Policy is Better than Obama's Was," *Foreign Policy*, April 13, 2018.

53. Andrew Roth, "US Confirms Withdrawal from Nuclear Arms Treaty with Moscow," *The Guardian,* October 23, 2018.

54. Peter Baker, "For Trump, a Focus on US Interests and a Disdain for Moralizing," *New York Times*, April 4, 2017.

55. Dov Zakheim, "Sisi's Meeting with Trump Was a Success," *Foreign Policy*, April 6, 2017.

56. Statement by President Trump on Jerusalem, The White House, December 6, 2017.

57. Julie Hirschfield Davis and Eric Schmitt, "Senate Votes to End Aid for Yemen Fight over Khashoggi Killing and Saudis' War Aims," *New York Times,* December 13, 2018.

58. Walter Russell Mead, "Trump's Iran Gambit," *Wall Street Journal*, June 8, 2018.

59. Remarks by President Trump on the Joint Comprehensive Plan of Action, The White House, May 8, 2018.

60. Statement by President Trump on Syria, The White House, April 13, 2018. See also Kori Schake, "Trump's Syria Strategy Actually Makes Sense," *Foreign Policy*, April 16, 2018.

61. Missy Ryan and Karen DeYoung, "Trump, Denying Any Shift, Embraces Revised Plan for Syria Exit," *Washington Post*, January 7, 2019.

62. Remarks by President Trump on the Policy of the United States Towards Cuba, The White House, June 16, 2017.

63. Remarks by President Trump to the 72nd Session of the United Nations General Assembly, New York, New York, September 19, 2017.

64. Azam Ahmed and Paulina Villegas, "Lopez Obrador, an Atypical Leftist, Wins Mexico Presidency in Landslide," *New York Times*, July 1, 2018.

65. Thomas Kaplan, "Congress Approves $1.3 Trillion Spending Deal, Averting a Showdown," *New York Times,* March 22, 2018.

66. Michaela Dodge, "Trump's Plan to Protect America's Nuclear Capabilities," *The National Interest*, February 16, 2018.

67. Jim Mattis, *Summary of the 2018 National Defense Strategy of the United States of America*, Department of Defense (January 2018), 1–2, 4.

68. The White House, *National Security Strategy of the United States of America* (December 2017), 2–3, 8–10, 18–20, 22–23, 26–28.

69. Wesley Morgan, "Trump Reverses Course, Tells Pentagon to Boost Budget Request to $750 Billion," *Politico*, December 9, 2018.

70. Remarks by President Trump on the Strategy in Afghanistan and South Asia, The White House, August 21, 2017. For commentary see John Allen and Michael O'Hanlon, "Trump Made the Right Move on Afghanistan," The Brookings Institution, August 23, 2017; Zalmay Khalilzad, "Why Trump Is Right to Get Tough with Pakistan," *New York Times*, August 23, 2017; Daniel Markey, "Pakistan Is Feeling US Pressure. Now What?" *Cipher Brief*, March 21, 2018; and Meghan O'Sullivan, "Trump's Afghan Strategy Is Different, and Braver, Than Obama's," *Bloomberg*, August 23, 2017.

71. Don Lamothe and Josh Dawsey, "Trump Wanted a Big Cut in Troops in Afghanistan. New US Military Plans Fall Short," *Washington Post*, January 8, 2018.

72. Statement by President Trump on the Paris Climate Accord, The White House, June 1, 2017.

73. David Shepardson, "Trump Administration to Propose Dramatic Reductions in Foreign Aid," *Reuters*, March 4, 2017.

74. Adva Saldinger, "Congress Again Rejects Steep Cuts to US Foreign Assistance in New Budget," *Devex*, March 22, 2018.

75. Remarks by President Trump to the UN General Assembly.

76. Karen DeYoung, "Trump Takes a Selective Approach to the Promotion of Human Rights," *Washington Post*, April 25, 2017.

77. Other contributions on the possible outlines of a Trump foreign policy doctrine include: Michael Anton, "The Trump Doctrine," *Foreign Policy*, April 20, 2019 Peter Baker, "The Emerging Trump Doctrine: Don't Follow Doctrine," *New York Times*, April 8, 2017; Michael Bender, "The Art of the Foreign Policy Deal," *Wall Street Journal*, June 10, 2018; Hal Brands, *American Grand Strategy in the Age of Trump* (Washington, DC: Brookings Institution Press, 2018); Ross Douthat, "The Trump Doctrine," *New York Times*, January 29, 2019; Niall Ferguson, "Donald Trump's New World Order," *The American Interest*, November 21, 2016; George Friedman, "The Trump Doctrine," *Geopolitical Futures*, July 11, 2018; Caroline Glick, "The Donald Trump Negotiations Academy," *Jerusalem Post*, June 15, 2018; Jeffrey Goldberg, "A Senior White House Official Defines the Trump Doctrine," *The Atlantic*, June 11, 2018; Haines, "Divining a Trump Doctrine"; Victor Davis Hanson, "Reciprocity is the Method to Trump's Madness," *National Review*, July 12, 2018; Arthur Herman, "The Trump Doctrine: American Interests Come First," *The Hudson Institute*, December 19, 2017; John Ikenberry, "The Plot Against American Foreign Policy," *Foreign Affairs* (May/June 2017), 2–9; Anatole Kaletsky, "Trump's Victorious Retreats," *Project Syndicate*, August 9, 2018; Harry Kazianis, "The Trump Doctrine Has Foreign Policy Elites Pulling Out Their Hair," *The American Conservative*, August 1, 2018; Laderman and Simms, *Making of a World View*; Bruno Macaes, "The Trump Doctrine," *The American Interest*,

March 29, 2018; Walter McDougall, "Art of the Doge," *Foreign Policy Research Institute*, January 9, 2017; Walter Russell Mead, "How Trump Plans to Change the World," *Wall Street Journal*, July 9, 2018; Henry Nau, "Trump's Conservative Internationalism," *National Review*, August 24, 2017; Mackubin Owens, "Is There an Emerging Trump Doctrine?" *American Greatness,* November 25, 2017; Barry Posen, "The Rise of Illiberal Hegemony: Trump's Surprising Grand Strategy," *Foreign Affairs*97, no. 2 (March/April 2018), 20-27; Ionut Popescu, "Conservative Internationalism and the Trump Administration," *Orbis* 62, no. 1 (2018), 91–104; Gideon Rachman, "The Trump Doctrine—Coherent, Radical, and Wrong," *Financial Times*, July 16, 2018; Kori Schake, "The Trump Doctrine Is Winning and the World Is Losing," *New York Times*, June 15, 2018; Randall Schweller, "Three Cheers for Trump's Foreign Policy," *Foreign Affairs* 97, no. 5 (September/October 2018), 133–43; Stephen Sestanovich, "The Brilliant Incoherence of Trump's Foreign Policy," *The Atlantic,* May 2017; and Thomas Wright, "Trump's 19th Century Foreign Policy," *Politico*, January 20, 2016.

78. Jamie Fly, "Why Europe Should Heed Trump's NATO Warning," *Handelsblatt Global*, July 19, 2018.

79. For an excellent taxonomy of allied responses, see Hal Brands and Peter Feaver, "Living in Trump's World: The Global Reaction to America First," *War on the Rocks,* March 27, 2018.

80. Stephen Brooks and William Wohlforth, *World Out Of Balance* (Princeton, NJ: Princeton University Press, 2008); Zachary Selden, *Alignment, Alliance, and American Grand Strategy* (Ann Arbor: University of Michigan Press, 2016).

81. Two usefully contrasting views on this matter are Noah Feldman, "Pros and Cons of Trump's Random Foreign Policy," *Bloomberg*, March 18, 2018; and Jerry Hendrix, "Donald Trump and the Art of Strategic Ambiguity," *National Review*, March 21, 2018.

82. Dimitri Simes, "A Trump Foreign Policy," *The National Interest*, June 17, 2018.

83. Mattis, *National Defense Strategy*, 5.

84. Peter Nicholas, Paul Vieira, and Jose de Cordoba, "Why Donald Trump Decided to Back off NAFTA Threat," *Wall Street Journal,* April 27, 2017.

CHAPTER 5

1. For a good example, see Dylan Matthews, "Trump Has Changed How Americans Think About Politics," *Vox,* January 30, 2018.

2. Pew Research Center, *Political Typology Reveals Deep Fissures on the Right and Left* (Washington, DC: Pew Research Center, 2017), 63.

3. Chicago Council on Global Affairs, *What Americans Think About America First* (Chicago: Chicago Council on Global Affairs, 2017), 8.

4. Ibid., 13.

5. Ibid., 33.

6. Chicago Council on Global Affairs, *America Engaged: American Public Opinion and US Foreign Policy* (Chicago: Chicago Council on Global Affairs, 2018), 26–27.

7. David Weigel, "GOP Voters Warm to Russia, Putin, Wikileaks, Poll Finds," *Washington Post*, December 14, 2016.

8. David Byler, "The Republican Party in the Age of Trump," *The Weekly Standard*, February 16, 2018.

9. Kristen Bialik, "Putin Remains Overwhelmingly Unpopular in the United States," *Pew Research Center*, March 26, 2018.; Chicago Council, *America Engaged*, 24.

10. Kathy Frankovic, "Americans See Russia as a Threat—But Aren't Sure Trump Does," *YouGov*, March 23, 2018.

11. Megan Brenan, "Americans, Particularly Democrats, Dislike Russia," *Gallup*, March 5, 2018.

12. Emily Elkins, "The Five Types of Trump Voters," Voter Study Group (June 2017), 9, 20.

13. Pew, *Political Typology*, 64.

14. Chicago Council, *What Americans Think*, 22–23.

15. Chicago Council on Global Affairs, "The Foreign Policy Establishment or Donald Trump: Which Better Reflects American Opinion?" (April 2017), 4.

16. Craig Kafura, Dina Smeltz, and Lily Wojtowicz, "Seven Examples Where Partisan Divisions on Foreign Policy Widened in 2018," Chicago Council on Global Affairs, January 3, 2019; Diana Mutz, "Free Trade Is Becoming More Popular—Especially Among Republicans," *Washington Post*, November 17, 2017; Dina Smeltz and Karen Whisler, "Pro-Trade Views on the Rise, Partisan Divisions on NAFTA Widen," (Chicago: Chicago Council on Global Affairs, August 2017), 6.

17. See for example *The Economist/YouGov Poll* (April 8–10, 2018), 184; Lydia Saad, "Trump Rated Best on Terrorism, the Economy; Better on Taxes," *Gallup*, February 22, 2018.

18. Chicago Council, *What Americans Think*, 10, 35; Pew, *Political Typology*, 4, 63; Saad, "Trump Rated Best on Terrorism."

19. Chicago Council, "The Establishment or Trump," 3–6, 8, 10.

20. Frankovic, "Americans See Russia As a Threat—But Aren't Sure Trump Does"; Kafura, Smelz, and Wojtowicz, "Seven Examples"; Mutz, "Free Trade Is Becoming More Popular—Especially Among Republicans"; Smeltz and Whisler, "Pro-Trade Views on the Rise," 6.

21. See for example, Chicago Council on Global Affairs, *Foreign Policy in the New Millennium* (Chicago: Chicago Council on Global Affairs, 2012); Scott Clement, "Majority of Americans Say Afghan War Has Not Been Worth Fighting," *Washington Post*, December 9, 2013; Jeffrey Jones, "Americans Oppose US Military Involvement in Syria," *Gallup*, May 31, 2013; Andrew Kohut, "American International Engagement on the Rocks," Pew Research Global Attitudes Project, July 11, 2013; Frank Newport, "Americans Disapprove of US Decision to Arm Syrian Rebels," *Gallup*, June 17, 2013; Pew Research Center, "In Shift from Bush Era, More Conservatives Say 'Come Home,' America," June 16, 2011; Rasmussen Reports, "28% Say Libya Important to US National Security Interests, 42% Disagree"; and Brian Rathbun, "Steeped in International Affairs? The Foreign Policy Views of the Tea Party," *Foreign Policy Analysis* 9, no. 1 (January 2013), 21–37.

22. Ole Holsti, *Public Opinion and American Foreign Policy* (Ann Arbor: University of Michigan Press, 2004 edition); Eugene Wittkopf, *Faces of Internationalism* (Durham, NC: Duke University Press, 1990).

23. Ronald Inglehart and Pippa Norris, "Trump, Brexit, and the Rise of Populism: Economic Have-Nots and Cultural Backlash," Harvard Kennedy School Faculty Research Working Paper Series, August 2016. See also David Goodhart, *The Road to Somewhere: The New Tribes Shaping British Politics* (London: Penguin, 2017).

24. Alan Abramowitz, *The Great Alignment* (New Haven, CT: Yale University Press, 2018), x–xi.

25. Madeline Albright, *Fascism: A Warning* (New York: Harper, 2018); Sheri Berman, "Populism Is Not Fascism: But It Could Be a Harbinger," *Foreign Affairs* 95, no. 6 (November/December 2016), 39–44; William Galston, *Anti-Pluralism: The Populist Threat to Liberal Democracy* (New Haven, CT: Yale University Press, 2018); Yascha Mounk, *The People vs. Democracy* (Cambridge, MA: Harvard University Press, 2018); Jan-Werner Muller, *What Is Populism?* (Philadelphia: University of Pennsylvania Press, 2016); Mario Vargas Llosa and Alvaro Vargas Llosa, "The Challenge of Populism," *Cato's Letter* 16, no. 1 (Winter 2018).

26. Roger Kimball, "Populism, X: The imperative of freedom," *The New Criterion* 35, no. 10 (June 2017).

27. Michael Kazin, *The Populist Persuasion: An American History* (Ithaca, NY: Cornell University Press, 2017).

28. The classic study is Lawrence Goodwyn, *The Populist Moment: A Short History of the Agrarian Revolt in America* (New York: Oxford University Press, 1978).

29. James Sundquist, *Dynamics of the Party System: Alignment and Realignment of Political Parties in the United States* (Washington, DC: Brookings institution Press, 1983), chapter 7.

30. David Mayhew, *Electoral Realignments* (New Haven, CT: Yale University Press, 2002), 8–32; Sean Trende, *The Lost Majority* (New York: St. Martin's Press, 2012).

31. George Mayer, *The Republican Party, 1854–1964* (New York: Oxford University Press, 1964), 519–20; Sundquist, *Dynamics of the Party System,* chapters 10–12.

32. Byron Shafer and William Claggett, *The Two Majorities: The Issue Context of Modern American Politics* (Baltimore: Johns Hopkins University Press, 1995).

33. Edward Carmines and James Stimson, *Issue Evolution: Race and the Transformation of American Politics* (Princeton, NJ: Princeton University Press, 1989); Sundquist, *Dynamics of the Party System,* chapters 16–17.

34. Nicol Rae, *The Decline and Fall of the Liberal Republicans* (New York: Oxford University Press, 1989).

35. Kevin Phillips, *The Emerging Republican Majority* (New Rochelle, NY: Arlington House, 1969), 25, 38, 105, 186, 471–74.

36. Edward Carmines and Michael Wagner, "Political Issues and Party Alignments," *Annual Review of Political Science* 9 (2006), 67–81; David Leege, Kenneth Wald, Brian Krueger, and Paul Mueller, *The Politics of Cultural Differences* (Princeton, NJ: Princeton University Press, 2002), 27–28, 254–58.

37. Gary Miller and Norman Schofield, "The Transformation of the Republican and Democratic Party Coalitions in the US," *Perspectives on Politics* 6, no. 3 (September 2008), 433–50.

38. Jacobson, "The Triumph of Polarized Partisanship in 2016."

39. Lee Drutman, "Political Divisions in 2016 and Beyond," Democracy Fund Voter Study Group, June 2017.

40. Emily Ekins, "The Five Types of Trump Voters," Democracy Fund Voter Study Group, June 2017; Pew Research Center, *Political Typology Reveals Deep Fissures on the Right and Left* (October 2017), 1–3, 13, 19, 21–24, 48, 61–65, 74–76, 79, 84, 88, 95–98.

41. Sean Trende, "The Emerging Democratic Majority Fails to Emerge," in Sabato, *Trumped*, 222.

42. John Sides, Michael Tesler, and Lynn Vavreck, *Identity Crisis: The 2016 Presidential Campaign and the Battle for the Meaning of America* (Princeton, NJ: Princeton University Press, 2018).

43. Holyk, "Foreign Policy in the 2016 Presidential Primaries Based on the Exit Polls"; Rapoport and Stone, "The Sources of Trump's Support," in *Trumped*, ed. Sabato, 139–40. See also Salena Zito and Brad Todd, *The Great Revolt* (New York: Crown Forum, 2018).

CHAPTER 6

1. Hesiod, *Theogony, Works and Days, Shield,* trans. Apostolos Athanassakis (Baltimore: Johns Hopkins University Press, 2004 edition), 65–85.

2. John Ikenberry, "The Plot Against American Foreign Policy: Can the Liberal Order Survive?" *Foreign Affairs* (May/June 2017), 2–9. For similar concerns, see Ivo Daalder and James Lindsay, *The Empty Throne* (New York: Public Affairs, 2018); Richard Haass, "Liberal World Order, R.I.P.," *Project Syndicate*, March 21, 2018; John Ikenberry, "The End of the Liberal International Order?" *International Affairs* 94, no. 1 (2018), 7–23; Robert Kagan, *The Jungle Grows Back* (New York: Knopf, 2018); Hans Kundnani, "What Is the Liberal International Order?" German Marshall Fund, April 2017; Michael Mazaar, Astrid Stuth Cerallos, Miranda Priebe, Andrew Radin, Kathleen Reedy, Alexander Rothenberg, Julia Thompson, and Jordan Willcox, *Measuring the Health of the Liberal International Order* (Santa Monica, CA: RAND Corporation, 2017); Joseph Nye, "Will the Liberal Order Survive," *Foreign Affairs* 96, no. 1 (January/February 2017), 10–16; and Kori Schake, *America vs. the West: Can the Liberal World Order Be Preserved?* (Sydney: Penguin, 2018).

3. Stephen Brooks and William Wohlforth, *America Abroad: Why the Sole Superpower Should Not Pull Back from the World* (New York: Oxford University Press, 2018), chapters 2, 5–6, 10; Jakub Grygiel and Wess Mitchell, *The Unquiet Frontier: Rising Rivals, Vulnerable Allies, and the Crisis of American Power* (Princeton, NJ: Princeton University Press, 2017), chapter 5.

4. Chicago Council on Global Affairs, "The Foreign Policy Establishment or Donald Trump: Which Better Reflects American Opinion?" (April 2017), 3–5.

5. Richard Baldwin, *The Great Convergence: Information Technology and the New Globalization* (Cambridge, MA: The Belknap Press of Harvard University Press, 2016); Francois Bouguignon, "Inequality and Globalization: How the Rich Get Richer as the Poor Catch Up," *Foreign Affairs* 95, no. 1 (January/February 2016), 11–15; Branko Milanovic, *Global Inequality: A New Approach for the Age of Globalization* (Cambridge, MA: Harvard University Press, 2018), chapter 1.

6. Mazaar et al., *Health of the Liberal International Order*, 126–29; National intelligence Council, *Global Trends: Paradox of Progress* (January 2017), 11–15.

7. The Editors, "Vladimir's Choice: Whither Nationalism?" *The Economist,* December 19, 2017; Freedom House, *Freedom in the World 2018: Democracy in Crisis* (2018), 2–10; Mazaar et al., *Health of the Liberal International Order,* 136–46; NIC, *Paradox of Progress,* 17–19; Stewart Patrick, "Trump and World Order: The Return of Self-Help," *Foreign Affairs* 96, no. 2 (March/April 2017), 52–57.

8. Yoram Hazony, *The Virtue of Nationalism* (New York: Basic Books, 2018); Samuel Huntington, *Who Are We? The Challenges to America's National Identity* (New York: Simon and Schuster, 2005), 362–65; Julian Koo and John Yoo, *Taming Globalization: International Law, the US Constitution, and the New World Order* (New York: Oxford University Press, 2012); Eric Posner, *The Perils of Global Legalism* (Chicago: University of Chicago Press, 2011); Jeremy Rabkin, *Law Without Nations? Why Constitutional Government Requires Sovereign States* (Princeton, NJ: Princeton University Press, 2007); Roger Scruton, *The Need for Nations* (London: Institute for the Study of Civil Society, 2004); Matthew Spalding, *We Still Hold These Truths* (Wilmington, DE: Intercollegiate Studies institute, 2010), chapter 9.

9. Saul Cohen, *Geopolitics* (Lanham, MD: Rowman and Littlefield, 2014 edition); Jakub Grygiel, *Great Powers and Geopolitical Change* (Baltimore: Johns Hopkins University Press, 2006); Francis Sempa, *Geopolitics: From the Cold War to the 21st Century* (Piscataway, NJ: Transaction Publishers, 2007); Geoffrey Sloan, *Geopolitics, Geography and Strategic History* (London: Routledge, 2017).

10. Halford Mackinder, *Democratic Ideals and Reality* (Washington, DC: National Defense University Press, 1996 edition); and "The Geographical Pivot of History," *The Geographical Journal* 23, no. 4 (April 1904), 421–37.

11. Nicolas Spykman, *America's Strategy in World Politics* (New York: Routledge, 2007 edition); and *The Geography of the Peace* (New York: Harcourt, Brace, 1944).

12. Barry Buzan and Ole Waever, *Regions and Powers* (New York: Cambridge University Press, 2004), 34–35.

13. Michael Brown, Owen Cote, Sean Lynn-Jones, Steven Miller, and Graham Allison, eds., *Primacy and its Discontents* (Cambridge, MA: MIT Press, 2009); Eric Edelman, *Understanding America's Contested Primacy* (Washington, DC: Center for Strategic and Budgetary Assessments, 2010).

14. Michael Beckley, *Unrivaled: Why America Will Remain the World's Sole Superpower* (Ithaca, NY: Cornell University Press, 2018); Stephen Brooks and William Wohlforth, *America Abroad: Why the Sole Superpower Should Not Pull Back from the World* (New York: Oxford University Press, 2018 edition), chapter 2; Nuno Monteiro, *Theory of Unipolar Politics* (New York: Cambridge University Press, 2014), chapter 2. Regarding the international geopolitical implications of the US shale gas revolution, see Meghan O'Sullivan, *Windfall: How the New Energy Abundance Upends Global Politics and Strengthens America's Power* (New York: Simon and Schuster, 2017). On US demographic advantages, see Susan Yoshihara and Douglas Sylva, eds., *Population Decline and the Remaking of Great Power Politics* (Washington, DC: Potomac Books, 2011).

15. Robert Kaplan, *The Return of Marco Polo's World and the US Military Response* (Washington, DC: Center for a New American Security, 2017).

16. Bruno Macaes, *The Dawn of Eurasia* (New Haven, CT: Yale University Press, 2018); Kishore Mahbubani, *The New Asian Hemisphere* (New York: Public Affairs, 2009); William Overholt, *Asia, America, and the Transformation of Geopolitics* (New York: Cambridge University Press, 2008); Dale Walton, *Geopolitics and the Great Powers in the 21st Century* (Abingdon, UK: Routledge, 2009). For a cautionary note on Asia's continued rise, see Michael Auslin, *The End of the Asian Century: War, Stagnation, and the Risks to the World's Most Dynamic Region* (New Haven, CT: Yale University Press, 2018).

17. Larry Diamond, Marc Plattner, and Christopher Walker, eds., *Authoritarianism Goes Global* (Baltimore: Johns Hopkins University Press, 2016).

18. For various perspectives on Chinese foreign policy, related power shifts, and their implications for the United States, see Graham Allison, *Destined for War: Can America and China Escape Thucydides' Trap?* (Boston: Mariner Books, 2018); Victor Cha, *Powerplay: The Origins of the American Alliance System in East Asia* (Princeton, NJ: Princeton University Press, 2018), chapter 8; Steve Chan, *Trust and Distrust in Sino–American Relations* (Amherst, NY: Cambria Press, 2017); Thomas Christensen, *The China Challenge* (New York: Norton, 2016); Jonathan Fenby, *Will China Dominate the 21st Century?* (Cambridge: Polity, 2017 edition); Aaron Friedberg, *A Contest for Supremacy: China, America, and the Struggle for Mastery in Asia* (New York: Norton, 2012); Lyle Goldstein, *Meeting China Halfway* (Washington, DC: Georgetown University Press, 2015); Sebastian Heilmann and Dirk Schmidt, *China's Foreign Political and Economic Relations* (Lanham, MD: Rowman and Littlefield, 2014); Andrew Nathan, *China's Search for Security* (New York: Columbia University Press, 2012); William Norris, *Chinese Economic Statecraft* (Ithaca, NY: Cornell University Press, 2016); David Rapkin and William Thompson, *Transition Scenarios: China and the United States in the 21st Century* (Chicago: University of Chicago Press, 2013); Nadege Rolland, *China's Eurasian Century? Political and Strategic Implications of the Belt and Road Initiative* (Seattle: National Bureau of Asian Research, 2017); Robert Ross and Oystein Tunsjo, eds., *Strategic Adjustment and the Rise of China* (Ithaca, NY: Cornell University Press, 2017); David Shambaugh, *China Goes Global: The Partial Power* (New York: Oxford University Press, 2014); Oriana Skylar Mastro, "Ideas, Perceptions, and Power: An Examination of China's Military Strategy," in *Strategic Asia 2017–18*, ed. Ashley Tellis, Alison Szalwinski, and Michael Wills (Seattle: National Bureau of Asian Research, 2017); Robert Sutter, *Chinese Foreign Relations* (Lanham, MD: Rowman and Littlefield, 2016); Ming Wan, *The Asian Infrastructure Investment Bank* (Basingstoke, UK: Palgrave Macmillan, 2015); Toshi Yoshihara and James Holmes, *Red Star Over the Pacific* (Annapolis, MD: Naval Institute Press, 2018 edition).

19. On Russian foreign policy under Putin, see Leon Aron, "The Kremlin Emboldened: Putinism after Crimea," *Journal of Democracy* 28, no. 4 (October 2017), 76–79; Fiona Hill, *Mr. Putin: Operative in the Kremlin* (Washington,

DC: Brookings Institution Press, 2015); Mark Katz, "Putin and Russia's Strategic Priorities," in Tellis, Szalwinski, and Wills, eds., *Strategic Asia 2017–18*; Bobo Lo, *Russia and the New World Disorder* (Washington, DC: Brookings Institution Press, 2015); and James Sherr, *Hard Diplomacy and Soft Coercion: Russia's Influence Abroad* (London: Chatham House, 2013).

20. Bobo Lo, *Axis of Convenience: Moscow, Beijing, and the New Geopolitics* (London: Chatham House, 2008).

21. Richard Ellings and Robert Sutter, eds., *Axis of Authoritarians: Implications of China–Russia Cooperation* (Seattle: National Bureau of Asian Research, 2018); Gilbert Rozman, *The Sino–Russian Challenge to the World Order* (Stanford, CA: Stanford University Press, 2014); Bob Savic, "Beyond China and Russia's Special Relationship," *The Diplomat*, December 7, 2016. For Bobo Lo's continuing skepticism regarding the full extent of Sino–Russian cooperation, see his book *A Wary Embrace: What the China–Russia Relationship Means for the World* (Sydney: Penguin, 2017).

22. Victor Cha, *The Impossible State: North Korea, Past and Future* (New York: Ecco Press, 2013), 297–305; Nicholas Eberstadt, "The Method in North Korea's Madness," *Commentary* (February 2018).

23. Brian Fishman, *The Master Plan: ISIS, Al Qaeda, and the Jihadi Strategy for Final Victory* (New Haven, CT: Yale University Press, 2016); Gilles Kepel, *Terror in France: The Rise of Jihad in the West* (Princeton, NJ: Princeton University Press, 2017); Shiraz Maher, *Salafi-Jihadism: The History of an Idea* (New York: Oxford University Press, 2016); Assaf Moghadam, *Nexus of Global Jihad* (New York: Columbia University Press, 2017); Michael Ryan, *Decoding Al Qaeda's Strategy* (New York: Columbia University Press, 2013); Graeme Wood, *the Way of Strangers: Encounters with the Islamic State* (New York: Random House, 2016); and Katherine Zimmerman, "The Salafi-Jihadist Movement is Winning," *RealClearWorld*, February 12, 2019.

24. Eric Trager, *Arab Fall: How the Muslim Brotherhood Won and Lost Egypt in 891 Days* (Washington, DC: Georgetown University Press, 2016).

25. Daniel Goldhagen, *The Devil that Never Dies: The Rise and Threat of Global Antisemitism* (New York: Little, Brown, 2013), 131–33, 219–20, 236–37.

26. For a broader discussion of political Islam, see Shadi Hamid, *Islamic Exceptionalism* (New York: St Martin's Griffin, 2017); Charles Hill, *Trial of a Thousand Years: World Order and Islamism* (Stanford, CA: Hoover Institution Press, 2011); and Peter Mandaville, *Islam and Politics* (Abingdon, UK: Routledge, 2014 edition).

27. Some of the leading realist texts since World War II include: Raymond Aron, *Peace and War* (New Brunswick, NJ: Transaction Publishers, 2003 edition); Robert Art, *A Grand Strategy for America* (Ithaca, NY: Cornell University Press, 2003); Robert Gilpin, *War and Change in World Politics* (New York: Cambridge University Press, 1983); George Kennan, *American Diplomacy* (Chicago: University of Chicago Press, 2012 edition); Henry Kissinger, *Diplomacy* (New York: Simon and Schuster, 1995); John Mearsheimer, *The Tragedy of Great Power Politics* (New York: Norton, 2014 edition); Hans Morgenthau, *Politics Among Nations* (New York: McGraw Hill, 2006 edition); Reinhold Niebuhr, *The Children of Light and the Children of*

Darkness (Chicago: University of Chicago Press, 2011 edition); and Kenneth Waltz, *Theory of International Politics* (Long Grove, IL: Waveland Press, 2010 edition).

28. Christopher Layne, *The Peace of Illusions* (Ithaca, NY: Cornell University Press, 2007), 159–203; John Mearsheimer, "Imperial By Design," *The National Interest* (January–February 2011), 16–34; and *The Tragedy of Great Power Politics* (New York: Norton, 2014), 163–64, 236–64, 387–90; John Mearsheimer and Stephen Walt, "The Case for Offshore Balancing," *Foreign Affairs* 95, no. 4 (July–August 2016), 70–83; Robert Pape and James Feldman, *Cutting the Fuse: The Explosion of Global Suicide Terrorism and How to Stop It* (Chicago: University of Chicago Press, 2010), 12–13, 333–35; and Stephen Walt, *The Hell of Good Intentions* (New York: Farrar, Straus and Giroux, 2018), chapter 7.

29. Notable arguments in book form favoring a strategy of restraint include John Mearsheimer, *The Great Delusion* (New Haven, CT: Yale University Press, 2018), chapter 8; and Barry Posen, *Restraint: A New Foundation for US Grand Strategy* (Ithaca, NY: Cornell University Press, 2014).

30. The Editors, "Of Course NATO Is Obsolete," *The American Conservative*, February 28, 2018; Trevor Thrall and Benjamin Friedman, eds., *US Grand Strategy in the 21st Century: The Case for Restraint* (New York: Routledge, 2018).

31. This definition of primacy is drawn from Buzan and Waever, *Regions and Powers*, 34–35.

32. Gilpin, *War and Change*, 194.

33. Art, *Grand Strategy for America*, 42–43, 172–222; Hal Brands, *American Grand Strategy in the Age of Trump* (Washington, DC: Brookings Institution Press, 2018), chapter 2; Brooks and Wohlforth, *America Abroad*, chapters 4–8.

34. On the uses of foreign assistance, see Daniel Runde, "Foreign Aid Is About US Interests," *Foreign Policy*, June 26, 2017.

35. Leon Aron, "Putin's Goal: Revenge and Restoration," *Wall Street Journal*, August 8, 2017; Laura Rosenberger and Jamie Fly, "Shredding the Putin Playbook," *Democracy Journal* 47 (Winter 2018); and Nikolas Gvosdev, "America Must Drop Its Delusions About Dealing with Russia," *The National Interest*, March 30, 2018.

36. Aaron Friedberg, "Competing with China," *Survival* 60, no. 3 (June–July 2018), 7–64; Michael Green and Andrew Shearer, "Countering China's Militarization of the Indo-Pacific," *War on the Rocks*, April 23, 2018.

37. Simon Tisdall, "Donald Trump Attempting to Play Nixon's China Card in Reverse," *The Guardian*, December 12, 2016.

38. Evan Medeiros and Michael Chase, "Chinese Perspectives on the Sino–Russian Relationship," and Eugene Rumer, "Russia's China Policy: This Bear Hug in Real," *NBR Special Report #66* (Seattle: National Bureau of Asian Research, 2017), 2–25; Robert Sutter, "America's Bleak View of Sino–Russian Relations," *Asia Policy* 13, no. 1 (January 2018), 39–45.

39. Michael Doran, "Trump Needs to Be More Trumpian on Syria," *New York Times*, April 10, 2018; Charles Hill, "Rolling Back Iran," *The Hoover Institution*, December 13, 2017; Kenneth Pollack and Bilal Saab, "Countering Iran," *Washington Quarterly* 40, no. 3 (October 2017) 97–108; Ray Takeyh, "Trump Pulled Out of the Iran Deal. What Now?" *Politico*, May 8, 2018.

40. Dan Blumenthal, "The Clock Is Ticking for Trump to Dismantle North Korea Weapons," *The Hill,* June 14, 2018; Nicholas Eberstadt, "Talks with North Korea Are a Zero-Sum Game. Here's How to Play It," *Washington Post,* March 9, 2018; John Yoo and Jeremy Rabkin, "No-One Wants an Arms Race, But High-Tech Weapons Are America's Best Shot at Containing North Korea," *Los Angeles Times,* August 18, 2017.

41. Eric Edelman and Gary Roughead, co-chairs, *Providing for the Common Defense: The Assessments and Recommendations of the National Defense Strategy Commission* (Washington, DC: United States Institute of Peace, 2018).

42. Seth Cropsey and Bryan McGrath, *Maritime Strategy in a New Era of Great Power Competition* (Washington, DC: The Hudson Institute, 2017); Mackenzie Eaglen, "Recommendations for a Future National Defense Strategy," statement before the US Senate Armed Services Committee, November 30, 2017.

43. Robert Gates, *Duty: Memoirs of a Secretary at War* (New York: Knopf, 2014), 590.

44. Douglas Irwin, *Free Trade Under Fire* (Princeton, NJ: Princeton University Press, 2015 edition), chapters 1–3.

45. Thomas Duesterberg, "Trump Needs Allies on Trade," *Wall Street Journal,* April 23, 2018.

46. Glenn Snyder, *Alliance Politics* (Ithaca, NY: Cornell University Press, 2007), 181–86.

47. Grygiel and Mitchell, *Unquiet Frontier,* chapters 2–3.

48. Ibid., chapter 4.

49. John Gaddis, *On Grand Strategy* (New York: Penguin, 2018); Ionut Popescu, *Emergent Strategy and Grand Strategy* (Baltimore: Johns Hopkins University Press, 2017).

50. Peter Rodman, *Presidential Command: Power, Leadership, and the Making of Foreign Policy from Richard Nixon to George W. Bush* (New York: Vintage, 2010), 289; Dale Walton, *Grand Strategy and the Presidency* (New York: Routledge, 2013), chapters 4–5.

51. Michael Mandelbaum, *Mission Failure: America and the World in the Post–Cold War Era* (New York: Oxford University Press, 2017); Tony Smith, *Why Wilson Matters: The Origin of American Liberal Internationalism and Its Crisis Today* (Princeton, NJ: Princeton University Press, 2017), chapters 6–7.

52. Aaron Friedberg, *The Authoritarian Challenge* (Tokyo, Japan: Sasakawa Foundation, 2017); Azar Gat, "The Return of Authoritarian Great Powers," *Foreign Affairs* 86, no. 4 (July–August 2007), 59–69; Grygiel, *Great Powers and Geopolitical Change,* chapter 7; Robert Kagan, *The Return of History and the End of Dreams* (New York: Vintage, 2009); Kaplan, *The Return of Marco Polo's World*; Walter Russell Mead, "The Return of Geopolitics," *Foreign Affairs* 93, no. 3 (May–June 2014), 69–79; Alexandros Petersen, *The World Island: Geopolitics and the Fate of the West* (Santa Barbara, CA: Praeger, 2011); Walton, *Geopolitics and the Great Powers in the 21st Century*; and Thomas Wright, *All Measures Short of War: The Contest for the Twenty-First Century and the Future of American Power* (New Haven, CT: Yale University Press, 2017), chapters 1–4.

For the benefit of digital users, indexed terms that span two pages (e.g., 52–53) may, on occasion, appear on only one of those pages.